MW01053690

OUTING THE SENATOR

OUTING THE SENATOR: SEX, SPIES, AND VIDEOTAPE

DAVID O'TOOLE

Library of Congress Cataloging-in-Publication Data —

O'Toole, David, 1945-

Outing the Senator: Sex, Spies, and Videotape / David O'Toole. 1st ed.

p. cm.

Includes bibliographical references and index.

ISBN 0-9771970-0-X (Hardcover) — ISBN 0-9771970-1-8 (paperback) — ISBN 0-9771970-2-6 (e-book)

1. Walsh, David I. (David Ignatius), 1872-1947. 2. Legislators—United States—Biography. 3. United States Congress. Senate—Biography. 4. Outing (Sexual orientation)—United States— 5. Espionage—United States—History—20th century. 6. World War II, 1939-1945— 6. Anti-war movements— United States. 7. United States—Politics and government—1913-1946. 8. Political corruption—United States—History—20th century.

A self-published book

For information, contact: James Street Publishing, 65 James Street, Worcester, Ma 01603

Front Cover: Portrait studio photo, undated, of David I. Walsh courtesy of the Dinand Library, Special Collections Division, College of the Holy Cross. Cover art work design by Kerin Molly O'Toole and Marlyn Rodriguez. Collage of newspaper headlines is a composite of actual headlines run by the New York Post in days leading up to the Nazi Spy Nest Trial, and is not an actual replication of each.

Printed in the United States

I dedicate this book to a whole generation of O'Tooles, whose stories of love and life made this book possible. Without their endless political stories at family gatherings, accompanied by laughter, this book would not have been possible. To Maurice and Mary O'Toole, Margaret O'Toole, Bill O'Toole, Evelyn and Tom Martin, and especially to my parents, "Jed" and Mary O'Toole, whose passion about everything had a profound impact on me. The oral story telling tradition of the O'Tooles passed this story down to me.

To my wife, Dotty, and my son and daughter, Ryan and Kerin, who are the loves of my life.

To the Town of Clinton, where the American dream for the O'Tooles first took root.

And finally, to a man I never met, a son of Clinton, a friend of David I. Walsh, and a son of the College of the Holy Cross, my grandfather, William Francis O'Toole.

Acknowledgments

The search for facts regarding David I. Walsh seemed longer than the Oregon Trail, and at times the trail could become pretty obscure. I would like to thank the College of the Holy Cross, especially the staff of the David I. Walsh Archives, for their many kindnesses. Access to the Walsh papers provided a valuable insight to what was happening on Main Street, as letters from his constituents show Walsh as he really was, a Jeffersonian Democrat. I would particularly like to thank Jo-Anne Carr and Lois Hammill, Archivist, for their always helpful suggestions.

I received excellent assistance from the staff of the FBI Reading Room which, indeed, is a national treasure. Thank God for the Freedom of Information Act. Without the FBI files, I could not have cleared the good name of David I. Walsh.

The staff of the National Archives in Washington, College Park, and New York City were always helpful and are also a national treasure.

The staff of the New York Public Library was particularly helpful in allowing me access to the Dorothy Schiff Collection.

The staff of the Worcester Public Library has a longstanding reputation for providing good service. Penelope Johnson has every right to be proud of her staff and the magnificent new library. My apologies to trustee Lenny Cooper for saying that rebuilding the old library was a mistake. Occasionally, an Irishman is wrong. And it is highly accessible!

To Tammy Catinella, Marlyn Rodriguez, Susan Matos, and Lillian Figueroa for all their support in preparing the text, and patience with me as I paced the office.

And to the Boston Red Sox, who finally, just once, did not drive me to distraction.

TABLE OF CONTENTS

INTRODUCTION

David Ignatius Walsh was a man of clichés, a solitary man not given to introspection. A son of immigrants, he was enamored of all things American, particularly the quintessential American item: the automobile. The automobile would be a metaphor for Walsh's life as it enabled him to travel life alone, and at times it could be a lonely life, indeed.

Walsh's enthusiasm for America shows through in his speeches that are peppered with references to the founding fathers. All his studies of US history came alive for him when he heard William Jennings Bryan, the "Silver Tongued Orator," speak at Boston Common when Walsh was a student at Boston University. He was hooked on politics for life.

Walsh was a little different from his peers. While his supposed allegiance to the pope was constantly thrown in his face, it mattered little what popes or presidents thought, for he marched to the tune of his constituents. If he disagreed with a constituent, he took the time to explain his position; but if he disagreed with presidents or pontiffs, they might have to read about it in a newspaper. Senator David Ignatius Walsh was not a contrary personality, but a firm believer that he worked for the citizens of Massachusetts. His belief in Jeffersonian Democracy put him out of step with his own party leaders, two presidents, Wilson and Roosevelt, who showed a vindictive side seldom seen by the public. Walsh never cared if he was in Washington's inner circle, and never succumbed to Potomac Fever. His life became a story of courage; a solitary journey, a patriot's journey.

Walsh became the longest tenured United States Senator Massachusetts had ever produced (until Edward M. Kennedy broke his record). He advocated for Philippine independence in 1900, as a student, and got a chance to vote for it in the Senate in 1946. He participated in the debate over the League of Nations and voted for the suffragettes in the campaign for women's right to vote. He authored the first minimum-wage law in US history, the Walsh-Healy Act, and supported the workers' right to organize in a less than genteel era in labor-management relations. He battled with Woodrow Wilson over the League of Nations and became an ardent opponent of FDR's Court Packing Plan.

David Walsh entered public life in 1899 when he was elected to the Massachusetts House of Representatives. By the outbreak of World War I, he was already a United States Senator. His senate career ended in 1946, and he was never heard from again. He was the victim of a political assassination.

His assassins used printed words, not bullets. They used the rumor mill, fantasy, and harmony, as they orchestrated a campaign of vilification playing all the instruments of propaganda. The story they concocted may seem like overkill, a story no one would believe, but it worked.

The campaign to destroy David I. Walsh worked because he could not defend himself. His assassins knew that. David I. Walsh was gay. He had conducted his life with dignity and honor while representing Massachusetts in the United States Senate, and he left his sex life in the bedroom, where most citizens of Massachusetts thought it belonged. His sexuality was not an issue in the US until Great Britain decided to make it one. Walsh, a strong anti-war leader, had spoken out strongly against US entry into World War I while on the campaign trail (although he ultimately fell in line with Wilson's change of heart), and he did it again in World War II. But, Walsh was not a pacifist. A strong supporter of veteran's issues, he was appalled at their treatment upon returning from World War I. He constantly fought to strengthen the US Navy and enjoyed the support of every veteran's organization in the United States.

Walsh was also strongly anti-colonialist. He advocated Philippine independence in 1900, warning his own government against colonialism. The greatest colonial empire in the world, Great Britain, took note. Anti-colonial rhetoric did not sit well with the British diplomatic class. They also noted that his parents were from that irritating British colony, Ireland. Walsh had taken an active organizational role, galvanizing the Boston Irish in raising funds for Irish independence during the 1920s. He also opposed the formation of the League of Nations, which he believed simply recognized the colonial status quo; but his opposition would be chalked up to "that Irish thing."

As World War II approached, Walsh played an active role in America First, the leading anti-war organization. Gallup Polls showed the popularity of America First's anti-war position as high as 80%, but by the time British propaganda was geared up, the anti-war movement was marginalized. The story of David I. Walsh is not about battles fought in World War II. He never wore a uniform. It is a story about his valiant attempt to keep the US out of European politics and off the battlefields of Europe. He did not succeed. Yet his fight was of heroic proportions and his ending one that no single playwright could invent. It was an invention, but (as some scholars believe is true of Shakespeare's plays) it would take the minds of many to concoct it, perhaps some of British tabloid genre, and it would take a conspiracy of Americans to execute it.

Americans may be startled and saddened to see how willing the country was to participate in the political execution of David I. Walsh. Walsh's story raises serious questions about the silencing of the United States Congress during perilous times. What was done to Walsh was certainly done to others. America's ally, Great Britain, went to extremes to destroy Walsh because he could not be silenced. His moral character was something the British could not deal with. Other congressmen were bought, like Congressman Sam Pryor of Connecticut. Many were blackmailed. It is clear that sentiment in congress was changed and they voted for the war even though the populace still opposed it. Military conscription passed by only one vote.

No president, certainly not Franklin Delano Roosevelt, would send a bill to congress unless the votes had already been counted. Were the British doing the vote counting for him? When David I. Walsh was yanked out of the closet in the Nazi Spy Nest Case, FDR told Senate Majority Leader Alben Barkley that his case should be handled the way the military did it, by leaving a loaded revolver next to the individual and having the accused kill himself. However, this book will prove that the charges were fraudulent and that FDR knew it. His complicity in the case is troubling. Walsh was an unabashed liberal, father of the first minimum wage law in America; he was "outed" not by a reactionary but by a New Deal liberal.

FDR had been working feverishly to silence congress, and he largely succeeded with the help of his British allies. Any criticism of FDR in the press was invariably attributed to right-wing reactionaries. While British propaganda pitched a pro-war line as the last hope for saving democracy, when the hot war actually began, American generals would find themselves in pitched battles with Churchill, whose task and obsession was to save the British Empire. European democracies would have to wait. While Churchill dominated US policymaking, US troops were sent to save the colonies in Africa and the Middle East. In the meantime, tens of millions of people died in Europe.

The ghastly ending of World War II could have been different. Churchill's constant delay of a cross-channel invasion cost incalculable lives — an invasion that George Marshall, with typical American optimism, proposed in May 1942, only six months after Pearl Harbor. The delay further embittered an already jittery

Joseph Stalin and set the stage for the Cold War. What if Soviet Russia had been a democracy? It is doubtful that an elected leader, after suffering the loss of twenty million people, could have simply announced the battle was over and retreated to its former borders. After all, the states of Europe were all colonial powers, and subjugation of non-native peoples had been part of the rules for centuries. Democracy only existed for the ruling class, and only for the mother country.

This story also raises serious issues of the role of a free press. Is there really a free press in the US? Has there ever been one? The concentration of media ownership can threaten democracy, as it did in World War II. Yet, the restraint demonstrated by the Washington media in David I. Walsh's critical hour provides a glimmer of hope for the media horde.

What is even more disturbing is the role of the American Civil Liberties Union in the Nazi Spy Nest Case. The ACLU General Counsel, Morris Ernst, ran the slanderous campaign against Walsh and destroyed this anti-war senator's career. While liberals sent in their membership dues, they would have no idea that Ernst was having dinner every Friday night at the Stork Club in New York with J. Edgar Hoover and that he provided the ACLU membership files to Hoover for over twenty years. ACLU members were being spied on from within.

As depressing as this story can be, it is also uplifting. It demonstrates an unwavering commitment on the part of David I. Walsh to the cherished ideals of Thomas Jefferson. The British Empire treated Walsh as just another Irish colonial; they never could bring themselves to view Walsh as a United States Senator. While the House of Representatives is usually described as "the people's house," Walsh felt strongly that his place in the United States Senate was to watch out for his constituents back in Massachusetts. As a member of the 'freshman class' of senators first directly elected by the people in the famous 1918 election, as a result of the 17th amendment, he felt a special obligation to represent the voter.

It is a story that will satisfy taxpayers that West Point and Annapolis did a good job. The best graduates of the service academies led the country out of a morass created by weak civilian leadership. Once the hot war began, they wrestled back control of United States foreign policy from Churchill by always asking the tough questions, and more important, waiting until they got answers. Like the civilian Walsh, they would always "question authority."

Walsh's story is a story of a great American patriot who happened to be gay. He did not intend to tell his story; Great Britain forced the issue.

PREFACE

The story you are about to read is not an objective one. It is a story about prejudice, vindictiveness and pettiness. It is a story about World War II. The story is told through the life of United States Senator David Ignatius Walsh. Almost no one has heard of him, even among those who might well be expected to revere him as a hero. He was the first Irish Catholic elected to the United States Senate and he served longer than any Massachusetts senator but Ted Kennedy. Yet, even Boston's Irish Catholics don't know who he was.

David I. Walsh's life tells a much larger story. As the first Catholic governor in Massachusetts and the first Catholic elected to the US Senate, Irish Catholics (and other Americans as well) should be able to look back on him proudly. However, he has been purged from the pages of history. His story has not been passed from one generation to the next. It is just too complicated to explain to children that your hero's career ended in a brothel for homosexuals in New York City under the stain of Nazi collaboration.

The Nazi Spy Nest Case ended Walsh's distinguished career, but only because he was the victim of a massive propaganda campaign; he was not the only victim, but perhaps its ultimate personal victim. On a larger scale, American democracy was a victim as well. The story is worthy of George Orwell's *1984*. It is so bizarre and twisted that the public in 1942 rejected many aspects of it as false. Walsh's supporters had charged that Franklin Delano Roosevelt was behind the smear campaign. To the credulous voters, that appeared preposterous. Unfortunately, it was true. Not only was FDR involved, he ran the campaign from his home in Hyde Park.

Senator David I. Walsh, the very liberal senator from Massachusetts, was targeted by the liberal wing of the Democratic Party because of his opposition to United States entry in World War II. He had opposed FDR every step of the way from 1937 to Pearl Harbor, and was the author of the Neutrality Act, whose purpose was to keep the US out of war. While he did not trust Germany, he trusted Great Britain even less. This anti-colonial senator was not popular in London, whose territorial reach was so vast that they liked to brag that the sun never set on the Union Jack.

The campaign to destroy Walsh was carried out by British spies in the United States and the instrument used was the liberal wing of the Democratic Party. FDR was having a tough time selling his strategy to support Great Britain, and powerful Senator David I. Walsh, Chairman of the Senate Naval Affairs Committee, was his biggest nemesis. The liberal wing of the party could be counted on to help Roosevelt any way possible, even if it meant destroying a fellow liberal. Walsh ardently fought to secure funding for the United States Navy, only to watch Roosevelt send new ships and planes to Great Britain.

The manipulation by the British Secret Service was so complete that the scheme could not have gained the support of Washington if the leadership had come from a mixed heritage. It was so pro-Britain, the perpetrators of the scheme would have been charged with treason. However, it was run by rabid Anglophiles, a group whose loyalties to the "old country" were stronger than their loyalty to America. The Anglophile elite disdained America as a cowboy country having none of the refinements of London, or Rome, or Paris, or Berlin.

While Anglophilia was important, it was not the only criterion; money and class were also important. Money could overcome the fact of national origin; why, with enough money, you could even get away with being Catholic, only on a quota system. You might even get ahead if you were Jewish, as long as you knew your place and had plenty of money.

When World War II started, the British Secret Service was run by Vernon Kell, a man who had served since World War I and who refused to hire Catholics. United States Senator David I. Walsh had been the mortal enemy of Kell, and Walsh's support for Irish freedom would not be forgotten. Great Britain hated to lose a colony, even one as small as Ireland. For, if Ireland was successful in fighting for freedom, what next? Would the crown jewel, India, with many more millions of people than Ireland, demand its freedom next? Boston had been the US fundraising capital for Irish freedom and no one gave more freely than Boston's Irish. But the Boston Irish also had power and influence, even among their Yankee brethren — a group that also distrusted Great Britain.

David I. Walsh was powerful, outspoken, and strongly anti-colonial. He preached for Philippine freedom and insured it was a party plank at the 1900 State Democratic Party convention. He attacked the plundering of China by Great

Britain, and when World War I ended, he bitterly criticized Britain's awarding its ally Japan a mandate in China. But, when the Rape of Nanking occurred, Japan would be blamed; the public's short attention span for all things in Asia would cause them to forget that this was a gang rape.

The involvement of FDR in the scheme to pillory Walsh may come as a surprise, but only because Americans have read a tremendous amount of propaganda that passes for history. When wars break out, propaganda is a necessary component for mobilizing a populace. Much of it is benign and much of it is immediately recognized as propaganda; loyal citizens usually comply cheerfully and pitch in to help the cause. When wars end, it is historians' job to sort out propaganda from reality. With Franklin Delano Roosevelt, historians have not done a very good job.

There are reasons for that. FDR died at the conclusion of the war and his death was untimely for several reasons. Roosevelt's critics had agreed to withhold numerous investigations until the conclusion of the war for the sake of national unity. For the duration of the war, FDR was able to invoke national security as reason for not fully divulging information that in peacetime should be made public. Another reason was that FDR did not experience leaks among those closest to him because he used his fellow Columbia graduates as surrogates. A committed band of Anglophiles, many of them did not even work at the White House, although they clearly were on the payroll in one fashion or another. They were united by class, religion, money and, often, a disdain for the brawny, brawling young nation called America. They could be trusted to keep the confidence of FDR because the loyalty was not necessarily a personal one, but a loyalty based on class. They firmly believed that they were the chosen ones, destined to rule America. They were the forerunners of today's political consultants, whose purpose is to tell as little about a candidate as possible while establishing focus groups to determine what the voter wants to hear, instead of what the voter should be hearing. FDR's small band of Columbia graduates brought the worst of Madison Avenue techniques, with sloganeering from the Columbia Classics Department to manage FDR's campaigns and write his speeches.

This sorry tale will shatter any faith one may have had in "New Deal" liberalism; it goes a long way towards explaining what is wrong with liberalism today. Franklin Delano Roosevelt destroyed the roots of liberalism when he destroyed the careers of David Ignatius Walsh, Gerald Nye, Burton Wheeler and many other senators. Virtually all of the senators FDR targeted were rooted in Main Street or the prairie Midwest. They reported to the voter; therefore, they could not be controlled. Their liberalism was not the liberalism of the elite. What FDR wanted was top-down liberalism. American liberalism has lost touch with the working man and woman, and the destruction of liberalism as a politically viable force in the American electorate began with FDR. The purge of the liberal faithful was so devastating and complete that it would leave a vacuum of liberal leadership for an entire generation, and it resulted in a surge by Republicans upon the death of Roosevelt. Harry Truman was a man from Main Street, a man who liberals disdained; he was able to ride out a Republican rebirth but he could do little but watch the resurgence in Congress.

While this story is told through the "eyes" of Senator David I. Walsh, he was a man with cataracts. He could see shapes and shadows, and he knew what was happening to him. He just could not discern the names and faces of all the assassins. He clearly understood who the commanding general was; but he did not have an army of researchers at his disposal to counter the charges against him. He went to his grave without knowing all the details. He deserves clear answers. This book might otherwise be titled *David I. Walsh's Revenge*.

Many of the women in FDR's life help to tell the story, for their presence at intimate moments provide insight that is priceless. FDR's shabby treatment of women was well documented. His obsessive interest in sex created a coterie of women who could provide valuable insights about FDR. Since Roosevelt did not perceive them as a threat, he let his guard down in front of them.

With the publication of *The Roosevelt's of Hyde Park, An Untold Story*, in 1973, Elliot Roosevelt begged historians to tell the truth about his father. "Since the passing of my parents, I have read a steady flow of appraisals of their lives. Some of these books were conscientiously researched by able historians. Other books have been written by haters or lovers of one or the other. From all this writing I have experienced a feeling that a kind of cardboard, one-dimensional image was emerging that did not tell the full story of the development of these two human beings." It was Elliot Roosevelt, not an historian, who revealed FDR's long affair with his secretary, Missy LeHand.

It is ironic that much of the perspective on FDR comes from his numerous sexual partners; but he was so profligate, there is plenty of material to draw upon. On the other hand, you will not read much about Senator David I. Walsh's sex life, although the public did read about it in the 'Summer of 1942'. What the public read was false. Walsh kept his sex life in the bedroom. FDR's smear campaign did not tell Massachusetts voters anything they did not already suspect: that Walsh was gay. They did not care what he did in private, as long as he kept it private. It was FDR who exploited the prurient curiosity of some segments of the public. Walsh's hometown newspaper, the conservative *Worcester Telegram &*

Gazette, was appalled at those making the charges. They originally refused to print the story, and did not do so until Senator Alben Barkley, the Senate Majority Leader, released a statement on the story many weeks later. The editor revealed the tremendous pressure he received to run the story in the heart of Walsh's political base, thus confirming a shadowy conspiracy to smear Walsh. He stood firm.

FDR's early political career ended in disaster in the Newport Sex Scandal, forcing him to resign as Assistant Secretary of the Navy. Yet his appetite for sex would continue lifelong, even as he entered a wheelchair. Jonathan Alter, writing on the 2004 presidential campaign for *Newsweek*, says that party bosses and the media early in the 1932 campaign saw Roosevelt as an "unprincipled lightweight" and thought he would be unable to overcome his poor image to gain the nomination. When the party bosses think a candidate is unprincipled, there certainly is an image problem. When they think you are stupid, it is time for a spin doctor. In this case the best and the brightest were found at Columbia University. However, FDR would remain the "unprincipled lightweight", and as World War II approached, his limited mental capacities would be further diminished by exceedingly poor health. FDR was known for his non-existent loyalties, and the best talent surrounding him had left his administration long before the war. Franklin Delano Roosevelt lacked the personal qualities and character to lead an important nation at a critical time.

In the end, it fell to the best and the brightest at the military academies to bail out a weak civilian team in the White House; and, after Roosevelt's death, Harry Truman gained the White House — a man loathed by the liberal elite. Yet it would be Truman who would propose the Marshall Plan and national health insurance in the same budget. Congress gave Truman his choice, and would not fund both.

Historians have had a long time to tell the truth about World War II, yet they have failed to do so. There were reasons why clear answers were not available during and immediately after World War II. But, all the excuses historians have had are no longer valid. So, call me a revisionist, if you will, but please, do not call me a historian.

CHAPTER 1. AN IRISH MILL TOWN

David I. Walsh, an Irish Catholic, was a United States Senator. In Massachusetts, in 1918, that meant something. No matter what side of the tracks they came from, the citizens of Massachusetts revered their public representatives, like Paul Revere, whether at a Massachusetts town meeting or the exalted position of United States Senator. Recent immigrants were immensely proud that one of their own might make it to the United States Senate. While Walsh's family had been in Massachusetts for over 60 years, this was the land of the Pilgrims. Anyone who could not trace their ancestors back to the Mayflower was a nobody in the political arena. Getting elected statewide seemed impossible. Outside of Boston, Massachusetts was mostly WASP, White Anglo Saxon Protestant. One may wonder whether he might have had an easier time of it if he had been a Protestant from Northern Ireland. All those Yankees in towns like Leicester, Southampton, Westminster, and Amherst (named after Lord Amherst) were not likely to vote for an Irishman, much less a Catholic. There are no towns in Massachusetts named Dublin, or Kerry, or Galway. The Irish did not get there early enough.

How did David Ignatius Walsh pull it off? While Massachusetts today considers itself a liberal state, or certainly an enlightened one, it wasn't always so. The state voted for Senator George McGovern in the Presidential race in 1972 and sprouted bumper stickers during the Watergate era that said, "Don't blame me, I'm from Massachusetts." Yet an earlier generation faced signs on factories that stated, "Irish need not apply." It wasn't until the United States entered World War II that such signs began to disappear. The Office of Wage and Price Controls played no small role in the issue. Federal contracts with factories that produced goods for the war effort were required to sign anti-discrimination agreements.

David I. Walsh crossed from the world of small, mill town Clinton to the Yankee "Brahmin" world of Beacon Hill in Boston. He cobbled together two very different constituencies, and went on to a powerful position in the US Senate. He did not openly proclaim that he was gay.

Being Catholic was far more of an offense than being Irish. And, while open homosexuality was not an option, being gay did not hurt him. No one was going to accuse him without proof. At the turn of the century, there was a strong belief that one's sex life belonged in the bedroom. If one conducted a discreet private life, the electorate would never know. Being single, and with no family commitments, worked to his advantage. He could move about the state more freely since he was not tied down to the home front, with no family to attend to. In the era when he entered politics, Massachusetts had no state highway system and statewide campaigning was not easy.

David I. Walsh joined a gentlemen's club on William Street in Worcester. A posh address, its membership was mostly Yankee and rich; it was an unlikely place to be raided by police. Besides, its members had nothing to gain by gossiping about indecent affairs. The membership gave him an entrée into a powerful group of independently wealthy individuals who possessed two valuable commodities: money and time. Being gay would actually work to his advantage. One wonders if he would have enjoyed the same access if he were happily married.

Walsh was not the only Irish Catholic politician in Massachusetts. James Michael Curley, "The Rascal King," served as Mayor of Boston, congressman, and governor. Curley, the inspiration for Edwin O'Connor's best selling novel, *The Last Hurrah*, was in many ways more powerful than Walsh. But the longtime Mayor of Boston had run into trouble when he ran statewide. As a consequence, his stints as Governor were much shorter than his stints as mayor and congressman. Perhaps he was too Catholic. He certainly was too Irish! This larger than life character contrasted greatly with Walsh's statesman-like demeanor. As a result, when Curley took his case to a Yankee electorate, he fared poorly. Curley and Walsh were bitter enemies. Sharing the same political base did not make relations any easier. Maurice V. O'Toole, who was appointed Chairman of the State Appellate Tax Board by Governor Curley, was David I. Walsh's county campaign coordinator in Worcester County; Curley's, too! Friends with both men, he could not mention one man's name in the presence of the other.

Increasing the bitterness in later years was the resentment Curley felt when his son Francis, a Catholic priest, was essentially exposed for homosexuality. While the term "outing" did not exist in that era, Curley's son had periodic run-ins with the local police because of his continuous affairs. Meanwhile, Walsh remained discreet.

17

James Michael Curley may have resented the ease in which Walsh moved from a Catholic to a Protestant world. For two decades, Walsh was easily reelected statewide, racking up large margins in mostly Protestant towns outside of Boston where it was said a Catholic could not win. Walsh was elected statewide in every election, save one, from 1918 until 1946.

David Walsh's hometown of Clinton might have been a small town, but it was a political powerhouse in the early 20th century and remained so for years. It was an early destination for the Irish coming to America, even before the great waves of immigration to Boston. In the era of canal digging, the Irish were hired for their strong backs and willingness to work for low wages. When builder Tobias Boland won a contract to build the Blackstone Canal from Providence to Worcester, he imported Irish laborers; they were allotted temporary housing in Worcester. Many eventually settled in the nearby town of Clinton, just one town away.

Another large public works project would take place in Clinton itself around the turn of the century. When the City of Boston was running out of water it looked westward towards Worcester. Two rural towns of Boylston and West Boylston were chosen as the site for the new Wachusett Reservoir. At the time, this was viewed as enviable "pork barrel" legislation for any district, and it certainly provided jobs for "out of work" Irishmen. Walsh's constituents would get jobs on this project, although Walsh himself played no role in delivering the bacon. His political career had not yet started, but he would be a beneficiary.

From the reservoir itself to the enormous aqueduct that carried water forty miles to Boston, the project was labor intensive. David Walsh may have grown up in a poor town, but he clearly had connections to the "lace curtain" Irish. A dapper dresser, his family provided him with every advantage possible. His family was preparing him for a life outside Clinton, though they could hardly have realized how far he would go. A lawyer's life in the county seat may have been fine. At the turn of the century, Catholics were not going to college. David Walsh did, with significant help from his whole family. Whether his family had political aspirations for David are unknown, but nothing that happens in Clinton, Massachusetts is remote from politics. By mid-century, the town had produced two of the most powerful politicians on Capitol Hill. Walsh would become Chairman of the Senate Naval Affairs Committee in an age when the Air Force didn't exist, and Congressman Philip Philbin would become Chairman of the House Armed Services Committee.

At the turn of the century, Clinton had not yet made its political mark. David Walsh would change that. Clinton voters were courted regularly in district and congressional races, as well as statewide contests. It was expected that candidates would court the vote, and for the town of Clinton that meant "pressing the flesh." Candidates had better be seen in Clinton, early and often, for citizens regularly reported to one another on who attended and who missed various events around town.

David I. Walsh was born on November 11, 1872 in Leominster, Massachusetts, one of ten children born to Bridget Donnelly and James Walsh. David's father would later take in an orphaned nephew, too. James Walsh was a hard worker. He would end up owning two houses in Leominster; not bad for an Irishman. His good fortune would not last, however. He lost one house to a fire and the second one to a court judgment when the family dog spooked a horse, which overturned a buggy. The man driving the buggy sued James Walsh for damages and the Walsh home was sold at auction. "David remembered all his life, with the bitterness of a child's heartbreak, the crowds of strangers milling through the rooms, the wooden hammer banging out its knell — going-going gone!...David and his mother were the last to leave, staying until the furniture had been loaded on a wagon, walking tearfully out of the door of the Leominster house for the last time and taking the train to their new home."[1] James Walsh's hard work was not treated to an equal measure of Irish luck.

And so, they moved to the town of Clinton, settling into a tenement on Old Pond Court. When David was twelve, his father died. Bridget moved the family to a house near the Catholic Church, and started taking in mill workers as boarders to make ends meet. Bridget Walsh made sure everyone got to Sunday mass. David Walsh would become an altar boy. While Bridget attended to his religious upbringing, his older brother John got him involved in local politics. He began attending town meetings as a young teen. His brother John, assisted by other family members, enrolled at the College of the Holy Cross in nearby Worcester.

John Walsh was admitted to the bar in 1880. He established a law practice in the neighboring town of Fitchburg, and soon had a thriving practice. It was unusual for a Catholic to succeed in a professional practice in the 1880s, primarily because of existing laws. In those days, you did not even have to go to law school to practice law, if you could serve an apprenticeship in a law office. Those spots were saved for the sons of lawyers, and the lawyers happened to be Yankee. Neither was Harvard University accepting many Catholics. For John Walsh, success came quickly. However, the family's run of bad luck would continue.

---

[1] Wayman, Dorothy G, *David I. Walsh, Citizen-Patriot*, Bruce Publishing Milwaukee, 1952, 5.

David's role model and unquestioned leader of the Walsh clan died of tuberculosis on August 12, 1887. The older brother, the beacon of hope for this immigrant family, was suddenly gone.

The family now turned their attention to David. He was helped by his cousin, John Corcoran, the older brother of the nephew David's parents had taken in. John Corcoran was appointed a justice of Superior Court in 1892, again very unusual for an Irish Catholic. The 1880s were a Gilded Age only for a select few. A Superior Court judgeship was a start, but the golden years for the Walsh family were yet to come.

In 1890, David Walsh graduated from Clinton High School, winning a competition as class orator. That September, Walsh enrolled in Holy Cross College. Walsh was a determined student, and in consideration of his family's dire economic straits he finished four years of course work in three years, graduating in June 1893. For the few students who were not from wealthy families, it was far more common to graduate in five or six years, taking time off to work to help pay for the tuition. And, like those others, Walsh went to work. Construction had finally begun on Wachusett Reservoir. While David I. Walsh could take no credit for landing this political plum for his hometown of Clinton, he would quickly learn the benefits of participation in public life. He could thank the activism of the entire town of Clinton.

His first full time employment was as clerk of the Clinton Water Board. The Wachusett Dam was being built right on the edge of town. Walsh became the paymaster, handing their pay to hundreds of Italian immigrants who were now replacing the earlier Irish laborers.

One year later, Walsh entered law school at Boston University in 1894. He was a top student, finishing in 1897 with the public speaking prize, and also as Class President. While at Boston University he would get a chance to see politics outside the prism of his hometown. Boston University was within sight of Fenway Park and Braves Field, which, with the departure of the professional baseball team, would become part of his school's campus. It was a short walk to Boston Common, a site that had been accommodating rabble rousers since the American Revolution. Walsh would walk to the common to hear the "Silver Tongued Orator," William Jennings Bryan, as he campaigned for President. Bryan's oratorical skills would enthrall Walsh. He was hooked for life.

Upon graduating from Boston University, he immediately opened a law practice in Fitchburg, following in his brother John's footsteps. Since the court-house was there, he did not have much choice. He did, however, keep evening hours in his hometown of Clinton. The establishment of his law practice would

20

define the man David I. Walsh would become. Rather than seek out the corporate interests of Yankee mill owners, Walsh began by representing poor and itinerant laborers in suits against mill owners. He handled personal injury cases before the advent of workers compensation laws. Factories were often hellholes, with no regard for worker safety or working conditions. Buildings and equipment were not maintained from a safety standpoint, only a production standpoint. One wonders what the mill owners thought of him. He was a pioneer on the legal frontier, and not in a way that helped the moneyed classes.

Because he was fighting corporate interests, he was facing the best legal talent in Massachusetts. He was opposed by prominent attorneys, one of whom would later become Chief Justice of the Massachusetts Supreme Court. His representation of the poor within the Massachusetts legal system became the launching pad for his political career. Walsh was elected to the state legislature as a state representative in 1899. He not only represented poor Irish, Italian, and French laborers, but poor Yankee farm owners as well: Swamp Yankees. With a declining farm base in Massachusetts, Swamp Yankees felt as disenfranchised as anyone else. They held no kin with their rich, mercantile Yankee cousins. This would give Walsh a good political base. With the industrial revolution in full bloom, there were many small struggling farmers who could not leave the farm very often — but they did so, to vote. Yet, their voice was not being heard in Boston.

Shays' Rebellion had occurred not too far from Walsh's home base of central Massachusetts. Farmer Daniel Shays rallied his neighbors in 1786 to refuse to pay their taxes. As late as the 1930s, two tax collectors sent to Cape Cod were never seen again. Walsh's cultivation of the Swamp Yankee voter was based on his sense of natural kinship for anyone who felt disenfranchised. He strongly believed that the poor workingman, including the small farmer, was underrepresented in the halls of justice. Indeed, in the 1890s, the term "halls of justice" was a misnomer. Lawyer-lobbyists patrolled the halls of the state house, on retainer for those who could pay. Public interest groups, other than anti-saloon league and good government types, barely existed. The "good government" movement started to flourish after the turn of the century, with groups from both major parties insisting on the replacement of commissioner boards that were politically appointed; boards that voted on each executive decision. They were to be replaced by one powerful commissioner who was professionally trained. Colleges began offering education and training for people who wanted to become professional bureaucrats.

In 1899, his first year running for public office, Walsh's early political phi-

21

losophy began to take shape, as well as an indication of what he would be up against in launching his political career. The Democratic ticket that year was headed by Robert Treat Paine, a descendant of the signer of the Declaration of Independence; and this was the party of the immigrants, or rather, would soon become one. Walsh's candidacy would be a radical departure from the usual plain fare in Pilgrim country. To illuminate how different Walsh was in that era, a reading of the Democratic State Party platform is necessary. In regard to foreign policy, one plank termed the acquisition of the Philippines as criminal aggression. Walsh was a driving force behind the party plank, but the fact that it became one highlights the political era as much as Walsh himself. If the state Democratic Party of the 1960's had tried to include a plank characterizing Viet Nam as criminal aggression, the petitioners would have been considered fringe members of the party. Walsh was a strong supporter of Philippine independence. He would remain a friend of the Philippine people for life. Walsh's views had the support of the rank and file in the Democratic Party and were actually shared by many conservatives in the Republican Party, who agreed that the United States should not emulate Great Britain's colonial empire.

He would later speak out against Japanese aggression in China in what, in later years, would be described as the "Rape of Nanking." Walsh could only be described as an anti-imperialist. His isolationist views were clear from an early age. His anti-colonial views would be established early in his career, even before he got to the US Senate. His antidote for colonialism would be isolationism. Not only should the United States stay home, he suggested, but so should all the European powers. His support for the right of all peoples to "self determination" was heartfelt, but perhaps naïve in a world of imperial ambitions. Even in its most overt forms, colonialism would not go to its grave easily. This did not stop Walsh from being a thorn in the side of the colonial powers, and he relentlessly preached an anti-imperialist message. His commitment to his early beliefs was not poll driven. One particular colonial power, Great Britain, would take early note.

David's younger brother Tom followed him into law practice and the firm Walsh & Walsh worked quite well. David I. Walsh was generating publicity as a state representative and Tom Walsh was in the office every day. The brothers were becoming successful, and now was the time to thank their mother, Bridget Donnelly Walsh, who had toiled so long to give her brood a good start in life. The brothers purchased a fourteen-room house. Bridget Walsh was finally getting her just reward.

Death struck the family again on the very day they were to have occupied the new home. Bridget Walsh died on May 16, 1904. Her wake was held in the new house, a practice common before the advent of funeral homes. David Walsh had seen untimely death too often. This was a particularly cruel blow, for David had now witnessed the death of his father, his older brother, and his mother in a relatively short span of years.

Death came visiting often to that generation, and particularly so for immigrant families, many of whom lacked adequate nutrition and health care. Life without the immunization and antibiotics later generations took for granted was tough on all social classes. Yet, as tough as it was for Walsh, his legal clients had it worse. They also often had to deal with illness and injuries that were a direct result of their factory jobs. Corporations lacked the incentive to improve conditions of workers. Without any threat of liability, conditions would not improve. Walsh & Walsh, attorneys-at-law, would provide that threat. David I. Walsh could do little to protect his family from disease but he made a living trying to prevent occupational illnesses and injuries to the working class, and seeking just compensation when injuries did occur.

CHAPTER 2. ON TO BEACON HILL — BRAHMIN COUNTRY

In the election of 1912, Walsh began to establish his political identity on the national level. He was out of office at this time; the law practice was thriving, and his brother Tom was doing a fine job. This gave Walsh the opportunity to dabble in politics. The idle rich Yankees had been doing it for years. At this point in his life, politics wasn't a necessity — not a way out of poverty — but a passionate interest. Progressive ideas were beginning to take root, as illustrated by "Fighting Bob" La Follette in the prairie Midwest. "Fighting Bob" became a national figure, and Walsh's political background fit into this mold. Walsh was not tied to any political machine in Massachusetts at the time. There were two major Democratic machines: those of James Michael Curley and John F. Fitzgerald. Called "Honey Fitz," he was the grandfather of President John Fitzgerald Kennedy. James Michael Curley was four times Mayor of Boston, served one term in the House of Representatives, and one term as Governor. John F. Fitzgerald was Mayor of Boston whenever Curley was not. Their perennial rivalry could be counted upon, like the swallows returning to Capistrano.

The election of 1912 marked the clear beginning of Walsh's political identity. Walsh was also captivated by Theodore Roosevelt's candidacy. His "Bull Moose" Movement, with attacks upon political machines, was just the hot button for Walsh. Machine politics were as big an issue within the Republican Party as it was in Democratic circles. Coming from a small town, he had no machine to belong to. He was now rubbing elbows with reformers who had connections. These were serious times for third party movements, and the leaders were politically experienced people with strong followings. Better government movements were springing up everywhere, particularly in big cities, and were a natural feeder into the national third party movements.

In Boston, Harvard University President Charles Eliot was involved, as were Edward Filene, Robert Wood, and Joseph Eastman. The Boston "do gooders" were out in droves, but not to support the usual suspects in Democratic or Republican circles. New parties and candidates were emerging from the left and the right. Walsh had previously served in the Massachusetts legislature with two Socialists. Walsh was now seeing political fervor at the national level, but most of it was outside the mainstream of both major political parties, which were viewed with suspicion — the parties of "smoke-filled rooms" dominated by back-room deal making.

Walsh's generation offered some exciting political choices. The Bull Moose Party and the Progressive Party were grassroots movements. The prairie liberals were focused on the plight of the small farmer — something even an eastern city dweller could relate to. The liberalism espoused by La Follette could not be easily branded as European socialism or communism, because no one doubted the patriotism of the small farmer.

Roosevelt, on the other hand, played to discontent over corruption and cronyism within the Republican Party. That discontent ran deep. Roosevelt's "Rough Rider" style appealed to people, and Roosevelt was no mere "talking head." He had strong political credentials as former Governor of New York, as well as military credentials; and the Roosevelt family was rooted in political life. Teddy Roosevelt could generate his own publicity in an era when national media barely existed. Whatever national political reporting existed consisted mainly of one large city newspaper reporting on what was being said in another city, i.e., a quote from another city newspaper.

This was an ideal era for David I. Walsh to launch his own political career within the Democratic Party. Without any political machine of his own, he could declare his independence without being branded an outsider. The Republican and Democratic parties were desperately trying to hold onto their political base. They did not need to drive anyone out of the party, particularly an ethnic who was attractive to a growing base of Catholic voters. He couldn't be Italian, French, and Polish, too, but he was Catholic; something that united those groups.

This unsettled time in US politics was a perfect backdrop for the launching of Walsh's political career. Walsh had been defeated for reelection; he saw the power of money in politics, and understood it was essential. He still was not independently wealthy; however, his law practice did put him in regular contact with wealthy individuals. Unfortunately, they were mostly on the other side of the aisle from David I. Walsh in the courtroom, and most often of another political persuasion. However, Walsh was being noticed by the Boston Brahmins as an "up and comer." Webster's Unabridged Encyclopedic Dictionary defines a Brahmin as "a person of great culture and intellect, esp. a member of a New England family that is aristocratic." The Irish definition was snob. Walsh was rubbing elbows with the Brahmins within the legal system, albeit usually as an adversary. By the time he was done with his legal career, he had befriended some of the finest minds in Massachusetts, and persons of pedigree to boot. Adversarial relationships can build respect, and that was all Walsh wanted. He would, in many cases, get lifelong friendship from people in the opposition party as a by-product of his legal career.

There was as much disaffection within the ranks of the Republican Party as there was in the Democratic Party. It was not unusual for wealthy donors to contribute to both parties. Gradually, David I. Walsh built his own machine, and donors only had to deal with David. He was smart, educated, and proper, not like those other "ethnics," Curley, and "Honey Fitz," et al.

Being from a small town helped Walsh remain free of the entangling alliances that city politics engendered. It also gave him one advantage that Boston politicians lacked. Being so close to the central part of the state, he could easily organize the smaller cities of Worcester, Fitchburg, Leominster, and Gardner. The political world ended here. Worcester County was the last populous county in the state. West of Worcester, the counties were very rural, and with the exception of the City of Springfield, had no population base; and they remain so today. Visitors to New England have an image of Massachusetts that reflects Boston. They are often surprised, when they leave the beaten path, by the small, rural farm towns of western Massachusetts. The last edge of the political frontier would be controlled by Walsh.

Walsh was well positioned coming out of a Democratic primary. Now, he had to figure out how to present himself in a general election campaign. He had an advantage in a state that was about to become heavily Democratic. Until Walsh's political ascendancy, that advantage had been enjoyed by the Republican nominee. Walsh could safely assume his opponent in the final election would be a machine-supported candidate. Walsh needed no approval from party bosses to change positions and outflank his opponent. Immigrants were coming from Catholic countries in Europe and there was an influx of French Canadians, people most likely to be attracted to the Democratic Party. David I. Walsh's legal work among poor Irish, Italian, and French working class families, coupled with his representation of less than affluent Yankee farmers, would provide Walsh with the ideal political base for the times. This political base plus his perceived independence from big city machine politics made a potent combination.

James Michael Curley's favorite political trick was to thumb his nose at the Yankee establishment; that played well only with the ethnic vote. It often came across as "Too Irish," and did not resonate well with Italian, French, and Polish voters. Curley's remarks against the establishment made great press, but they were not always sufficient motivation to vote. And Curley was not going to get the Swamp Yankee vote, nor the Yankee establishment vote, either.

Honey Fitz, John F. Fitzgerald, was as Irish as they come, "as Irish as Paddy's pig." He did not have to crack any one-liners to alienate the Yankee vote; he simply had to open his mouth. John F. Fitzgerald had the same effect on voters as his grandson, Sen. Edward M. Kennedy, has today. People either loved him or hated him. Honey Fitz would not be able to expand his base beyond Boston.

The Democratic Party in Massachusetts was in tumult in 1912. Walsh decided to run for Lieutenant Governor. Governor Foss was running for reelection in the Democratic primary. Like most candidates for Lt. Governor, Walsh was unknown statewide. This would be his first attempt at name recognition. It was, as they say, a balanced ticket: Foss, the Yankee, and Walsh, the Catholic. Both Foss and Walsh won the primary, but Walsh ended up losing in the final election by 4,000 votes, 204,000 to 200,000; not bad for someone who is just starting to establish name recognition.

Who was David Ignatius Walsh? The politicians were all asking that question. This "up and comer" was a hot commodity. The Democratic Party of 1911-12 was not in the usual "wait until it's your turn" mode. Foss himself had switched from the Republican Party to the Democratic Party just two years earlier. The party was in flux, and almost any candidate had a chance. To add to the turmoil, this was a period when candidates served one-year terms. Campaigning was a permanent thing.

In 1912, Walsh was chosen as a delegate to the Democratic National Convention. He was a supporter of William Jennings Bryan. The battle for the presidential nomination, between William Jennings Bryan and Senator Bennett "Champ" Clark from Missouri, made the history books. Walsh was to witness a titanic struggle whose ending would dovetail nicely with Walsh's political identity. This would become one of a number of deadlocked conventions that Walsh would witness in the Democratic Party. Walsh would witness how deadlocks were broken; with deal making. Walsh would see the "Silver Tongued Orator" abandon his campaign with a dramatic announcement of his support for Woodrow Wilson, while he attacked the power brokers of Wall Street. Bryan's reference to Wall Street was indicative of the feeling prevalent at the time that both major parties, not just the Republicans, were tools of big business. The voters in both parties felt the eastern banking and finance establishments headquartered in New York City controlled both major parties by paying off the big city power brokers who dominated party and convention politics. Now Bryan was playing the role of power broker. Wilson promised Bryan the position of Secretary of State.

Bryan had broken the deadlock by throwing his support to Woodrow Wilson; thus, Walsh was now supporting the reformer, Woodrow Wilson, a former college president at Princeton, no less. Wilson may not have gotten Walsh's support unless Walsh had been drawn to the candidacy of Bryan first. He had his first chance to witness the politics of convention deal making, and he ended up supporting an Ivy Leaguer. Bryan could not have done Walsh a bigger favor. This would play well back in Boston. Walsh's "do-gooder" image was being reinforced. Walsh returned to Massachusetts, and in the fall was elected Lt. Governor by 40,000 votes over the incumbent. While the Lt. Governorship would not give Walsh any real power it would give him the statewide stage he needed to project his image as a reformer. He was already drawing the attention of the do-gooders on the fringe of the party, and would soon be enjoying the support of the party regulars, who, above all else, wanted a winner.

They say timing is everything in politics, and timing seemed exceedingly kind in these early years of David Walsh's political career, in great contrast to the tragedies in his family life. Everyone knew that the lieutenant governor's slot was a steppingstone. But to what? Governor or US Senator? Governor Foss was on his third one-year term, and could not run again. Law did not prevent Foss from running, but custom did.

US senators, at that time, were not elected by the people but rather by the state legislature. This was a horse trading environment, and Walsh had no horses to trade. Without powerful backers, he could deliver nothing. In the convention he had just witnessed, for instance, William Jennings Bryan would eventually become Wilson's Secretary of State, as his payback for supporting Wilson.

But Theodore Roosevelt, absent the Rough Riders, would ride to Walsh's rescue. Roosevelt had proposed the direct election of US senators through a constitutional amendment and the idea was catching on across the country. This was an era of reform and apparent decentralization of power. Smoke-filled rooms still existed, but the way things happened was beginning to change. State legislatures were quickly endorsing the change, and it appeared that the direct election of US senators would be a reality by the 1918 election. Walsh had time, but not much.

He would have to run for the open seat as governor, and that would serve as his springboard. Walsh's other options were to run for Senator in 1916 against the incumbent, Henry Cabot Lodge. In Massachusetts, the Lodges and the Kennedys were the two dynastic forces of the twentieth century. No other political families made honorable mention. Walsh was not about to challenge Lodge; but John F. Fitzgerald was.

As titans clashed, David I. Walsh was wise to stick to the sidelines. Walsh had no troops to commit to battle; the other side of the coin was that he had no "entangling alliances." He was on the verge of running for governor, yet had the freedom of being his own man. Without troops, he made no enemies.

While Walsh prepared to run for governor from his lieutenant governor's seat, the dynamics between he and Governor Foss heated up. After all, Foss, a millionaire, was planning to run again. With no statutory requirement against a fourth term, only a party rule, Foss could run as an Independent. Foss had a taste for power and with his money, he could indulge his tastes. He would not go quietly.

Walsh prepared to capture the Democratic nomination, and he won it easily. The fight would not be at Fanueil Hall, the site of the Democratic State Convention, since Foss could not run as a Democrat. The fight would be later, in the general election, against a Republican and the newly Independent Foss. This would be the third party Foss represented in five years.

Walsh was concerned that this third-party candidacy would hurt him. Foss, as sitting governor, had the pulpit. Walsh therefore mounted his campaign using new technology: the automobile. Boston politics were neighborhood politics; one might not even need a subway or trolley. But Walsh's base was central Massachusetts, and the use of the automobile was required: even if it meant changing three flat tires a day. Walsh would be the first candidate to make an attempt to blitz the towns west of Boston. A progressive-thinking campaigner? Hardly. A practical one, yes. Millionaire candidates like Foss or Lodge were unlikely to undergo the hardships of canvassing the towns outside of Boston; they would see little value in traveling such great distances for so few votes in sparsely populated towns.

Dorothy Wayman, in *David I. Walsh, Citizen Patriot*, recounts Walsh's methods of reaching the electorate, particularly the vast, rural areas outside of Boston. "Walsh with his lieutenants Frank Donahue and State Representative John F. Meaney of Blackstone quietly set about personally visiting every one of the more than 350 cities and towns of the state. It was grueling work, over dirt roads in primitive automobiles. An example was a trip during which a punctured tire beyond Webster forced him to walk two miles in the dark and the mud to Charlton, where he took a trolley car to the home of the nearest owner of an automobile; there he got a man out of bed to drive him, and finally reached a rally at Mechanics Hall, Worcester, at eleven o'clock that night, with a crowd of two thousand patiently waiting to hear him speak. Even on election day, motoring from Boston to Fitchburg to cast his vote, he was delayed by two punctures, was an hour late to dinner with the sisters in Clinton, and had to take a train back to Boston to receive the returns at his Hotel Lenox headquarters." [1]

Walsh had used the horse and buggy in his first campaign for state representative. The horseless carriage era had arrived, but not with the amenities that are now associated with the automobile. His trips more resembled Lindbergh's flights at the dawn of the aviation age, but without the glamour.

Walsh took to the automobile out of necessity. He was not rich. He would suffer the indignities of breakdowns, which were many, and endure long walks on muddy roads to the nearest farmhouse. The problem was scheduling rallies. It was difficult when no one knew when the candidate might arrive. Walsh had a powerful message to deliver in defense of labor and the workingman, and that was a message that would resonate with the poor Yankee farmer trying to eke out a living from the soil even if it was a Catholic doing the talking. And he would not run into the likes of Foss, or Lodge, or Curley, or Fitzgerald, toiling along in the dust. He had the audience to himself. The small towns were used to covering political events by reading the newspaper. They loved the attention Walsh gave them.

Walsh was sure that Foss would cut into his vote. The question was how much. However, a bigger question was a split in the Republican vote. The Republican primaries of that era were fiercely competitive, and a split at the national level caused by Teddy Roosevelt's Bull Moose Party was reflected at the state level as well. Indeed, Roosevelt's bid could not have been possible unless similar conditions existed at the local level. Perhaps the Republican split would outweigh the third-party candidacy of Foss. If Foss drained off too many Democratic votes, Walsh was in trouble. The Republican split in Massachusetts was not a mirror image of the split at the national level.

Good Government voters tended to congregate within the liberal wing of the Republican Party. The "Goo Goos," as James Michael Curley was fond of calling them, would be supporting Republicans in most primaries. This year, the split in the Republican Party had most of those votes going to the Progressive, Charles Sumner Bird. The Republican standard bearer was Augustus Gardner, Congressman, and just incidentally son-in-law of Henry Cabot Lodge. Political dynasties are not a recent thing in Massachusetts politics. The political "machine"

---

[1] Ibid., 48.

was only a modern version of the family dynasty.

David Ignatius Walsh was standing bare-handed, no party machine and no prominent family name. The "Goo Goos" within Democratic circles tended to be supporters of William Jennings Bryan; but Democratic politics had little room for "good government" types. Democrats were interested in jobs, not reform. Democrats were interested in economic opportunity, and quite often that meant pork barrel politics. Bringing home the bacon was far more important to Democrats, the party of immigrants, than Republicans.

Walsh's positioning in the election could not have been better. Today's "spin doctors" or pollsters could not have created a more perfect union. Walsh would get a large share of the good government vote, usually reserved for a Republican. Walsh would get the labor vote, usually reserved for a machine candidate. Walsh would get the Swamp Yankee vote, a vote never reserved for a Catholic. And poor Joe Foss would be ousted from his chair in humiliating fashion, garnering just 20,000 votes!

Foss's career ran its course long before term limits became fashionable. However, he ran into a political maelstrom when he violated the custom of the day by seeking more than three terms. The term limit issue had little to do with good government, and everything to do with many candidates waiting in the wings. Foss showed bad form and bad judgment — he would have no idea how bad until election night. Gardner, the Republican, would garner 116,000 votes; Bird the Progressive candidate, would take 127,000 votes; and Walsh, the Democrat, would take the election with 183,000 votes. If such records were kept, Foss may have turned in the worst record by an incumbent since Caesar's last day in the senate.

"David I. Walsh found himself Governor-elect of the Commonwealth of Massachusetts by the largest plurality ever polled by a Democrat in the preponderantly Republican, Yankee, and Protestant state — 57,558 votes. He was the first of his kind to reign under the golden dome of the State House on Beacon Hill. Moreover, the victory had come to him against the opposition, open or tacit, of the old-line Democratic machine politicians of Boston. He had campaigned for clean politics, honest administration, and progressive legislation; and the people had given him their accolade. He had run ahead of every man on the Democratic ticket in votes, though he had brought the whole ticket through with him in victory... the political cartoon of the day...showed him, Roman profile, and figure clad in toga, guiding a spirited team behind a Roman chariot to victory, in a race in which Charles S. Bird was driving a gawky Bull Moose, "Gussie" Gardner was a diminutive mahout on a G.O.P. elephant, and the mustached Governor Foss in the distance came tearing along like a messenger boy on a motorcycle."[2]

By Bush-Gore standards, this was an absolute rout. To win a four-way race by this margin was unthinkable. To have such a margin result in the election of the first Catholic in Massachusetts' history is even more remarkable. The mold had been broken. The year was 1913.

Walsh could take great credit later in his career for the role he played in barring discrimination in federal contracts. He would never forget the discrimination that many Irish, Italians, French, Poles, and Jews faced as recent immigrants. Walsh was fully aware that he was able to leap the great divide of religion, while many of his countrymen and women could not. In later chapters, the prominent role of Walsh on defense issues will be discussed. The Irish of today have largely forgotten the early steps taken to bar discrimination based on religion or ancestry. Rather than sympathize with many Black leaders in their efforts to bar discrimination based on the color of one's skin, today's Irish barely seem to realize the battles fought by a previous generation.

As David I. Walsh began his first term as Governor, Woodrow Wilson was in the White House. Walsh had a smorgasbord of choices as he set off for Boston. Having run a la carte, he had plenty of choices without ever having to leave the Democratic Party.

When he arrived in Boston, he was prepared to govern as a reformer. He was unprepared for the social scene. While he anticipated exercising his gubernatorial duties, he did not anticipate the endless gossip about his private life. He could not simply rule from the golden dome; he had to be out and about, and Boston was a demanding social scene. As a highly eligible bachelor his personal life would be subject to speculation. "The few occasions when Walsh, being human, yielded to social invitations, stirred up a furor of gossip in Boston. The society columnists were forever alternately speculating that the handsome bachelor's engagement would soon be published, or else authoritatively denying it. The most persistent of these rumors centered on Mrs. Horatio Nelson Slater, a very wealthy widow who occupied a brownstone chateau in Back Bay at Beacon and Gloucester Streets. The Slater estate had been a lucrative client of Walsh & Walsh, which probably explains why David Walsh accepted an invitation to a ball to be given by Mrs. Slater on February 19." The gossip continued in the Boston newspapers. The town of Clinton was small; but Boston was a fishbowl. "The last straw was when Mabel Slater remodeled her Beacon Street library into an 'oratory' like Isabella Stuart Gardner's palace chapel in the Fenway; and all the

---

[2] Ibid., 51.

world said knowingly that Mrs. Slater must be turning Catholic to marry Dave Walsh."[3] Walsh soon found the publicity stifling.

Walsh would be a champion of women's rights long before such a cause was popular, and signed the first law allowing the appointment of women police officers. He actively courted the women's vote even before suffrage. On May 2, 1914, Walsh had the opportunity to review over ten thousand women marching in Boston in support of the suffragette cause. Having signed the bill regarding women police officers, he was immersed in the most liberal cause of the moment. He had the pulpit as governor, which made burnishing his liberal credentials that much easier. He would now have entrée into the progressive Boston social scene, one that was not at all divorced from politics. It was a well entrenched social movement dating as far back as the abolitionist cause, and currently encompassed the good government types, women's groups, the Anti-Saloon League and, lest one forget, the peace advocates that were often more rooted in churches than in the political parties themselves. In this era of peace, they were not the hottest cause in Boston, but in a few years would become so.

---

[3] Ibid., 56.

CHAPTER 3. A TIME TO GOVERN

Walsh's term as governor would mark the transformation of state bureaucracy from appointive commissions to full time commissioners. This marked the beginning of professional administration of government agencies. This was heartily endorsed by the "good government" proponents but was met with tepid endorsement in Democratic circles. The prior approach, with many members of a commission running a state agency, and voting as a committee, resulted in more frequent and numerous opportunities for patronage.

This new approach would mean the appointment of one single administrator, a powerful commissioner appointed by the Governor. The professional staffing movement was well under way when Walsh arrived in the Governor's office. Walsh's timing was right again. His reformer image was now being polished, with brickbats coming only from the Democrats. These Democratic salvos, coming from the likes of the Curley machine, only helped burnish his image more. Republican opposition was more muted, based mostly on their desire to regain the governor's seat. It was difficult for Republicans to criticize Walsh, for the good government types within the Republican Party had been preaching this kind of reform for years. The professional bureaucrat was about to make an appearance in Massachusetts, and it might even be a Harvard graduate.

In Walsh's first term he had to grapple with infrastructure issues, particularly the railroads, but Walsh would also be turning the page on transportation. Governors had been wrestling with problems regarding railroads since the iron horse was invented. Walsh would not forget his love affair with the automobile and the role it played in his election; his love of the automobile would become both personal and political. He asked to increase state borrowing to build highways to the western part of the state. This was a pioneering move, very early in the age of the automobile and, in a sense, Walsh could claim to be father to the state highway system. The fact that his own political fortune was linked to the western part of the state should not diminish his legacy. Leadership and personal self-interest often intersect. Other candidates could have taken advantage of the roadways; the fact that they did not helped Walsh.

On the national scene, Walsh's hero, William Jennings Bryan, was having a falling out with Woodrow Wilson. Bryan was opposed to the possible entrance of the United States into World War I. He felt strongly that America should keep out of this European war and when it was apparent that Woodrow Wilson was determined to go forward, Bryan resigned as Secretary of State. Massachusetts Republicans derided Bryan as a way of indirectly attacking Walsh. Walsh was strongly identified with Bryan, and Bryan's oratory kept him in the news.

The irony in these attacks is that the Republican Party was as strongly isolationist as Bryan, particularly in the West; but they were not about to pass up an opportunity to tie Walsh to Bryan, particularly since they were soul mates on so many issues.

The patronage politicians within the Democratic Party were squeezing Walsh. They were not getting what they had come to expect. The professionalization of the state agencies was limiting patronage opportunities. Patronage is what keeps a machine going, and Walsh was not playing the game. Progressives of all stripes were supporting Walsh, but the 'Goo Goos' could not deliver the votes. The President of Harvard University, Dr. Charles Eliot, publicly endorsed Walsh.

Walsh had established university extension courses for working people, and educators took note. The university extension system would provide opportunities to people who did not have the financial wherewithal or the connections to get into Harvard. While the courses were primarily career-related, this would provide a way up for thousands of Massachusetts citizens. Walsh was fully appreciative of the opportunities that had been afforded him at Holy Cross College, and thankful for the help his sisters had provided. Not all families could do that. Sen. Henry Cabot Lodge had invited Walsh to speak to the Harvard Alumni Association. "Walsh was glad to make the acquaintance with the Harvard men, because he was desirous of enlisting their support and co-operation in the project nearest and dearest to his heart, university extension courses....The suggestion, contained in his inaugural address, had been broached in detail at the banquet of the Massachusetts Institute of Technology alumni in January, with President Richard C. MacLaurin listening as Walsh spoke." [1]

Perhaps Walsh's greatest satisfaction was passage of a workers compen-

---

[1] Ibid., 62.

sation bill in 1914 that had languished in the legislature since he had introduced it in 1900 when he was a representative in the House. Walsh had spent his career defending the rights of the worker. The Bill provided that in all actions seeking damages, whether civil or criminal, the persons killed or injured should be presumed to have been in the exercise of due care, with the burden of proving contributory negligence put on the defendant. The unions were inspired to march their Labor Day parade past the State House, cheering Walsh, in 1914, after purposely routing it away from Governor Foss the year before.

Walsh would also face calamity in 1914. He had reorganized the Massachusetts National Guard, which had been in disarray, and the Yankee Division would shortly go on to fame in World War I. When the infamous Salem fire broke out, the town was destroyed and over 20,000 were left homeless but Walsh's deployment of the reorganized Yankee Division stopped a witch hunt. Walsh's response left a good impression with the voter, and raised the image of the Yankee Division at the same time. Walsh had demonstrated that he could act under crisis. Many political officeholders are judged by their personal response to calamity, but Walsh was seen as neither a grandstander nor as a Governor who offered a tepid response. His measured response struck the right chord with the public, and President Wilson soon followed with a promise of federal aid. Walsh faced the worst crisis any Governor in Massachusetts had ever faced, a nightmare for any politician, but generally received high marks for handling of the situation.

In a strange irony, during his first term as governor Walsh would encounter a person who would become his lifelong nemesis. Their lives would be intertwined from the very beginning of their public careers to the bitter end. Their paths first crossed when Governor Walsh was to christen the Cape Cod Canal. A project originally envisioned by George Washington, the canal was finally completed in Walsh's first term. Once the canal was completed, commercial ships from Rhode Island could sail directly into the outer reaches of Boston harbor without having to round Cape Cod. A festive ceremony was planned to inaugurate the new route. Governor Walsh and Mr. and Mrs. Belmont, guests of honor, rode through the Buzzards Bay entrance onboard the steamer *Rose Standish*, escorted by the US Navy Destroyer *MacDougall*. Among the spectators on the *MacDougall* were Franklin D. Roosevelt, Assistant Secretary of the Navy, and several ladies. This last detail foreshadows something of FDR's personal life that was hidden from public view, but was hardly a secret in Roosevelt's insular social life.

Riding with Walsh at the time was Augustus P. Belmont, a New York financier whom he praised for combining money and public interest in the construction of this vital opening. (Walsh would go on to support two New York

Governors, Al Smith, and later, Franklin Delano Roosevelt.) On this beautiful July day, Walsh certainly could not foresee that the man on the destroyer would become his mortal enemy, and that his own sex life would later explode on the front pages while FDR's "ladies parties" would be hidden from public view.

Walsh's good fortune regarding political timing was about to change. Few governors could expect to have their first year studded with such accomplishments. While circumstances of the state and national political scene had always seemed to benefit Walsh as an independent candidate, he would soon find out that independence meant standing alone. Squeezed on one side by Republicans and from within the Democratic Party by the big city bosses, James Michael Curley and Martin Lomasney, Walsh was vulnerable. The split in the Republican Party between Republicans and Progressives had already led to the third-party candidacy of Charles Sumner Bird as a Progressive. The split in 1913 helped Walsh. In an era when governors had to run every year, alliances had to be rebuilt continually. Now, the year was 1915. There would be no Republican split this time. Samuel McCall secured the Republican nomination. An amiable man, he would not have to deal with the split in the Republican Party, and he would get indirect help from the Democratic city bosses who withheld their support from Walsh.

Walsh would lose by 6,000 votes, a respectable showing under the circumstances. Walsh learned how quickly political currents could change, and he realized that job performance often had very little to do with being returned to office. Yet, Walsh would remain an incurable idealist his entire life.

Walsh could not have changed his political strategy even if he wanted to. No matter how organized he was, he was no match for the Boston machines of James Michael Curley and 'Honey Fitz' Fitzgerald. He had traveled his own road to power, and would have to continue down that road. He would simply have to take advantage of the solo traveler routine. He could change directions without getting anyone's approval. He had finished two one-year terms, served with distinction, and now he had a chance to earn some money. He also would have a chance to travel on his own, without carrying the state's agenda with him. Now was the time to see the world he had only read about.

In 1916, the Senate Judiciary Committee was holding hearings on a Supreme Court nomination. Woodrow Wilson had nominated Boston jurist Louis Brandeis for the Supreme Court. The long knives were coming out. The former Princeton professor (and President) had dared to nominate a Jew. Highly regarded in legal circles, no one questioned Brandeis's credentials. David Walsh would travel to Washington to confer with the Chairman of the Senate Judiciary

Committee, Senator Thomas Walsh from Montana, and offer testimony in support of Brandeis' confirmation. This was not the beginning of the two Walshes' friendship, but perhaps it was the first public issue that they worked on together.

This Senator Tom Walsh was a firebrand; not someone easily pushed around. Later in his career, he stood up to politically-inspired investigations by J. Edgar Hoover, and survived them all. In 1933, he was nominated to be Attorney General by Franklin Delano Roosevelt, which meant he would become J. Edgar Hoover's boss. But, that was not to be. Thomas Walsh died on a train, traveling to the presidential inauguration in Washington, D.C. Strangely enough, there was an FBI agent on the train at the time of Walsh's death. Maybe that was just J. Edgar Hoover's method of greeting his new boss. Walsh had his new and quite young Cuban wife in tow. There is no doubt that Hoover received a juicy report. What the public received was rumors, rumors "that the president-elect intended to name Senator Thomas Walsh of Montana attorney general... [and that] Walsh had confided to friends that his first act on taking office would be to fire J. Edgar Hoover." And, indeed, on February 28, 1933, Roosevelt announced Tom Walsh's appointment. That same day Walsh, located by the *New York Times* in Daytona Beach, Florida, confirmed that he had accepted the appointment and stated that "he would reorganize the Department of Justice when he assumed office, probably with almost completely new personnel."[2] The implication was that Hoover was about to be fired. Hoover had to have seen this coming; he was not one to be caught unawares. While candidates for public office in those days used "advance men," Hoover was using his field agents in a similar capacity.

But in 1916, this was the man presiding over the nomination hearings of Louis Brandeis. Thomas Walsh faced a barrage of negative testimony against Brandeis and the confirmation process dragged on for months. Thomas Walsh's temperament was perfect for the job. He did not give a damn; and he was Chairman of the Senate Judiciary Committee.

David I. Walsh went on record to support Brandeis. He addressed his statement, written in Washington after his inquiry into the situation, to the chairman: "It seems to me a public duty to write to you in regard to the appointment of Mr. Louis D. Brandeis of Massachusetts, as a Justice of the Supreme Court of the United States. During the two years that I was Governor of Massachusetts, and the years preceding them, I had repeated occasions to observe this man and his high ideals and common sense; his wide practical knowledge of

---

[2] Gentry, Curt, *J. Edgar Hoover, The Man and the Secrets*, W.W. Norton, New York, London, 1991, 153.

the law; his extensive understanding of the business, economic, and social problems of our time; his sound judgment and ardent devotion to the public welfare." David Walsh followed his conscience, and for the next twenty years would have an appreciative and warm friend on the Supreme Court bench."[3] Walsh and Brandeis were the two most prominent ethnics in the Massachusetts political and government arena during that era. While much of their friendship was based on a common set of political beliefs, their shared professional experiences cemented their relationship.

The Brandeis confirmation hearings signaled that ethnic minorities were gaining some influence. Religious bigotry from the Boston bluebloods, forever touting their connections to the original Mayflower crowd, was starting to sound out of place. It is ironic that a group that left England for religious freedom had become the most intolerant group in America, with anti-Catholic prejudice extending well into the 1960s, especially in manufacturing and banking. Indeed, the formation of the other New England states, particularly Rhode Island and Connecticut, was due in large part to a break away from the religious intolerance of the Pilgrims. Walsh and Brandeis well understood what the other faced.

A proclamation signed by ex-President William Howard Taft and many other political, judicial and business leaders, including the President of Harvard, A. Lawrence Lowell, called Brandeis "not a fit person" for the job. They might as well have said "Jew," since they did not question his qualifications. Walsh, as a self-made man, had sidestepped the effects of religious discrimination but was keenly aware that others could not. Walsh's support of Brandeis was not geared to the opinion poll. His Jewish constituency was infinitesimal. His political base was Irish, French, Italians, Polish, and Swamp Yankee; anti-Semitism could be found amongst those groups as well. Walsh was proving his independence once more. He may have been out of office, but he still was exercising leadership, far more leadership than the President of Harvard, A. Lawrence Lowell, who had stood against him.

---

[3] Wayman, Dorothy. *David I. Walsh, Citizen-Patriot.* Bruce Publishing, Milwaukee, 1952. p. 89.

CHAPTER 4. THE INTERREGNUM

Back in Massachusetts, religious intolerance was still strong. A heated debate was occurring regarding public aid to parochial schools. Since the middle of the 19th century, Catholic parishes had been springing up all over the Commonwealth, particularly in the medium-sized cities of Worcester, Fitchburg, Springfield, Lowell, and Lawrence. Many of these towns were textile towns, reflecting the economy of the times. These Catholic parishes were building schools that fully met the standards of the public school curriculum. The descendants of the Pilgrims thought it made good sense to keep Catholic youth — mill urchins — in their own schools, since it did not cost the taxpayer a dime.

However, as Catholic schools grew in the 1800s, the Protestant majority got nervous. Since they had been funding private schools for years, most notably that Protestant bastion, Harvard College, concern was growing that Catholics might soon request funds. In 1855, the state constitution was amended to prohibit the use of public funds for any private school. Harvard would have to go it alone. The Catholics were coming, and Katie, bar the door!

The issue would be revisited in 1917. A Constitutional Convention had been convened. David I. Walsh was a delegate. Aid to parochial schools was a hot issue, raising strong feelings on both sides. Sensing the strong possibility of sectarian strife, at least within the political arena, Walsh voted against the measure, invoking the ire of the Catholic clergy. He was not the only Catholic voting against the measure, but his leadership on this issue must have been extremely painful, since he was so close to his Catholic roots, particularly his Jesuit teachers at Holy Cross College. While Harvard College had fed at the public trough for over two centuries, Holy Cross College would never see a dime. But, Walsh wanted to ensure that religious intolerance was not enflamed. One could argue that his position was politically expedient. After all, his constituency cut across the religious chasm, in that he represented the heavily Catholic labor vote, as well as the Swamp Yankee, a group that had no great love for their rich Protestant brothers in Boston. The groups were united by class, but divided by religion. Walsh was the first politician in Massachusetts to establish this broad a political base.

He would not lose the Catholic vote over this issue, for Catholic voters had nowhere else to go. Many Catholics agreed that it was not worth enflaming religious intolerance by continuing the fight. Given Walsh's established record for tough votes, one has to give him a free pass on this. He had demonstrated at this point in his career that his convictions governed his decisions. While separation of church and state had not been an issue during two centuries of funding Protestant schools, it now became one.

Walsh had not given up his plan to run for the US Senate in 1918. Being out of office had some advantages in preparing for the next move. This election would be the first direct election of a United States Senator. He could have run earlier, against Henry Cabot Lodge, but sidestepped that election. He knew how popular Lodge was, for after the Fitzgeralds and the Kennedys, no family had as tight a grip on Massachusetts's politics as the Lodge clan.

While Lodge would not be a factor in the 1918 race, already having secured his own senate seat, he would have an indirect effect. His clashes with Woodrow Wilson about World War I were prominently covered in Boston newspapers. The debate of the day was whether the US should enter World War I, and Walsh would switch gears.

Walsh's earlier stances on foreign policy could only be described as isolationist. His hero, William Jennings Bryan, had resigned as Wilson's Secretary of State because of his deeply held belief that the United States should not involve itself in the affairs of Europe. Walsh's other hero, "Fighting Bob" La Follette, was also opposed to the United States participation in the war.

Walsh would cast his lot with Wilson and support the US entrance in the war. This gave him a stark contrast with Lodge's position, and continued his alliance with the progressive Wilson. While distancing himself from Bryan and La Follette, he still was identified with the most important progressive of the moment: the President of the United States. As history shows, a certain degree of political opportunism may be necessary if one is to win, or stay in, office; Walsh was judicious in choosing when and how much he displayed.

The position of Walsh on the eve of the United States entry into the war runs counter to all his prior positions, and that of his political idols. However, by that time, it was clear that the United States would soon enter the war, no matter what anyone did. Walsh strongly believed in Wilson's domestic policies, and it would be awkward, to say the least, to align himself with Wilson's domestic initiatives and yet oppose him on his most important foreign policy decision. As a freshman senator, he would have little say, anyway. Wilson, himself, had been neutral earlier in the war, and a change in position on Walsh's part could be chalked up to changing circumstances. Walsh could not be accused of changing positions because his prior job as governor did not require him to speak out on foreign policy issues. Walsh strongly believed in Wilson, and did not view him as a war hawk. And by that year, with the war virtually at an end, it was widely believed that US entry would quickly terminate the conflict.

Walsh was being branded as a "follower of Wilson" — not a bad moniker to carry around, since Walsh already had a strong identity as a progressive from his prior stint as governor. There is no record that Wilson and Walsh orchestrated political announcements, but Wilson was openly campaigning for the election of Democrats. It is probable that White House staffers were making Walsh aware of any presidential announcements, and it was up to Walsh to take advantage of them any way he could. Walsh was about to make his first and only pronouncement concerning intervention in European affairs.

Walsh campaigned for senator in 1918, with the same fervor and zeal as Harry Truman did for president in 1948, only using a different mode of transportation. A whistle-stop campaign in Massachusetts would not get one very far off the beaten path. Walsh aimed to visit once more every city and town in the Commonwealth. That meant over 350 stops. Walsh would heavily work the areas not covered by big politics. He was counting on the fact that the city machines would not openly attack him. Because of Walsh's strong support by labor, the city machines would not go public in their attacks. The firm of Walsh & Walsh had a long tradition of representing the interests of the workingman. This could help Walsh offset the antipathy of the machine politicians.

The automobile would remain Walsh's closest ally. From his earlier campaign, Walsh's supporters had perfected the routine. The automobile of the day, and the roads, were not built for long distance driving; go too fast, and you were sure to end up with a punctured tire as you hit the next pothole. Walsh would be ferried from town to town, and transferred from one vehicle to the next to assure his timely appearance at a rally.

One of the major issues in the campaign was veterans insurance following World War I. Walsh had championed veterans insurance, while his opponent, John Weeks, had proposed cutting the benefit. Walsh had identified with the veteran very early in his career, before veterans had become a significant voting bloc.

Veterans groups greeted him warmly, and counted on his almost automatic support for issues those groups championed.

In November 1918, Walsh was the winner by 20,000 votes, the first US Senator elected directly by the people of Massachusetts, and the first Catholic as well. Walsh benefited again by a third party candidate, Thomas Lawson who garnered 21,000 votes, just about the margin of victory. The automobile and the city vote did it for Walsh.

Walsh became the first Democrat elected in Massachusetts since the formation of the Republican Party. Massachusetts was no liberal state at the turn of the century. Any choice between liberal and conservative occurred in the Republican primary. The ultimate tribute to Walsh's victory was paid by Frank B. Hall, Chairman of the Massachusetts Republican Party. Hall said, frankly: "The loss of the election by Senator Weeks was the greatest calamity that has befallen the Republican Party in Massachusetts history. There is no one to gainsay that he, Walsh, is the greatest vote-getter the Democratic Party has ever produced in Massachusetts — they did not dream that even with his great personality and his strong appeal to the ordinary citizen, Walsh could possibly defeat Weeks who typified the ideal Republican with an unassailable public record."[1] Apparently, the Republicans did not expect to lose. The WASP vote for Walsh in the central and western parts of the state stunned the Republican Party, and the realization that they could not take the WASP vote for granted was driven home by Walsh's performance at the polls.

The House of Representatives had always been called "the people's house," but a reform championed by Teddy Roosevelt would now make the Senate a domicile for the voter. Walsh's election signaled to the party regulars that this new reform was more than window dressing, and was a step that weakened the grip of party bosses.

---

[1] Ibid., 101-102.

CHAPTER 5. MR. SMITH GOES TO WASHINGTON

With the election of David I. Walsh to the United States Senate, Massachusetts politics had changed forever. The Republican Party would remain strong, and its strength would help Walsh. The liberal wing of the Republican Party would remain a potent force, and serve to split the party. Up until Walsh's election, the Republicans did not have to worry about the general election. Whatever split occurred in the Republican primary had no consequences in November. Now the Republican liberals had something else to worry about. They would have to battle to win the soul of the Republican Party in September, and then face a Democrat who had captured the imagination of liberals of all stripes, particularly those of the working class. "Mr. Smith," albeit a Catholic, was going to Washington.

On March 4, 1919, Senator David Ignatius Walsh was sworn into office. He was escorted to his oath by the senior senator, Henry Cabot Lodge. Lodge, short and frail, and a member of the old guard introduced the tall, robust newcomer up the aisle, inaugurating an era when the old families had to begin sharing the levers of power — at least, to some extent.

World War I ended shortly after the United States arrived on the scene, and events were moving at a fast pace. Woodrow Wilson proposed ratifying the founding of the League of Nations. World War I was supposed to have been "the war to end all wars." The covenant of the League of Nations was sent to the Senate in July 1919. Wilson's vision of a new world would have the League of Nations resolving disputes around the globe and maintaining an era of peace. This grand idea was a tough sell, however. Wilson was trying to pull the United States away from its isolationist roots. Americans, by and large, were afraid of entangling alliances and most immigrants were more than willing to leave European troubles behind.

In February 1919, Walsh gave a speech that showed early indications of his foreign policy views. Speaking on the topic of China and Japan, he expressed outrage that Britain and France had handed Shantung and the German possessions in the Orient to Japan as a reward for its role in the war. In a country that was obsessed with Europe, Walsh was showing an interest in Asia. He would remain among only a handful of senators who would be concerned with the fate of yellow-skinned people. Walsh's concern for the rights of foreign peoples would become even clearer during the peace treaty sessions of Versailles. While the public would come to believe that the "rape of China" should be placed at Japan's doorstep, Walsh was angrier at Japan's partners in crime in the Pacific. Japan and Great Britain would remain close allies throughout the 1920s. Walsh did not believe that Great Britain had any right to give away China's sovereignty to Japan. The "peace table" would remain a euphemism for "war table" for years to come.

Woodrow Wilson was about to find out that this freshman senator was a little different. While Walsh may have been on the other side of the tracks, he, like the Yankees, was strongly isolationist. Walsh may have been a liberal and they may have been conservative, but when it came to foreign policy they were on common ground. Wilson was counting on Democrats for support and hoped to win enough support from Republicans to pass the League of Nations. Wilson was reading the Democrats wrong, and in particular, David I. Walsh. Many liberal Democrats had questions about the League of Nations, and it was already stalling in the Senate when Walsh came out strongly against it. Wilson was expecting support, and was stung by Walsh's outspoken opposition.

The citizenry assumed Walsh's opposition to the League of Nations was based on "the Irish thing." The United States had helped liberate the peoples of Europe from subjugation, but with the League of Nations the Irish would remain subject to British rule. The Easter Uprising in 1916, with all its bloodshed, had been put on hold because of Britain's involvement in World War I. Walsh was painted as anti-British because of his Irish heritage. Surely he did not act so strongly, most thought, because of his concern for Asians; but Walsh's recent trip to the Philippines was still fresh in his mind. Either way, his standing with the mainstream Protestant voters in Massachusetts would not be diminished at all, for they had little interest in the affairs of Europe or the Pacific region.

Walsh spoke strongly against the League of Nations with a fervor that stunned Wilson. Freshman senators usually took a backbench. Taking on the President of one's own party was not to be done lightly and certainly carried political risk. Walsh was incensed at Article 10, which dealt with colonial possessions. Not only would Ireland remain under colonial rule, but also the Philippines, Korea, Shantung, and Egypt.

Walsh never got much support in the Senate for any concern for the Pacific. His fellow senators had the same level of interest as Walsh's constituents in Massachusetts: none. The Anglophile bent in the Senate meant that Europe was all that mattered. Walsh would find a broader view in academia, and particularly from his Jesuit friends who had traveled the world. It was the Jesuits that convinced Walsh to visit the Philippines. Walsh had already gone on record as supporting Philippine independence. He was genuinely concerned about the China question and, in general, the question of "self determination" of peoples around the world.

Walsh had always leaned towards isolationism. On the campaign trail Walsh had supported Wilson's preparedness for entry into World War I. However, Wilson was playing a game too. On the campaign trail, Wilson had campaigned for "preparing for war" — not going to war. He waited until after the elections to do that.

There was nothing in the League of Nations document to win Walsh over. Walsh questioned why Great Britain had six votes and the United States one: a British dominance that bothered many people. The freshman senator from Massachusetts was not following his party leader, and Wilson was furious. Walsh may not have expected the intensity of the reaction. The Democratic leadership pounced. The religion card would be played with a viciousness Walsh had not seen in his political life. Politics back in Massachusetts was a 'blueblood sport' not a blood sport, but the bluebloods there were a genteel sort, not given to open name-calling. Walsh had expected that the Democratic Party, the party of the immigrant, led by a former college president and a progressive, no less, would treat dissent in a more professional manner.

Walsh's opening remarks indicate that he did expect some retaliation from President Wilson.

> "My objection to Article Ten is that it perpetuates a status quo condition and removes the opportunity in the future for the readjustment of boundary lines or the evolutions of races or peoples....I approach this question of a League of Nations with great sympathy, with exceedingly great sympathy. I expect to vote for a covenant for a League of Nations...I have supported President Wilson in every political campaign. I have been in hearty sympathy with his views and opinions. I think he is the greatest political leader with the most progressive and forward looking thought and political program upon public questions of our time. I well know what would happen by taking an attitude contrary to the opinion of the administration. I know that it is purposed by some to take from me all political patronage that a Democratic Senator might have in the Commonwealth of Massachusetts...I know now more than ever that I was right, especially since I have not heard one Senator on this floor justify the Shantung provision of this covenant; and I have not heard one senator on this side of the chamber speak in justification of the inequalities of this treaty which gives in the

League six representatives to Great Britain and one to the United States..."[1]

Walsh had apparently been warned beforehand what would happen. His attack on Great Britain as the motivating force for the League of Nations brought the glare of publicity. Despite the pressure from the White House, Walsh was willing to give up all the patronage for his convictions. Wilson would hold him to the bargain, and even appoint Republicans in Massachusetts to embarrass Walsh. The split was permanent. Perhaps Wilson's training as college president had honed his skills at presenting a dispassionate exterior while the hand-to-hand combat went on behind the scenes. Perhaps Wilson was particularly upset that Walsh was raising a curtain, exposing the League of Nations as just another colonial relic and not the progressive idea that was being touted by Wilson. This was to be Wilson's legacy and a mighty sensitive issue for him. Wilson was counting on liberal votes; conservatives the likes of Henry Cabot Lodge were unlikely to buy it.

However, the day was not over for Walsh. What came from party leaders next was stinging. Walsh would see religious prejudice taken to new heights. The dignity of Boston Brahmins prevented the kind of exchange that other regions of the country would indulge in; there, prejudice against Catholics was widespread and needed no cloak of dignity. In his remarks objecting to the subjugation of peoples in the covenant, Walsh closed by saying: "If I believe, as I do believe, that the subject races of Europe are debarred from a hearing under this covenant, I ask what your opinion of me would be if I sat there, an offspring from people of a subject race, and did not cry out in protest…"

John Sharp Williams, a senator from Mississippi, provided that opinion. As Walsh closed, Williams interrupted. "If I took down this language correctly it was literally this, 'I stand here as the offspring of a subject race.' The senator ought to stand here as the Senator of the United States. He ought to stand everywhere in the United States as an American citizen in that single capacity and in no dual capacity. He ought to stand here as an American Senator regardless of all questions of love or hatred existing now or hitherto in Europe. He announces himself that he stands here…. as the subject of an offspring race. If every Jew in America…If every Jugo-Slav, every Hungarian…every German and every Austrian stood here in that capacity…we would have as hyphenates some ten or twenty million Irish- Americans, another twenty millions Slovak-Americans, some thirty million of some other sort of American, reducing the real plain 'Americans' not only to a minority but to a minor quantity. We would not be a nation

---

[1] Ibid., 116.

homogenous and of one history, aim and policy as fellow nationals, but as a pot-pourri of indigestible ingredients…." [2]

Walsh should never have asked for an opinion. While he truly thought it an important occasion to debate an important issue, he was not expecting an attack on his religion or race. Senator Williams accused Walsh of using 'Jesuitical pretense'. There is no record of what Walsh's Jesuit teachers thought of that reference, but Walsh was learning that perhaps Boston politics were more genteel than the national stage.

Walsh's arrival in the Senate in 1918 was akin to Harry Truman's first term as President. All kinds of issues were cropping up, and at breakneck speed. Out of the ashes of World War I, a new world order was coming, or, at least, such was believed to be the case. While the "War to end all Wars" was being fought, many issues had been put on hold. Now, the Senate would be a busy place. The British had put the Irish question on hold when they entered the war; America, too, had deferred certain domestic questions. The momentous issues now coming to the fore make dry reading in the pages of history books, but they were issues forged in the heat of the political arena and Walsh was an able blacksmith.

In June of 1919, the suffragettes had finally completed their lengthy crusade for the women's right to vote. The US Senate was considering the measure, and it was making its way through 48 state legislatures, and would need ratification by two thirds of the states. Walsh had championed women's right to vote, and now was in a position to vote for it in Washington. His timing could not have been better. Walsh was able to bask in the glow of the most progressive issue of the time, and it was only his first year as Senator.

As was the custom during times of war, organized labor could not press its demands too hard during the war lest it be accused of being unpatriotic. Now, the hottest labor issue in the land would happen back in Boston. Calvin Coolidge had been elected Governor of Massachusetts, and what was about to happen would catapult the taciturn politician to national prominence. It has been said (but not documented) that a loquacious female admirer approached Coolidge at a White House reception, and said that a female friend had bet her that she could not get three words out of the President. Coolidge replied, "She won."

Whether this story is true or not, Coolidge's lack of personality would help him during the Boston Police Strike. In September 1919, the strike began. The issue of the day was whether public safety personnel had the right to strike. Within a few days, looting and vandalism broke out. "Cool Cal" called in the National

---

[2] Ibid., 116-117

Guard to patrol the streets of Boston. The civilian rioting in the downtown business district made national news, and Coolidge was cast as the guardian of the gate, keeping the Vandals out of Rome..

This quickly became a national issue, and popular support was firmly behind Coolidge. The riots had been a public relations disaster for the American Federation of Labor, and as colorless as Coolidge was, he was credited with saving Western civilization. Coolidge had saved America from "creeping socialism" and "anarchy." Most of those labor types were ethnics, and mostly Catholic.

Timing was everything. Just three years earlier, Walsh had been receiving accolades for his performance as Governor of Massachusetts, the first Catholic and first Democrat elected since the formation of the Republican Party. While Walsh's career had been on a fast track, Coolidge's career was on a bullet train. Coolidge was a low-profile governor, but he would leapfrog ahead of Walsh to the Vice Presidency in 1921 and upon the death of Warren G. Harding in 1923, would become President of the United States.

As the 1920 elections approached, Walsh threw his support for the Democratic nomination for President to Governor Cox of Ohio, hardly a household name. His competition at the Democratic Convention was President Wilson's son-in-law, William McAdoo, an even less distinguished candidate. The giants of earlier campaigns were gone. Cox would get the nomination on the 44th ballot. The Democrats would be facing the Harding-Coolidge ticket. Despite the lackluster slate on both sides, the Republicans won in a landslide, by a 2 to 1 margin. The Republican victory was chalked up to a return to peacetime.

As Walsh was campaigning for the Democratic ticket, his strong speeches against the League of Nations were probably aiding Republicans; the Democratic Party was seen as the party in support of the League of Nations. The Republican Party was the party of peace, and the Democratic Party was the party of war. Without any towering personalities, the debates were muted. There would be little discussion of the socialism sweeping Europe. Calvin Coolidge was well equipped to handle any "pinkos," in the manner in which he handled the Boston Police Strike. The isolationist mood, which Walsh so strongly believed in, had benefited the Republican Party and the populace focused on local concerns.

In 1924, Walsh was a delegate to the Democratic National Convention held at Madison Square Garden. Franklin Delano Roosevelt was manager of Alfred Smith's campaign. Smith, the former Governor of New York, was a Catholic. As a member of the resolutions committee, Walsh would end up in a battle over a resolution to denounce the Ku Klux Klan. The Klan was spreading across the country, attacking Negroes, Jews, and Catholics. This issue was boiling over, just as a battle for the nomination was being fought. Al Smith was fiercely in contention; his competition was none other than William McAdoo, Woodrow Wilson's son-in-law.

The convention did not need a North/South split, and many resisted pressing this divisive issue; but Walsh would attempt to finish the battle with the Ku Klux Klan. The plank vote would have condemned the Klan, but the plank lost on a margin of 542 to 541. The split in the party would haunt them for years to come, culminating in the 1948 convention with the Dixiecrats. This marked the beginning of disunity in the Democratic Party in the South, with conservative Democrats threatening to bolt and form their own party. The issue thrust Walsh into the national spotlight once again.

On the floor, Walsh spoke eloquently. "When America drafted her sons to bare their breasts to the bullets of the enemies of civilization and of liberty, we raised no religious test. When the defenders of America fought side by side in the diseased trenches of glorious France, no soldier fighting and dying for you and for me asked his buddy if he was black or white, Jew or Gentile, Catholic or Protestant. The blood of Americans of every color, of every religious faith, mingled together in the common soil of France. Are we not recreant in our duty if we permit the children of those who died for us to be denied equality of opportunity, religious freedom and the right to fair trial before the law and to hold and enjoy the priceless privilege of serving their fellow man in office?"[3] Not everyone opposed to the plank was a bigot; some were merely cowards, and some pragmatists. Walsh was lauded in the press for his tenacious fight, and afterwards for his gracious manner that showed no trace of bitterness.

After 103 rounds, it still could not select a candidate. It was the convention nobody won. The two candidates released their delegates after 103 rounds. John Davis secured the nomination, with Governor Charles Bryan of Nebraska as his running mate. Charles Bryan was William Jennings Bryan's brother. Walsh was dueling with a political machine and with family dynasties as well. He truly was Mr. Smith in Washington.

A year that had started out so promising was ending miserably. The Democratic Party, the party of the "big tent," had room for everybody. The ethnics from the northern cities, labor, the big city bosses, and Southern, rural Democrats were all welcome. The trouble was keeping them happy. No one could foresee that a Southern Democrat would integrate the armed forces in 1948, the same year of the

---

[3] Ibid., 149.

Dixiecrats. Sometimes progress bypasses political conventions. Harry Truman would also be the first world leader to recognize Israel.

Back home in Massachusetts, Walsh had to seek reelection to his Senate seat. The badly divided national party would be of little help. And it was no help that Al Smith was defeated; had he remained on the national ticket, Catholic voters would have come out to support him. Furthermore, a "home grown" candidate was heading the top of the ticket: Calvin Coolidge was running for President, and the Massachusetts Republican Party was never more united. Alvan Fuller, the Republican candidate for Governor, was very attractive to voters, too, and his rival James Michael Curley was disliked enough that Republicans would flock to the polls to keep him out. The Democratic ticket was Walsh for Senator, and Curley for Governor, not a balanced ticket at all; and they could barely stand one another.

During the 1924 campaign, a letter written by Woodrow Wilson surfaced which bitterly denounced Walsh's failure to support the League of Nations. Wilson wrote, "I feel obliged to say, in reply to your letter of January 10, that Senator David I. Walsh has proved to be a great disappointment to all Democrats who sincerely believe in the high principles he so signally failed to maintain."[4] Wilson would die that year; he may have been in ill health when he wrote the letter. It was used against Walsh in the campaign, and this would not be the last time that Walsh would suffer personal attacks from the progressive wing of the Democratic Party.

While national press coverage of Walsh's accomplishments and leadership had been spectacular, nothing in Massachusetts was going his way. The campaign resembled his defeat as governor. Fuller would wage an impressive campaign against Curley. Curley could bring out the Irish vote, but Walsh could do that on his own. Curley could also bring out the opposition, the anti-machine vote, the 'Goo Goos' that Curley was fond of taunting. With Wilson's attack, good government progressive Republicans who were attracted to Wilson's progressive image would be less inclined to cross over and vote for Walsh. With the Republican Party united behind Fuller for Governor, and Coolidge for President, the Republican liberals had no reason to desert their party.

The candidate running against Walsh was Frederick Gillett, Speaker of the House of Representatives in Washington. Gillett was highly regarded, respected in both parties, and a political force in his own right. The changing political tides would overwhelm Walsh, but not the vote totals. Walsh was defeated for

---

[4] Ibid., 151-152.

reelection by 18,000 votes. Considering that Coolidge topped the ticket with a half a million plurality, Gillett barely slid to victory on Coolidge's generous coattails.

In defeat there was some solace. Walsh outpolled Curley in Boston by 15,000 votes, a remarkable achievement given Curley's political machine, which encompassed every precinct in Boston. Walsh outpolled Curley statewide by 50,000 votes. Curley must have been stunned by the magnitude of the defeat. How could David I. Walsh, with his little clubs in every city and town, beat Curley in nearly every precinct and ward, even in Curley's backyard, the neighborhoods of Boston? The Irish liked Curley, but Curley could not tell them how to vote. The proven vote getter in Irish Catholic politics was not the rascal Curley, but the gentleman Walsh. Even though Walsh lost to Gillett, he became the unavowed leader of his party because he outpolled Curley by such an astounding margin statewide.

In Boston Harbor, the tide goes out as quickly as it comes in. The Boston political scene had been changing fast. Coolidge had been catapulted from obscurity to the Presidency because of the Boston Police Strike. The Boston political scene was about to change again. Walsh had become quite close to Henry Cabot Lodge. Despite the difference in party affiliation, they both were committed isolationists. Senator Lodge had been cutting back on his workload for some time now, and was spending more time than ever in Boston. Rumors of his ill health had received prominent attention during the summer of 1924. On November 10, 1924, Henry Cabot Lodge died.

The Lodge dynasty at this point far outshone the Kennedys. The Kennedy dynasty was in its infancy, starting with Joseph Kennedy's marriage to Rose Fitzgerald, daughter of the Mayor of Boston, 'Honey Fitz' Fitzgerald. Six years into Walsh's tenure, the Republicans had snatched back the prize and restored Republican domination to the state: a Republican governor, and two senators. Four days after the election, Republicans lost a senator who had perhaps achieved more prominence than any senator in Massachusetts's history. Lodge was as known internationally as well as nationwide. The loss of the Lodge family name meant the loss of brand identity. It would be many years before Henry Cabot Lodge Jr. would appear on the front pages. It would be another generation before Massachusetts witnessed a battle between two dynasties: Henry Cabot Lodge, Jr. and John Fitzgerald Kennedy.

Four days after Lodge's death, Republican Governor Channing Cox named William Butler to fill the unexpired term. Thus, a political unknown was selected to fill Lodge's shoes. The public outcry was immediate. The Lodge family was furious. While Butler was Calvin Coolidge's campaign manager, he had never held public office. The public had no idea who he was; Butler had not been to Washington yet, and he was off to a terrible start. He would never be confused with William Butler Yeats.

It was Walsh's duty to introduce the new senator. Now, he had to introduce two new senators, plus deliver the eulogy for Henry Cabot Lodge in the Senate. Six years earlier, Lodge had escorted Walsh down the aisle, and introduced him to the senate. It was a sad occasion for Walsh, made doubly so by the fact that he would be returning to Boston immediately after the ceremony, having been turned out of office.

Walsh returned to Massachusetts to encounter goodwill from both parties. Massachusetts had just lost both incumbent senators. The manner in which the Republicans had handled Lodge's replacement, Butler, did not sit well with anybody. Voters were reminded just how much they would miss Walsh.

Walsh now had another chance to make some money. Walsh & Walsh was thriving in Boston and Walsh was not a threat to anybody. The press was having great fun with the fact that Walsh had bested Curley in Curley's hometown. Curley loved to taunt the establishment, and now he would have to take it. Curley loved running against wealthy Republicans. He was not used to being outpolled by an Irish Democrat.

Walsh had always enjoyed the indirect support of Republican liberals on those occasions when they were not entirely convinced by their own party's nominee. Walsh was about to get some endorsements from unorthodox quarters. His friendship with Henry Cabot Lodge was much deeper than the public suspected. Constance Lodge Williams, the daughter of the late Senator, was still irate about the Butler appointment. The Lodge endorsement of Walsh only served to remind the voter of troubles within the Republican Party. *The New York Times* wrote, "Direct election in 1926 will determine whether he [Butler] will be able to surmount the animosities which he has stirred in his own party in his own state to defeat that unrivalled fisher of votes, Senator Walsh...."

Endorsements were pouring in, and from some strange corners. Prohibition was becoming an issue, and Butler was dry. Dave Walsh was "wet." He did not believe that prohibition was the answer to the evils of alcohol. He did not believe that government could, or should, play a role in policing it. "Even some of the former Massachusetts Ku Klux Klan wanted their liquor enough to swallow Walsh along with it, declaring: Twenty-five thousand Klansmen in Massachusetts say the best interests of the state and nation will be served if the Democratic Party wins."[5]

---

[5] Ibid., 156-158.

While it does not mention Walsh's name, it is an endorsement. They may have not liked his Catholicism, but they were not about to do without their alcohol. Walsh may be the only candidate in history to have the Klan and the *New York Times* on his side

If Butler's support continued to erode, he would be in serious trouble. He had never stood election in his own right. His patron, "Cool Cal" Coolidge had benefited from his stern demeanor in the face of the Boston Police Strike. Butler's stern demeanor was killing him. Walsh would not need a spin doctor to paint a portrait of Butler, for the local newspapers would do it for him.

The decade of the 1920s would be turbulent in politics and the nation, and politicians would have to tack quickly. Prohibition was in place, and it had become a front-page issue. While Walsh's "wet" position had not always helped him in the past, it would begin to help now amongst all social classes. The progressives of an earlier generation were generally members of the Anti-Saloon League. They believed that the poor, huddled masses could be saved if only someone would take liquor away from them. The 'Goo Goos' were at it again. The problem, however, was that as Prohibition continued, it was obvious to the general public that it was not working. Speakeasies were everywhere. Walsh's "wet" position was becoming more respectable each day. His position was certainly not going to hurt him with the working class voter, and among Democrats, he still had a lock on the "good government" types.

As the campaign was winding down, Walsh made one apparent faux pas. The Bishop of Fall River took exception, although the public likely enjoyed it when Walsh noted, "If the reformers' argument are true, the Founder of Christianity set an awful example, for he drank wine...' Bishop James Cassidy responded: 'I am profoundly shocked that he, of all men, should make the comparison between Christ and the saloon... [he] walks mighty close to blasphemy.[6]

Walsh was busy burying the hatchet with important political operatives. While he would never bury the hatchet with Curley, in this particular election, he did not have to. Curley had no place to go. He could not possibly throw his support to the textile magnate Butler. He had been tweaking the nose of that type for years. Walsh was able to make peace with Martin Lomasney, the real power of Boston politics. While not as well known as a Curley or a Lodge, he had an impressive vote-getting record. Curley, in his autobiography, *I'd Do It All Again,* gives great credit for his own political career to Lomasney, "who taught me a great

---

6 Ibid., 159.

deal about the importance of constituent service."[7] Lomasney, perhaps Boston's most astute politician, had witnessed Walsh's strong vote in Boston in his loss to Gillett, despite the Republican landslide in 1924. In this election, President Coolidge journeyed from the White House to return to Massachusetts to cast a vote for his campaign manager. Walsh had been opposed by President Wilson in the previous election, and now another president was taking shots at him.

The symbolic visit by Coolidge was sure to generate considerable press coverage for Butler. Lomasney knew that if Walsh won, Lomasney would get all the credit for beating back the president's candidate. Martin Lomasney had nothing to lose; he was not going to get anything out of the Coolidge people, for he was viewed as the Boston machine politician. Whereas James Michael Curley held grudges, Lomasney did not. Politics was business to him, and he enjoyed putting an arm around down and out politicians. Console them today, and ask a favor tomorrow. Helping Walsh could only bring a return favor down the long road ahead.

Walsh repeated his large plurality in Boston. This time, with Lomasney's support, he swept Boston with a staggering 70,000-vote lead. While this election did establish ties to Lomasney, Walsh still was primarily on his own. Lomasney did not publicly endorse Walsh until the eve of the election. In this instance, it was Coolidge who got caught in changing currents, and this embarrassing defeat resonated nationally.

---

[7] Curley, James Michael, *I'd Do It All Again*, Prentice Hall, Englewood Cliffs, NJ, 1957, 13.

CHAPTER 6. THE ROAD BACK TO WASHINGTON

David I. Walsh was back on the political map, albeit filling an unexpired term of Henry Cabot Lodge. Walsh had tangled with two presidents and was back on his feet. In 1928, Walsh would have to run again. However, events on the national scene would again show how important timing was. Al Smith had been elected to a fourth term as Governor of New York. He would start his campaign for President early to insure there was no deadlock this time, and certainly he would team up with that Catholic, Walsh from Massachusetts.

If Walsh were to face re-election, what better way than to have a Catholic at the top of the ticket? Walsh would not have to work very hard to get out the Catholic vote. If Smith got the Democratic nomination, every Catholic would have their first chance to vote for a man of their own. The pews would be filled. Walsh would work hard for Smith, and not entirely for selfish reasons. He was very close to Smith, and firmly believed that Al Smith had a shot at the Presidency. Walsh was not naïve about anti-Catholic bias. He had seen enough of it himself, and was aware that in upstate New York Smith would have to overcome religious prejudice, too. Smith had always had large pluralities in New York City, and winning four terms as governor was not an insignificant accomplishment. A Catholic candidate who could win in upstate New York was a rarity, but if it could be done in New York, it could probably be done across the country. In two short years, Walsh and Smith would know for sure.

The year 1928 would be interesting in Massachusetts, and Boston would be the stage for national events as well. On October 12, Walsh introduced Franklin Delano Roosevelt as Al Smith's campaign manager; he addressed a crowd of 12,000 people at Mechanics Hall in Boston. Excitement was building. This was an era of participation politics. Al Smith was due to arrive in this heavily Catholic town, and the politicos had to decide where to hold the event. The cardinal rule is to hold such an event in a slightly smaller venue than is needed to give the appearance of an overflowing crowd. The Catholic vote was growing, as most immigrants to Boston during the last twenty years had been from the Catholic countries of Europe.

Back in 1918, Eamon de Valera had come to Boston to speak in support of Irish freedom. Fenway Park was used, and the crowd of 50,000 people filled it. De Valera would become the first president of a free Ireland. Born of a Spanish father and Irish mother in New York City, he may be the only New Yorker who ever received a warm welcome in Fenway Park. Walsh had introduced him to the multitude. The problem now, for event organizers, was what venue to use for the next New Yorker.

Al Smith would draw all Catholics, not just the Irish. There was actually no facility that could hold such a crowd. The event was scheduled for Boston Common, at the Parkman Bandstand. The Parkman Bandstand had seen every soapbox politician; every Socialist, Communist, Progressive, Anti-Saloon League, 'Goo Goos', Suffragette, Ku Klux Klanner, and even a few Republicans and Democrats. The papists were having a grand time. "Rum, Romanism, and Rebellion" was making a second tour. The event was going to be big because it was understood that this would be Smith's only visit to the state.

The event was energizing for Walsh and Smith; the national press people were covering it. With over 100,000 people, it was impossible to hear the speakers. Walsh benefited more from the appearance than did Smith. Smith had lost his voice on the campaign trail and asked Walsh to speak for him. With his booming voice, Walsh commanded attention — no matter that most people could not hear the words, anyway. Every photographer caught Walsh speaking, and that is what appeared in every big city newspaper. Walsh was back in the spotlight. News coverage of the day would give the impression that Walsh organized the event, but Walsh lacked a political machine to turn out a crowd of that magnitude. Walsh had also been unaware that Smith had lost his voice. Their friendship, and the circumstances, gave Walsh an opportunity that he would remember for the rest of his life.

The 1928 elections became a footnote in the history books. The country was not ready for a Catholic candidate. Another Republican landslide would carry Herbert Hoover to the White House. Al Smith would barely carry Massachusetts. What Smith accomplished in New York would not be replicated nationally.

Despite the national landslide, Walsh was unscathed. He turned in an astounding total of 800,000 votes. By any measure, the win was historic. Walsh was running against the national tide. He would outpoll Al Smith. He was clearly setting records; for Walsh, religion was becoming less a factor each time he ran. This lone wolf was winning in a game of pack mentality. He could alienate the President of his own party. He could alienate the machine politician, Curley. Always a loyal Democrat, he was yet a maverick. Walsh would go on to alienate the next Democratic president. No matter what campaign Walsh was involved in, he always seemed to be standing alone when the battle was over. While clearly a team player in the collegial senate, and certainly not a contrarian personality, Walsh nonetheless always seemed to end up on the outside looking in, sometimes to his benefit and sometimes to his detriment.

The election in New York produced a new governor, Franklin Delano Roosevelt. The national press had identified two Democrats that could be counted on in the future: Walsh, with his huge win in Massachusetts and Roosevelt in New York. Both thrived despite the Republican tide.

Walsh was now an acknowledged leader in the Senate. He was beginning to develop experience and expertise in a number of areas as his seniority in the Senate increased. One area of great interest would be naval affairs. As a member of the Senate Naval Affairs Committee, Walsh would eventually become a powerful player in the development of the modern navy. But in 1929, the United States did not have much of a navy. Great Britain still ruled the seven seas. The sun never set on the British flag, but it sure did set on appropriations bills in the Senate. The Senate Naval Affairs Committee could discuss naval affairs ad nauseam, but neither party was helpful when it came time to appropriate funds.

Walsh's interest in naval affairs was a natural fit with his isolationist views. Walsh felt that with a two-ocean navy, the United States could keep any enemy at bay and therefore would not have to become engaged in international affairs. Walsh was determined to build "Fortress America," using the natural advantages of geography to keep the United States safe. The Atlantic and Pacific would be his moat. Walsh may have been thinking of the New England farmer that poet Robert Frost wrote about in using his "walling in, and walling out" approach. He was not alone in his thinking. He simply was alone in his desire to spend money to achieve it.

The Kellogg-Briand Pact was before the Senate in 1929. The pact finalizing the end of World War I had taken over a decade to enact. The delay symbolized how reluctant the United States was to enter into any agreements with other countries that could complicate American interests. Walsh would vote for the pact, but took pains to explain to constituents that he did so reluctantly. He did not want his constituents to think that he believed it was a solution to Europe's problems, or that it would commit the United States in any way. It is not often a senator gets to vote on an issue using hindsight to guide him, but they were voting on the pact ten years after the war; and it was still unclear whether the pact would solve any problems. Walsh endorsed the treaty simply because it was long overdue.

In a speech before the Senate on April 17, 1939, Walsh shed some insight into his views on World War I. It is clear that he did not care if the Kellogg Pact was endorsed, and his deep distrust of America's allies is startling.

> History is repeating itself. Between 1914 and 1917, while war was raging in Europe, to which we were not a party, this country was flooded with every type of foreign propaganda. We were told that our blood cousins across the sea from whom we inherited many of our democratic and legal institutions and a common language were on the verge of annihilation, and we should rally to their assistance. We were threatened with the loss of billions of dollars our international bankers had loaned the allies unless we joined hands to defeat the Central Powers...at a total cost of $30,000,000,000. This money came from the pockets of the American people and much of it was loaned to our allies, who not only failed most dishonorably to pay us back but have scoffed when we asked them to do so, all the while quite proudly boasting of their balanced budgets as compared to our unbalanced one, and feverishly spending huge sums to rearm for another sacrificial offering to the gods of war.

> We have replaced the money lost in that fateful adventure even though the burdens and sacrifices required to do it have weighed heavily on our people. But we can never replace or restore grieving American mothers the country over the fine American boys who were butchered defending foreign soil, nor can we restore sight, limbs, health, or reason to the wounded and afflicted of the great World War. [1]

Walsh's comments in the Senate were a stinging indictment of the behavior of the British both during and after the war. Walsh went on from there.

> Which are the enemies of democracy and which are the democracies to thwart them? Are we as a government ready to set ourselves up as a judge between the simon pure democracy assumed by some nations which are and have been for centuries notorious imperialists and other nations obsessed with grandiose complexes and devoted to newer authoritarian theories and totalitarian systems?[2]

Walsh's language sounded like that reserved for the enemy, not an ally. He made no distinction between the "notorious imperialist" Great Britain and the newer totalitarian regimes. Yet the feeling towards Great Britain was shared by many in the senate, as well as many in the general populace. The failure on Great Britain's part to make any attempt at repayment had to be particularly grating on Walsh, who had been trying for a decade to get funding for a very outdated US Navy. Great Britain was facing a significant public relations problem of her own making.

---

[1] Dinand Library, Walsh Archives, College of the Holy Cross, April 17th, 1939 letter.
[2] Ibid

The damage Great Britain had done to itself in World War I, in terms of its credibility in the United States, went well beyond the Senate. The institutional memory of the senate leadership would remain a constant problem for Great Britain. In the period since the Great War, the public had voted into office a new breed of politician, largely in response to the Great Depression. The younger senators may have been less isolationist but the corollary was that they were usually anti-colonialist. As a result, both the old guard in the senate and the newly elected were just as likely to be suspicious of Great Britain, even with the naturally strong bond of language, skin color, and culture.

Understanding the British propaganda campaign during World War I requires some insight into how the British viewed Americans. One recurrent theme is the British view that America was a land of country bumpkins. The British could scarcely hide this conviction, and Lord Northcliffe made no attempt to hide it. Professor H. C. Peterson explains,

> The British campaign to induce the United States to come to their assistance affected every phase of American life; it was propaganda in its broadest meaning. News, money, and political pressure each played its part and the battle itself was fought not only in London, New York, and Washington, D.C. but also in American classrooms and pulpits, factories, and offices. It was a campaign to create a pro-British attitude of mind among Americans, to get American sympathies and interests so deeply involved in the European war that it would be impossible for this country to remain neutral.
>
> The problem confronting the directors of any such campaign was that of winning the sympathy of the general public. When Lord Northcliffe visited this country he remarked of Americans: "They dress alike, they talk alike, they think alike. What sheep!"[3]

Lord Northcliffe's publishing empire was perhaps the most influential in the United Kingdom.

Americans, indeed, did not follow events in Europe, certainly not on a regular basis. They had some respect for Germany but knew and cared little about her and less about her neighbors. There was a kind of affectionate rivalry with England.

Neither ordinary Americans nor the American ruling class had any particular financial interest in Africa, the Middle East, and Eastern Europe. Whatever knowledge Americans did possess of foreign affairs usually came from information gleaned from British sources. Prominent people did their foreign banking through London, too; and the press in New York reflected the views of

---

[3] Peterson, H.C., *Propaganda for War*, Univ. of Oklahoma Press, Norman, OK, 1939, 4.

this elite.

The J.P. Morgan connection with London, often the target of conspiracy buffs, was fairly open and Morgan actually held a contract with the British government for their services. It was commonly assumed among the working class that Morgan's financial empire was funding all the munitions makers and was the cause of all the world's problems. J.P. Morgan would have a heavy investment in the English-speaking world, and certainly would do what they he could to ensure that Great Britain's interests were protected. Not surprisingly, Von Papen, the German military attaché in Washington, charged that J.P. Morgan was a front for the British and generated propaganda to promote the British position.

Von Papen's statements also contrast with the British methods of handling propaganda. Great Britain would have assigned a seasoned professional in propaganda to handle the response, not a military attaché. Germany appeared clumsy throughout the war in all its attempts to respond to charges of German misconduct. Von Papen, while highly regarded in Washington, was no match on the propaganda front.

Complete censorship of the news was eventually achieved by British government officials, but it was done with great élan and style. British contempt for the American sheep gave way to another British excess: fawning. Writers and editors, and opinion leaders of every faith, class and color were courted shamelessly.

British propaganda efforts in World War I were far more advanced than any other country. The professional qualifications of its participants were at the highest level, and the mobilization of both governmental and nongovernmental resources for that purpose far exceeded any other country. There was a complete absence of trained German propaganda specialists or even pro-German writers.

Sometimes propaganda was not aimed at the enemy, but rather, was designed for home consumption. Propaganda was devised to bolster a specific government objective for domestic purposes. Such was the case of the "crucified Canadian," a soldier supposedly tortured by German soldiers. The tale variously mentioned a Frenchman or some other nationality, but it was generally considered to have served as a considerable stimulus to Canadian recruiting, particularly French Canadians.

Propaganda was certainly a cheaper way to boost a recruitment campaign, and produced quicker results. In a country that was trying to funnel troops to the front lines as quickly as possible, it is doubtful that British bureaucrats spent much time debating the morality of it.

As the propaganda campaign came under suspicion, Great Britain would undertake extraordinary steps to cloak it in respectability. British Ambassador Lord James Bryce, author of *American Commonwealth*, was asked to commission a study to determine the authenticity of alleged German atrocity stories. Bryce was highly thought of in America. He signed an atrocity report that convinced the nation that unspeakable evils were being perpetrated by the Germans. Bryce was very close to Woodrow Wilson, and only his reputation for veracity could overcome suspicion of Great Britain in America.

After the war was over it would become apparent that most of the British propaganda consisted of outright lies, and the remainder a shading of the truth so great as to make the original story unrecognizable.

The British propaganda machinery kicked into high gear with the sinking of the *Lusitania*. Generally considered the beginning of the US entry into the war, this Cunard liner was sunk by a German submarine. While the newspaper head-lines screamed "passenger liner," it was no secret that the ship was loaded with munitions. It was common knowledge at the time, and the newspapers even said so. While there were many Americans on the ship, this was a British liner. Yet even today, many Americans believe this was a US vessel. This was a classic example of the headlines saying one thing, and the bylines another.

What were civilians doing, traveling on a boat loaded with war materiel? General Leonard Wood, in spite of his pro-British conduct, is supposed to have said: "You cannot cover 10,000 tons of ammunition with a petticoat."[4] Secretary of State William Jennings Bryan declared that Americans were on their own when traveling to a battle zone. The usual posture and responsibility, for a Secretary of State is to defend the rights of US citizens abroad. However, the complicity of the *Lusitania* case was so great that Bryan felt he could not possibly defend an American traveling on a British ship. This would mark the falling out of Bryan and Woodrow Wilson, and soon Bryan would resign because he felt he could not support Wilson's policies, which were clearly leading America to war.

Yet when Robert La Follette rose in the US Senate to question the event, he got nowhere. The newspapers had whipped anti-German fervor to such a pitch that La Follette, despite his stature in the Senate, was whistling in the wind. "The anger of the American people [over the attack] made it possible for the American and British newspapers to gloss over their government's own shortcomings in this connection. After the first day the American press attempted to avoid discussion of the *Lusitania*'s cargo, and when Senator La Follette stated that the boat carried munitions, the indignant Anglophiles wished to throw him out of the Senate. The

---

[4] Ibid., 129.

prosecution of the senator was dropped only when Mr. Malone (Collector of the Port of New York) offered to testify on his behalf."[5]

The British were not done getting full propaganda value from the sinking of the *Lusitania*. A "second torpedo" story surfaced, which focused on the brutality of the German submarine commander preying on innocent civilians as they went to their watery grave. When critics countered that it was the munitions exploding, not a second torpedo, the British backpedaled diplomatically but continued full speed ahead on the propaganda front. The *Lusitania* sank in just eighteen minutes. The ship, like the Titanic, had been advertised as unsinkable.

For the Germans, it was a propaganda disaster. The details favored the Germans, but US newspapers had already been won over.

While Great Britain was not the only country engaged in questionable propaganda in World War I, they clearly were masters of it. This gives rise to the stereotypical view of the German as clumsy in social relations and diplomacy. The French were also making attempts to bolster their stereotype with bombastic statements throughout their propaganda. The French were not nearly as restrained as the British, therefore, their propaganda was not nearly as effective. British writers took propaganda and cloaked it in intellectualism, thus giving it an aura of credibility. French propagandists showed no restraint at all. While French writers cited "authoritative sources," no good propagandist would have approved of many of the French propaganda pamphlets. The effects of French propaganda on the US press would be nil, since the language barrier would provide very few French sources anyway. Much like the Germans, they were shut out, and much like the Germans, their message would not have carried anyway.

Harold Nicolson, the prominent British diplomat who served numerous British governments admitted British misconduct on the propaganda front, but it was many years after World War I. In the House of Commons, twenty years later, Nicolson had this to say: "I do not want to be self righteous, because in a national emergency we can be as untruthful as, or more untruthful than anybody else. During the war we lied damnably. Let us be clear about that. (An Honorable Member: 'Splendidly') No, damnably, not splendidly. I think some of our lies have done us tremendous harm and I should not like to see such propaganda again."[6] Harm could only come from those who understood the lies, and no greater damage to Great Britain's cause could have occurred than in the US

---

[5] Ibid., 121.

[6] Morgan Read, James. *Atrocity Propaganda*, 1914-1919, Yale University Press, 1941, p. 187.

Senate.

While Nicolson's honesty is refreshing, he would soon participate in the propaganda campaign to draw the United States into World War II. Churchill was a leading proponent and no doubt believed the end justified the means. While Britain controlled the seas, Germany controlled the under seas. The only viable approach to challenge British dominance in tonnage was stealth. While Churchill would attempt to characterize this kind of warfare as "unmanly," and it would certainly appeal to the commoner's sense of honor in the conduct of war, it was hardly an atrocity. As in Gallipoli, the British writers would ignore the barbarism of all war, if it were cloaked in heroic acts and manliness. The "come out and fight" mentality had all the aspects of a spaghetti western, but still served as effective propaganda.

While domestic propaganda was usually concentrated on preparing the masses for the coming campaign, British propaganda also focused on decision makers even at home in London. The British tabloids focused on preparing the masses, but even the respected journals and newspapers showed no more restraint. The *Financial Times* reminded its readers of the following: "It is worth while for us to remember that: (1) The Kaiser gave orders to German airmen that special efforts were to be made to kill King Albert's children. (2) He has ordered double rewards to be paid to sub crews whenever there were women and children among the victims. (3) He has personally ordered the torturing of three-year-old children, specifying the tortures to be inflicted."[7]

The German execution of nurse Edith Cavell for aiding and abetting escaping soldiers in Belgium marked the low-water point for achievements in propaganda, and needless to say, Germany won the prize. Edith Cavell would become perhaps Great Britain's leading hero in World War I. Germany had all the details right and everything else wrong. Edith Cavell admitted to the charges; they were punishable by death under international law, and her execution was not without precedent. The Allies would have no compunction about killing a woman, Mata Hari, as a spy.

While Edith Cavell would provide British propagandists with the appealing face they needed, in a nurse's uniform, at that, Mata Hari would be portrayed as an evil slut. This propaganda gift from the Germans could have been just as easily turned around by commuting nurse Cavell's sentence at the last minute and putting a human face on the German High Command. But the Germans missed an easy propaganda opportunity.

---

[7] Ibid., 189.

In the sinking of the *Lusitania*, Germany had a powerful ally. Secretary of State William Jennings Bryan agreed with the German position on this, and was so distressed by joint US-British conduct in the event that he resigned his position. If they could not take propaganda advantage in that situation, they would utterly fail to capitalize on any propaganda front.

The final piece of the propaganda puzzle was aimed at the war's conclusion: the peace table and the division of the spoils. Britain had its eyes on German colonies, and quickly portrayed themselves as compassionate colonial administrators. The Germans were portrayed as brutal masters who deserved to have their colonies taken from them. Some observers maintain that this was not propaganda at all, that the British actually believed it.

The British propagandists, throughout the propaganda campaign of World War I, appeared quite comfortable with their work except when it came to William Randolph Hearst. Hearst newspapers constantly cautioned its readers that any dispatch from London was only half of the story. His refusal to be a cheerleader for British causes would carry over into World War II, and as usual, the British would ascribe sinister motives to his actions. He must have been bought off by German money, they would charge. However, from one decade to another, selling newspapers seems always to have been his greatest motivation.

While Hearst was not the only worry of British propagandists in America, there would be insurmountable opposition from America's heartland; opposition that Great Britain could not overcome until Germany decided to give London a helping hand. Concerned that America was going to join the war, Germany made contact with the Mexican Government and promised that if Mexico allied them-selves with Germany, she would be given back the southwestern states. At least, so Great Britain alleged. They said they had intercepted incriminating messages.

With no confirming information coming out of Mexico, Americans assumed it was just another British allegation. A telegram was produced by the British, but no one believed it. When German Ambassador Zimmerman admitted he had authored it, everyone was stunned — including Great Britain. Zimmerman had brought the war home to America. This was certainly Zimmerman's Alamo in the diplomatic wars. Author H.C. Peterson, in Propaganda for War, points out that it killed the pacifist movement that had been strong in America's heartland. Reading other people's mail had paid off handsomely for Great Britain, but the propaganda coup could only have been delivered by bungling German bureaucrats.

David I. Walsh, despite his strong anti-colonial views, was not a target of British propaganda in World War I for several reasons. As a freshman senator, he had no power. He had supported Wilson's decision to enter the war, late, and apparently for pragmatic reasons. He thought it was inevitable, anyway. His rhetoric on the campaign trail was in opposition, but since the war was winding down, he decided to support Wilson. His vote served to mask his true leanings. The real David I. Walsh would not become apparent until the post war debate on the League of Nations; even Woodrow Wilson would see the real David I. Walsh stand up.

While Walsh was still trying to firm up his identity in regards to foreign policy, his domestic concerns remained constant. Always a friend of organized labor, Walsh served on the Committee on Education and Labor. He would be serving on this committee when workers faced their bleakest hour, as the "Roaring 20s" came to a screeching stop. Even before the stock market crashed, Walsh had been working on labor issues for years and had strong positions on what ought to be done. In 1927, Walsh held hearings on the unemployment problem. No one was listening then, but soon they would be listening intently.

Even during the good times, Walsh was disturbed about the number of people left behind, with no safety net. They were, indeed, visible, with the issue of homelessness apparent on every street corner. Coming out of the hearings, he recommended "aid to mothers with dependent children, as well as old age pensions."[8] Walsh was significantly ahead of the curve on social issues. His belief that government must step in where the private sector will not must have been inspired in the tiny town of Clinton, where everyone believed that government could make a difference. He carried these beliefs to Washington. It would take a Great Depression to find enough people to jump on Walsh's bandwagon and a slick President to sell the wares. Both would come along, in time.

It would be another ten years before unemployment insurance was passed in the form of the Wagner-Peyser Act. In 1936, the first federal wages and hours act would be passed, with Walsh as the primary architect. The Walsh-Healy Act would affect every working man and woman, not just organized labor. Organized labor could not possibly "organize" every sector. The resistance they were receiving from corporations was stiff. In the industries represented by organized labor, there were pitched battles.

Walsh's attempt to seek federal legislation to establish a minimum floor for all workers was extraordinary. It was easy to vote on the legislation in 1936, after all the country had gone through. But in 1927, it took an unusual vision — and it is surprising he was not branded a Socialist.

---

[8] Congressional Record, December 21, 1927, Dinand Library, Walsh Archives, College of the Holy Cross.

Walsh returned to the active social scene in Washington. While it was not quite the fishbowl that he had found Boston to be, it could be even more malicious. *Time* magazine ran the following in November 1929.

> A bachelor, he is tall and stout. A double chin tends to get out over his tight fitting collar. His stomach bulges over his belt. He weighs 200 pounds or more. Setting up exercises every day at a Washington health centre have failed to reduce his girth. He is troubled about it. His dress is dandified. He wears silk shirts in bright colors and stripes and, often, stiff collars to match. His feet are small and well shod. Beneath his habitual derby hat, his hair is turning thin and gray. Society is his prime diversion. Of secondary interest are motoring, sporting events, and the theatre. In Washington, he occupies an expensive suite of rooms at the luxurious Carlton Hotel on Sixteenth Street. A good and frequent host himself, he accepts all invitations and is one of the most lionized senators in Washington. Ironic comments are sometimes heard on the contrast between his political representation and his social activities. In senate debate, which he enters frequently, he is gruff and bull voiced...In private conversation his voice is soft and controlled.[9]

What was the aim of such an article? *Time* certainly knew about his interest in the automobile. It got him elected. The rest leaves just enough of a hint to lead savvy readers to speculate about his personal life. Of course, today, tabloid journalism leaves nothing to be guessed.

Would Henry Booth Luce, the owner of *Time*, engage in politics? FDR thought so. In 1939, Roosevelt ordered Henry Morgenthau, Secretary of the Treasury, to investigate the tax returns of the *New York Times* and *Time Magazine*. Morgenthau refused to do so. Roosevelt knew how to get even. "In 1943, FDR opposed giving one of Time's best correspondents, John Hershey, a Silver Star for assisting in the care and removal of wounded under fire on two occasions. This was not heroism, FDR argued, but something that 'any man....who had red blood in his veins would do.'"[10]

Clare Booth Luce was elected to the House of Representatives in 1942, so the line between journalism and politics was less than clear. When she criticized Roosevelt's lack of preparedness for the war, FDR had some nice things to say. "Roosevelt in cabinet referred to 'Clearly Loose, and Loose and Wild', and said 'You know she was Barney Baruch's girl. Yes, he educated her, gave her a yacht, sent her to finishing school, she was his girl'."[11] This is the side of Roosevelt that is not often portrayed in history books. His description of Clare Booth Luce sounds rather like Lucy Mercer, Roosevelt's lifelong mistress.

[9] Wayman, Dorothy, G., *David I. Walsh, Citizen-Patriot*, Bruce Publishing, 1952, 182.

[10] Morgan, Ted, *FDR: A Biography, Simon & Schuster*, New York, 1985, 562.

[11] Ibid., 563.

67

It is difficult to discern the motive for the less than flattering article about Walsh. It could have been motivated by his stand on domestic issues. Certainly, later in Walsh's career, Henry Booth Luce and Walsh's views about the Roosevelt foreign policy would be very similar; both expressed doubt about FDR's lack of preparedness for World War II. However, the liberal views of Walsh on domestic issues would set them apart. Walsh, the "dandified dresser," would get Luce's support as World War II approached, when Walsh would question FDR's foreign policy.

David I. Walsh enjoyed an active social life, and had entree into the most popular, if not the most exclusive, nightspots in the Washington-New York social scene. The Pullman from Washington to New York on a Friday night was a veritable who's who of Washington politics. The Stork Club in New York City was a favorite destination for luminaries like J. Edgar Hoover and Walter Winchell, who shared a table every weekend. Walsh was an active member. A letter in the Walsh Archives at the College of the Holy Cross acknowledges the renewal of his membership as offered by Sherman Billingsley. As World War II approached, he would carry a heavy burden of leadership in the US Senate; at least, he had no trouble getting a table at any of the finest clubs in New York City or Washington. The Washington of 1939 was hardly a "club" town, but World War II would change that somewhat, but it was no competition for New York.

While Walsh's isolationist views appear troublesome by today's standards, his views were entirely mainstream and it is difficult to ascribe them to any particular political leanings. The stereotype of the isolationist was a Midwestern or Western senator, conservative, and without defense installations in his or her home state. However, William Jennings Bryan, Walsh's hero of a prior generation, was an isolationist. Bob Lafollette was a liberal. Walsh was a liberal; Senator Burton Wheeler, too. While Walsh's criticisms of British imperialism were often unkindly attributed to his Irish Catholic background, Walsh's anticolonial view was consistent all over the globe. That was part of the problem. Britain did rule the seas, and Walsh saw no reason to jump to her defense every time they were involved in an incident. Walsh would champion the cause of Philippine independence, and, while those islands were not a British possession, this too, would be chalked up to his Catholicism.

The religion card would be played freely against Walsh by his opponents, and frequently that opponent would be the strong British lobby in Washington. Many people throughout the world questioned British imperialism, but it was not until generations later that they were able to force the issue. Arabs would rise up, strangely enough led by a Brit, Lawrence of Arabia. Jews in Palestine, led by the

Irgun; Blacks and Whites in Rhodesia; and that peaceful giant, China would finally ask Great Britain to leave. Michael Collins would do it in Ireland in the 1920s, asking with a gun. Yitzak Shamir would study Collins' guerrilla methods and adopt the code name, Mikhail, in honor of him, in the underground movement to drive Great Britain out of Palestine. Collins had the distinction of being the only colonial to drive Great Britain out militarily since the American Revolution. Winston Churchill, as Dominions Secretary, was on the losing end of that battle and would sign the peace agreement with Collins, granting Ireland independence.

Walsh set out to support his isolationist views with a strong navy; however, much like the rhetoric on social legislation regarding widows and orphans, there was not a lot of money. There was a great concern with the loss of life in World War I, where 52,000 Americans were killed. That was actually fewer than were killed in an undeclared war, Vietnam. But this was a simpler time. Entering World War I at the tail end saved countless American lives, but the Americans were still unprepared to accept the horrific loss of life. The Europeans had had more experience, and more recent, with losses on a much larger scale.

If anything, the isolationist movement, which was firmly entrenched before World War I, grew stronger after the war. The movement encompassed liberals and conservatives, Republicans and Democrats, Third party candidates, Big Business, and Big Labor. Woodrow Wilson was the candidate who "kept us out of war." That is the slogan that got Wilson elected to a second term. The United States entered the war shortly after the election.

This can be likened to Richard Nixon's "secret plan to end the war," only to keep it going four more years. Wilson may have been duplicitous, but he won the Nobel Peace Prize. By European standards, Wilson was the Prince of Peace. Perhaps Wilson should have shared the prize with the isolationists, whose pressure kept him from going to war before the election.

Because of America's late entry into World War I, veterans were not accorded the recognition they deserved. So few went to the front that World War I was not a generational experience. Between the wars, veterans were treated very shabbily. Harry Truman went to war, but few others did. While FDR would soon be leading American servicemen into battle, he had done little for them when the battles were over. As a consequence, there were few in uniform that had any love for their Commander in Chief. On the other hand, Walsh was revered by veterans. FDR's treatment of veterans, coupled with his lack of support for military budgets in the intervening years worked against him. There was no reason for a veteran to support FDR. FDR's close identity with the New Dealers also turned most veterans against him; the loathing of the president was almost palpable.

The Walsh Archives at Holy Cross College contain a letter from Dennis Haverty, Department Adjutant of the American Legion, dated May 25, 1928, thanking Walsh. His vote to override FDR's veto enabled the Tyson-Fitzgerald Bill to go forward, increasing veterans' compensation. The letter pays Walsh the ultimate compliment: the American Legion took it for granted that Walsh would defy the president, even though they were of the same party, and did not even bother wiring him to lobby for his vote.

May 25, 1928

Honorable David I. Walsh
United States Senator
Washington, D.C.

My Dear Senator:

We of the Legion in Massachusetts are deeply grateful to you for the vote in favor of overriding the veto of the president on the Tyson-Fitzgerald Bill, a most just piece of legislation with which the American Legion has been prominently identified for the past eight years. So certain were we of your favorable vote that we did not bother telegraphing you when the bill came up for Senate action yesterday. We knew you would be with us as you have always been in the past.

Regardless of the testimony of our opponents, the Legion was solidly behind this measure and we are all gratified that the biggest legislative fight which the Legion has had since the Adjusted Compensation Bill has come to a close favorably. Again let me say that we are grateful to you for your efforts and cooperation.

Sincerely yours,

Dennis H. Haverty,
Department Adjutant [12]

In 1930, President Herbert Hoover had asked the senate to endorse the London Armament Treaty. Walsh was disposed to vote for the treaty, which set limits on naval armament, but wanted a commitment from Congress to fund naval strength up to the treaty limits. The treaty only made sense if parity was achieved. There seemed to be no point in signing the treaty if America was not going to implement it. Walsh set about applying pressure on the Hoover administration, but found that he had no leverage. He was deserted by his closest friends in the Senate; the treaty was easily approved, but no appropriations were made, and the navy would remain seriously under funded for many years to come. While the

---

[12] Dinand Library, Walsh Archives, College of the Holy Cross, letter of Dennis Haverty, May 25, 1928.

treaty may have meant something to Europe, it meant little to the United States. Without naval parity, the treaty would receive scant attention.

Walsh also worked on the plight of widows and orphans in 1927; on this score, too, he received no support in the Senate; but things were about to change. The stock market crashed in October 1929. By the 1930 mid-term elections, the big debate in Washington had shifted from the London Armament Treaty (now seen as a relic of World War I) to the issue of the economy. The press had been widely reporting on the shenanigans on Wall Street after the collapse. Foreign policy would take a back seat for a long time, while unemployment, bank failures, and mortgage foreclosures haunted the voters.

The public consensus was that the unregulated business community was the cause of the collapse. The laissez faire legislative approach of the 1920s was about to be replaced with the most legislatively active decade in the history of the country. The public mood was changing, and Walsh's domestic legislative agenda was about to receive tremendous support. Republicans shortly would be swept from office.

The problems of funding the programs would remain. With unemployment rates at an all time high, the tax base collapsed, so that funding mechanisms were in short supply. Walsh would again witness a change in the political landscape. Roosevelt's election was two years away, in 1932. Yet Walsh's work on social welfare programs had begun almost ten years before FDR's most noteworthy domestic accomplishments.

There was very little difference between what Roosevelt proposed, once he was elected, and what the Committee on Education and Labor had been discussing all along. Walsh had proposed in 1927 to put the unemployed to work on government projects. FDR proposed the Civilian Conservation Corps. Walsh's first government job as paymaster for the Wachusett Dam project had impressed him; Walsh believed that government spending on needed public projects was worthwhile, especially to help the marginally unemployed.

The elections of 1932 marked a major shift in domestic policy concerns, much as entry into World War II would change America's isolationist views. The 1932 elections were looming as a colossal struggle, but it was still unclear who would be leading the Democrats. The string of Democratic losses went back unbroken to Woodrow Wilson's last term. Al Smith's landslide loss in 1928 was just the latest humiliation. The giants of the Democratic Party had been gone for some time now, as evidenced by the fact that Woodrow Wilson's son-in-law could be taken as a serious candidate after Wilson's demise. Walsh's huge win in Massachusetts was still fresh in everyone's mind. Walsh was in demand as a speaker throughout the country.

Addressing the American Federation of Labor, Walsh decried the miseries of unemployment. In the well of the Senate, in 1930, Walsh acknowledged the place of charity but called for opportunities to work, not hand-outs, and called on government to provide those opportunities. Thus, Walsh was calling for the federal government to be an employer of last resort two years before Roosevelt got elected.

Despite his occasional spats with John L. Lewis over the effects of coal strikes on Massachusetts, labor was recognizing the early legislative work that Walsh had attempted on behalf of all working people, not just the then narrowly organized labor unions. Walsh may have been the only senator at that time that could stand in a convention hall and tell labor what they did not want to hear. His stature with labor could not have been higher. Walsh was not going to be a candidate for president because of the Al Smith debacle — the Democrats were not about to try another Catholic. This fact gave him the freedom to speak his mind; a freedom he used frequently.

The Democratic Party was looking for a fresh face, and the new Governor of New York was a fresh face on the national scene. Most importantly, unlike the prior New York Governor, he was not Catholic. And the Roosevelt name had a certain ring to it. The rhetoric of Calvin Coolidge's campaign after World War I would come back to haunt Republicans. The "return to normalcy" campaign worked fine as the boys returned from World War I. The "business of America is business" theme would not sell well now. No one was calling for a smaller government. And no one was looking to help out the bankers; this was no time to be a banker's son in small-town America.

Organized labor had been portrayed in the newspapers as greedy. Whenever John L. Lewis called for a strike, the mine owners would raise prices, just in time for the heating season. Lewis would be blamed. Owner of a chain of newspapers, William Randolph Hearst, like Henry Booth Luce, made his views known; Hearst had even attended Democratic National Conventions on a regular basis, and always tried to play the role of kingmaker.

Labor strikes usually received poor coverage from local dailies for two reasons: one ideological, the other practical. The owners held conservative views and did not believe in helping labor. They were fearful of union organizing in their own newspapers; and labor did not advertise. Labor did not pay the bills, management did. In Walsh's hometown of Clinton, if someone was not reading the *Clinton Daily Item*, they were reading the county's largest newspaper, the *Worcester Telegram* & Gazette, which was owned by the Stoddard and Booth families. (They were still conservative, to say the least, in the 1960s, when Robert Stoddard was serving on board of the John Birch Society.) Newspapers were seeing "pinkos" under every tree, and were more than willing to associate them with labor unions. No one was charging "liberal bias" in the newspapers of the 1920s and 1930s. When Walsh himself spoke to newspapers about domestic issues, he always included a call to patriotism to ward off any suggestion he was a socialist. Walsh jousted with imaginary "pinkos" in a number of speeches, presumably to inoculate himself against attack by a conservative press, as his platform regularly included socialist-like provisions. And as a Catholic politician, he would make the "pledge of allegiance" often lest anyone claim he was reporting to the Pope. He was used to having his patriotism questioned.

At least, the time had come when Walsh could spend far less time defending his liberal views. The shoe was on the other foot, now. Business would have to defend why there should not be government regulation. Walsh had done a lot of work in his law practice at the turn of the century defending the rights of workers. Now he would be extending benefits to the unemployed when they were not working, and he would not be labeled a Communist for doing so. Even the press was changing.

In 1932, Walsh filed a bill in the Senate that called for the establishment of the Federal Trade Commission. Walsh got no support, but FDR had not been elected yet. His bill could go nowhere without a messenger. The idea of spending government money on regulatory or "pump priming" activities was still foreign to Congress. Rural America was still apparent in the makeup of the senate. While labor unions and city bosses had clout in the House of Representatives, they did not have nearly the clout in the senate. Many of the programs Walsh talked about were not well received in either party. However, as the Great Depression spread, the attitude in the Senate would finally change. The labor boss in the city now had an ally sitting atop a tractor, a farmer who was having a tough time keeping up with the farm mortgage. The WASP banker/financier crowd centered in New York City would be blamed for every conspiracy, both real and imagined, by every podium pounding politician from Huey Long to Franklin Delano Roosevelt. Social assistance programs might not be such a bad idea, after all.

If thoughts ever did stray back to foreign policy, most senators remained strongly isolationist. They resented being dragged into a war they had been told the country would stay out of; and Great Britain's unpaid bills rankled.

FDR campaigned for the Democratic nomination against Al Smith in 1932. Smith was still the acknowledged leader of his party, despite his loss four years earlier. The former four-term governor of New York would not slip away peacefully into the night, and for good reason. The political climate now favored a Democrat win. But he did not count on the Democratic thirst for victory; the Democrats had been out of office too long to take a chance again on a Catholic. Party stalwarts tried to convince Smith not to run, but he could not be dissuaded. Walsh was in a difficult position; he was very close to Smith. Walsh was now a power broker within the party. And Walsh was a realist. He felt a Catholic could not win. But he was not about to tell Smith. The race was on.

By Democratic standards, the race was over early. Roosevelt won on the fourth ballot by a 5 to 1 margin. Given previous Democratic Conventions, that was practically a rout. Much as Coolidge had leapfrogged over the previous incumbent governor in Massachusetts (Walsh) into the Presidency, Roosevelt would leap over the previous governor of New York. Roosevelt was a fresh face with a familiar name. That is what the Democrats wanted.

With the dawn of the FDR era came a sweeping majority in Congress. Walsh must have felt a wave of relief; the long run of Republican domination since World War I was over. Roosevelt's people were talking about many of the programs Walsh had previously sponsored in the Senate. Finally, there would be appropriations for social welfare legislation in the Senate. Walsh would have the president's ear.

Yet, as legislation was prepared in congress, debate on the senate floor showed some distance between the two. Washington insiders immediately noticed that Walsh was not in Roosevelt's inner circle. Walsh had laid out his support for increasing FDR's authority on budget matters, but also signaled his right to change his mind if he saw objectionable issues down the road.

"Because of the importance of doing that [balancing the budget], I am going, as far as I can, to support the President's views, after urging him modifica-tions as I have done, which in part have been granted. When I feel a serious injustice is being perpetrated, I shall not hesitate to vote to remove it even if I differ with the President." These words signaled a divergence of opinion, in which the President led one large element of the American population and Senator Walsh spoke for another element, whose convictions were no less firmly held. Walsh stood for the Jeffersonian Democratic position while Roosevelt, although nominally a Democrat, emerged more and more openly as an exponent of the Hamilton school of federal power."[13]

Whatever the academic debate, Walsh's split with his President was immediate. Walsh had not waited for years in the wilderness anticipating a

---

[13] Wayman, Dorothy, G., *David I. Walsh, Citizen-Patriot*, Bruce Publishing, 1952, 209.

Democratic majority, only to cede authority to the President when it arrived. There appears to have been nothing personal about it at this point in their relationship. Roosevelt evidently arrived in Washington with no plan to use the veteran senators and congressmen on the Hill. This would be the first of many misjudgments FDR would make. He would experience many difficulties enacting the programs that he proposed, and not all the opposition came from Republicans. Roosevelt brought his own inner circle with him, and they would prove to be somewhat clumsy on Capitol Hill. He would change legislative initiatives as frequently as he changed Vice Presidents.

The honeymoon between Roosevelt and Walsh was short. Walsh accepted the fact that his role in the senate was quite different than that of the President, and that, therefore, they would clash as a normal part of the process of checks and balances. Walsh was not the only legislator who felt left out, as FDR's first term was marked with a rocky relationship with Capitol Hill. Whether Walsh compared this with his sudden falling out with Woodrow Wilson is unknown, because there is little introspection in the Walsh Archives. When Walsh reflected and analyzed, it usually revolved around his foreign policy views or domestic policy initiatives, and quite often was read into the Congressional Record along with elaborate explanations. Perhaps Walsh felt uncomfortable recording his thoughts regarding his personal relationships; and essentially, his relationship with FDR would remain distant for years to come.

CHAPTER 7. THE LOYAL OPPOSITION

Walsh was in a familiar position. He had to go it alone during his whole career in Massachusetts. Now, even with a Democratic administration, Walsh was on the outside. Roosevelt was looking for a rubber stamp from Congress as a whole. Upon his entry to the Senate in 1918, Walsh had established a frosty (and later bitter) relationship with Woodrow Wilson. He got nothing out of Wilson for the remainder of his presidency, and now he was off to a rocky start with Roosevelt. Was there something in Walsh's background that stood in his way? Coming from a small town, he had proved somewhat clumsy in his dealings with big city operators — some said refreshingly so. He had served as a minority in the Massachusetts legislature and never had a majority as Governor of Massachusetts. He was in a minority within his own Democratic Party back in Massachusetts, a party dominated by the competition between political machines. As he ascended the Senate hierarchy, it would remain a solitary journey. But his was not a contrarian personality.

Neither were his clashes with his presidents, both of his own party, based on horse trading. He appears almost naive in thinking that neither Wilson nor FDR would hold it against him if he voted on the basis of his convictions. Aides to presidents do hold grudges; it is their job to corral votes. Certainly, the record is clear that both Wilson and FDR held deep grudges against Walsh. Throughout Walsh's long career, and his voluminous letters, virtually no other acrimonious correspondence appears, nor any suggestion of any other antagonistic relationships except those with Woodrow Wilson and Franklin Delano Roosevelt.

Walsh worked closely with FDR on many issues, despite not being a close confidant. As Chairman of the Committee on Education and Labor, Walsh was the point man on the Civilian Conservation Corps. Walsh had long championed the use of unemployed people on public works projects. While the CCC may have been a different model than Walsh had proposed in his 1927 US Senate hearings, the public purpose was the same.

The CCC employed urban youths on many public projects in rural areas. The alphabet soup of FDR's programs had its first ingredients. FDR's programs started to march across the political landscape of the 1930s, and some, like unemployment insurance and social security, would become permanent institutions. Both of those programs could trace their initial concepts back to Walsh's Committee on Education & Labor hearings in 1927; Roosevelt managed to sell the programs to the nation, with, of course, a little help from the Depression, and also from Walsh. It wasn't easy. Walsh was floor leader of the CCC Bill and Roosevelt's proposal was going nowhere. Even organized labor objected. William Green of the American Federation of Labor balked and it was Walsh who did the negotiating, redrafting the administration's bill, who got his Committee on Education and Labor to report it favorably, and got it passed into law on March 31, 1933. Walsh may have been the only person who could have overcome Green's reservations. FDR's aides assumed that only the business community would be opposed. Roosevelt's staff was unprepared, and almost allowed one of FDR's first major initiatives to fail. Walsh's relationship with organized labor helped bail them out. However, FDR's mistakes would continue.

In March 1934, Walsh had been fighting for more money for hospitalization of veterans from World War I. Like today's Gulf War or Vietnam veteran, these soldiers were denied health benefits because they could not prove that their ailments were service connected. Walsh also had been fighting for payment of the Veterans Bonus, which was not scheduled to be paid until 1945. In the middle of the Depression, the veterans needed payment now. Walsh had been advocating payment since 1921. He pointed out that if the Veterans Administration did not accept responsibility, the men became charges of state and local welfare agencies — something that governors surely understood. Roosevelt still hung back. Roosevelt said: "No person, because he wore a uniform, must thereafter be placed in a special class of beneficiaries over and above all other citizens....It does not mean that because a person served in the defense of his country, performed a basic obligation of citizenship, he should receive a pension from his government because of a disability incurred after his service had terminated and not connected with that service."[1]

FDR had a difficult relationship with the military; Walsh did not. A letter of December 15, 1937 from Josephus Daniels, former Secretary of the Navy, shows

---

[1] Ibid., 210.

how exceedingly close Walsh was to the Navy brass. The letter written while Daniels was Ambassador to Mexico illuminates a warm relationship, despite the fact that Daniels had not been Secretary of the Navy since World War I.

Mexico, Dec. 15, 1937

My dear Senator:

I thank you for your letter and the enclosure. I particularly appreciate the courtesy of having my address in Brest printed in the Congressional Record. During the years the Navy was engaged in its gigantic task of safeguarding American soldiers to France and performing other notable services, all of its activities were, of necessity, kept secret. As a result, the American people never fully apprehended the magnitude of the task or the great efficiency with which it was carried out. It seemed to be a matter of importance, even if belated, that the story of the greatest transportation job in history should be told at Brest, and be made a part of the permanent history of our country by being incorporated in the Congressional Record. I have already received a number of letters showing appreciation by those interested in the Navy.

I notice on your letterhead, which carried the names of the present members of the Committee of Naval Affairs, that of all the men who served on the committee in the days when I was Secretary of the Navy, only three remain, you and Fred Hale and Peter Gerry. Is it a coincidence or something else that all three of you represent New England and the Democrats have a two-thirds majority?

I recall with great pleasure our long association beginning when you were Governor of Massachusetts, and I always regard it as a privilege I had to have been able to speak in the campaign of 1918 in Massachusetts when you broke a long record of only Republicans in the Senate from your state and won by a wholesome majority.

With Christmas greetings and sentiments of esteem and warm regard, I am

Sincerely yours,
Josephus Daniels[2]

Daniels' relationship with FDR was quite different. FDR was Assistant Secretary of the Navy under Daniels in World War I; Daniels was FDR's boss when the Newport Sex Scandal broke. Daniels had disapproved of FDR's conduct in the affair, and FDR attempted to blame Daniels, or at least deflect criticism from himself. FDR was not successful, and the investigating committee, the very same Senate Naval Affairs Committee, would find FDR guilty as charged. Walsh did not serve on that committee since he had not yet been elected to the US Senate. The committee accused FDR of perjury. Dave Walsh became chairman of a committee that FDR loathed, a committee that was directly connected to the biggest professional and moral failure in FDR's entire career.

---

[2] Dinand Library, Walsh Archives, College of the Holy Cross, Josephus Daniels letter of December 15, 1937.

FDR misread the mood on Capitol Hill regarding veterans' benefits. The senate leadership, far more experienced than Roosevelt, had been wrestling with this issue since the end of World War I. The bill passed easily. FDR vetoed it. The bill passed anyway, 63–27. Roosevelt had shown himself to be no friend of the veteran, and had suffered a humiliating defeat in the process. Roosevelt should have known that Walsh had been working on this issue for years; given the margin of the vote, it seems that many other senators had, too. Walsh was an accomplished speaker on the senate floor, and it did not take much work to figure out how he would vote. Perhaps FDR and Wilson knew they could not dissuade Walsh, so they did not try.

Walsh continued his work on foreign affairs. Though he was the acknowledged leader in the senate on naval affairs, little had been accomplished in the way of funding a modern navy. On foreign affairs, Walsh and FDR approached most issues from opposite sides, but they often ended up on common ground. Walsh wanted a strong navy for defensive reasons. FDR wanted a strong navy to engage the allies. Walsh wanted no entangling alliances. Roosevelt was perhaps an optimist in regard to human behavior; Walsh a pessimist. Walsh trusted the British to do one thing: go to war again. He was determined that the United States would not be an instrument of Britannia's foreign policy. However, the success on the domestic policy front was not making it any easier for Walsh to secure appropriations to bring naval strength up to treaty levels. His earlier opposition to the London Naval Treaty had been based on congress's refusal to fund the navy up to treaty strength. Why make a commitment and sign a treaty, if the United States was not going to benefit by it? Great Britain could not have been unhappy when congress failed to appropriate funds year after year, for she was fearful of losing her naval supremacy to the United States.

In June 1934, Walsh turned his attention to reelection to a fourth term. He returned to Massachusetts, but there was no campaign. Walsh was nominated by the state Democratic convention by acclamation. No one would run against him in the Democratic primary. Walsh would face opposition from Robert Washburn, a Republican, but the outcome was unsuspenseful. Walsh won by 300,000 votes. Many prominent Republicans, including former Governor Alvan Fuller, endorsed him.

The relatively placid political waters in Massachusetts were in sharp contrast to the national political scene. Walsh was at the pinnacle of his career, wielding significant power in the senate. Adolf Hitler had risen to power in Germany in 1933. He was not on America's radar screen at this point, and Walsh returned to Washington to deal with domestic legislation. Walsh was never concerned about the armies of Europe; he assumed that the Teutonic tribes would fight again. Capitol Hill was trying to digest FDR's domestic agenda, and issues of the Great Depression were far more prominent.

General Douglas MacArthur would plead with Congress all through the 1930s to modernize an army that was still using horses in 1936. MacArthur resigned in disgust and left to become Commander of the Philippine Army. MacArthur was as concerned as Walsh about the situation in the Pacific. Washington was dominated by Anglophiles, and most of the country was of European stock. No one was interested in Asia. The Philippines had hired MacArthur for one reason. They feared the Japanese. Walsh's concerns lay with the navy. Britain had a strong navy to protect its far flung empire. Walsh wanted a strong navy for deterrent purposes.

MacArthur had a long history on Capitol Hill, yet even he could not get Congress to listen. His father, General Arthur MacArthur, had been commander of the Philippines during the Spanish-American War. Douglas MacArthur had spent his childhood in Manila when his father was stationed there, and he knew Asia well. Arthur MacArthur had also won the Congressional Medal of Honor as a young man in the Civil War; he, too, had also spent considerable time on Capitol Hill pleading for funding. If MacArthur could not command the senate's attention, it was unlikely that Walsh would do any better.

All of the armed forces had been neglected since World War I. America had no intention of going to war with anybody, and it was difficult to conceive that anyone was going to attack America. Many members of the senate (and others) felt that Great Britain had dragged the US into the last war to defend its empire; that was not going to happen again.

Walsh was enjoying great success in his domestic agenda. In 1935, he was the point man for passage of a bill that would require any bidder on a government contract to sign an agreement prohibiting child labor, setting an employee workweek of not more than forty hours, paying a specified minimum wage, and prohibiting convict labor. The Walsh-Healey Bill was landmark legislation.

FDR badly needed Walsh's help because the NRA (the National Industrial Recovery Act) had been declared unconstitutional. The NRA was a cornucopia of programs tossed together in an effort to get the economy moving again. Unfortunately, the bill was too complex; it was intended to satisfy unions, big business, and trade associations, and cure virtually every ailment that was dragging the economy down.

Author Ted Morgan, in *FDR, A Biography*, suggests that Roosevelt failed to appreciate the implications of the bill. "This was the Law of Unintended Consequences at its most dizzying, for FDR did not have a clue as to what the results of Section 7(a) would be. Casually, almost unknowingly, he committed himself to a policy of government protection of collective bargaining. It did not occur to him at the time, nor to anyone else, that it would make the Democratic Party the majority party."[3]

The law was struck down by the Supreme Court; but Walsh had already bailed out Roosevelt on the NRA by securing passage of a blanket bill that would retroactively validate all government contracts that had been made in good faith. Walsh reported the bill out of committee with the following comment: "Not my bill. This bill is here at the request of the administration. But I am for it…." Huey Long, the "Kingfish," tried to filibuster the bill; Walsh did not leave the Senate for four tense days. Walsh vigorously protected the President on a bill that he had little stake in; he could be counted on to fight for the President for issues that he believed in. For someone who was not in Roosevelt's inner circle, Walsh fought extremely hard. The bill passed, making all contracts signed during NRA legal.

The Walsh-Healy Act was up next. The bill would reduce the 48-hour workweek to 40. In an effort to defeat the bill, and knowing that Walsh had strong support from labor, Huey Long proposed a 30-hour workweek. The issue had been debated two years earlier, but the so-called Black Bill had died in committee. Huey Long dared Walsh to oppose the 30-hour bill; he interrupted Walsh, boasting that every senator who had opposed the Black 30-hour week two years before had been defeated for reelection. Walsh met him head on: "I am in favor of every reasonable means to reduce the hours of labor but personally I believe that in a general thirty-hour law there are the possibilities of the most destructive financial collapse this country has ever witnessed."[4] Walsh's reputation with labor was so reliable that he could afford to be frank. With so many people out of work, Walsh was not about to support a radical move that would jeopardize more jobs.

The opposition to the Walsh-Healy Act collapsed. The 40-hour week became law, on a voice vote. FDR could not have passed such a law; his dealings with Congress were shaky, and his aides had not proven adept at the grinding process of securing passage of any bill deemed controversial.

The basic argument against the law was powerful. With millions out of work, employers had no incentive to ease up on the lucky ones who remained employed. Why shorten the workweek? Walsh knew the ways of the Senate, and

---

[3] Morgan, Ted, FDR: A Biography, Simon & Schuster, New York, 1985, 387.

[4] Dinand Library, Walsh Archives, College of the Holy Cross, Congressional Record, Black Bill Hearings.

almost every item in the bill was something he had been fighting for since 1927. The rehearsals had been many. Despite this tremendous achievement for the worker at the heights of the Depression, today's generation has never heard of Walsh. It would be difficult to pass such a law today; doing it in the midst of the Great Depression was a miracle. While the Walsh-Healy Act only covered companies that did business with the federal government, it encompassed important parts of the economy and set the stage for a nationwide minimum wage.

While the mood of the country had become much more progressive, passing legislation did not get any easier. The issue of how to pay for the costs new initiatives entailed always remained. Walsh preferred working on social issues (in which he and FDR almost always agreed), or on naval issues, his main foreign policy interest, but he was about to get embroiled in a legislative battle that would leave no winners. The issue would bring no pork to Massachusetts, bring no jobs to the unemployed, provide no funding for the navy, and no unity to the Democratic Party.

Roosevelt's inability to work with Capitol Hill was by now well known, and his aides, rather than make up for this weakness, seemed to add to the problem. He was not good at taking criticism; this made it difficult to engage in the give and take of legislative action. His imperious demeanor left him vulnerable to critics. He stumbled once again with what has come to be known as the "court packing" plan. Capitol Hill first learned of this initiative at a press conference.

Stung by the Supreme Court's ruling that the NRA was unconstitutional, Roosevelt proposed expanding the Supreme Court. Roosevelt would appoint the new judges, and therefore would control the court. Walsh, who had just bailed him out after the mistakes of the NRA, was about to witness a chief executive gone awry. The Democrats controlled Capitol Hill and they were unwavering in their support for New Deal programs. FDR should have anticipated the reaction. Instead, he surprised the legislative leaders with a proposal for radical surgery; and now that the proposal was public, Congress had to respond in a very public way.

FDR was smarting over his losses before the Supreme Court. Unlike the Coolidge and Hoover years, Congress had entered a period of legislative activism the likes of which the country had never seen. If the opponents of FDR's social agenda could not win in Congress, they had every right to try in the courts. But FDR assumed he had a mandate from the people to cure the economic ills that faced the nation, and he was not going to be dictated to by the Supreme Court. This is sometimes referred to as the "messiah complex."

FDR's staff came up with the plan to add more judges. FDR had been laying the groundwork for it throughout 1936, but he did not want to go public until he felt he had lined up support. It was a delicate balancing act, selling the idea while keeping it out of the limelight. FDR seemed unprepared for Walsh's first public comments on the court-packing plan: a stinging denunciation. FDR expected support from his party leaders, or at least more circumspect public comments. Walsh, speaking at Carnegie Hall in New York, said:

> The bill now before the congress gives our President today, and to his successors, an elastic power, a discretionary authority, to appoint additional judges, or not, according to his own desires....In brief, it is proposed to give to the Executive, power to control future decisions of the court...Do you believe that this power once granted to an Executive will be surrendered by any future President willingly?...I submit that there can be no justification for such ruthless sabotage of the people's rights....Were it not for the independent judiciary that has blessed us since the birth of our nation, tyrannical interferences with the liberty of the individual would have prevailed, and they would have been multiplied. Who may say when some new hysteria may overtake us? Who may say when some majority of the moment may attempt to oppress the minority? What avail to us, our Constitution and our Bill of Rights, if our courts shall be subservient to the government, as the courts are today in Russia, Mexico, Germany, and Italy?.... My fellow citizens, let us not lose sight of the fundamental question — the question of the integrity of our courts...[5]

The speech made national headlines for four days. FDR appears to have been caught off guard by the passion Walsh displayed. He may have anticipated such a reaction from a conservative, but not from a member of the liberal wing of the party.

Walsh's longtime legal practice prepared him for only one decision: unwavering support for the court. Roosevelt should have known of Walsh's lifelong friendship with Justice Brandeis, since he was around Washington, serving as Assistant Secretary of the Navy, at the time of Brandeis' bruising confirmation hearings. Did Roosevelt know Walsh was a lawyer? As a politician, Walsh could have been more diplomatic. But, as in so many other instances, Walsh's comments here do not seem calculating. His senate seat was safe. There was nothing to be gained by attacking his party leader, especially someone as thin skinned as FDR. His decision would cause permanent enmity with Roosevelt. Walsh's decision was a decision of conscience, firmly held. Walsh went to extraordinary lengths to explain his position, as though he felt he owed it to the electorate; his explanations reveal his strong commitment to Jeffersonian democracy. The Walsh Archives at the College of the Holy Cross contain press releases prepared for all of Massachusetts newspapers, and all appear carefully crafted by him. Striking in its

---

[5] Wayman, Dorothy G., *David I. Walsh, Citizen-Patriot*, Bruce Publishing Milwaukee, 1952, 229.

absence is any attempt to explain his stand to FDR. It appears that Walsh did not even give it an afterthought.

In an article published in three leading newspapers on October 12, 1937, Walsh states:

> Since I have been in the Senate, no issue has arisen that has created more intense feeling, longer consideration, and sharper differences of opinion (excepting the League of Nations issue) than the President's plan of reorganization of the United States Supreme Court. This was as it should be. All suggestions dealing with fundamental changes to our institutions should be considered with the greatest deliberation....It is not generally realized by the general public, the extent of the power of the Presidential office in corralling votes to any cause it sponsors in congress. Apart from the natural inclination not to differ with one's party leader, except upon the strongest conscientious convictions, there is the knowledge on the part of members of the congress that opposition, no matter how conscientious, often means a loss of party prestige, denial of senatorial patronage, even some forfeiture of party standing among one's associates in the Senate, and in numerable other ways one is made uncomfortable.[6]

In other words, David Walsh knew what he was in for, and explained to his constituents that their representative in Washington may have diminished his own power, the power of patronage, by this vote of conscience. He clearly believed that FDR had enough control without packing the court; and he wanted to let the voters know how much power the President had over senators.

Walsh paid special tribute to his colleagues who likewise would stand up to Roosevelt. "What I want to emphasize, however, in this article is the indomitable courage and character and the extent of their personal sacrifices that I have witnessed on the part of 22 of the 76 democratic senators during this controversy in the recent session."[7]

Walsh could not be accused of waffling. His stand was clear and well articulated. He understood there was nothing to be gained by his position, and knew that penalties would follow. This vote would cost Walsh dearly.

Walsh, at this point in his career, was no political neophyte. He had grown accustomed to standing alone. The court-packing plan was a public relations disaster for FDR. It raised serious questions regarding FDR's aides who cooked up the scheme. As Walsh pointed out in his newspaper article, payback would be forthcoming. The staff around the President had been cheerleaders. Ted Morgan, in *FDR: A Biography*, describes the jocular attitude of the cabinet and the stunned silence of the assembled congressional leaders when Roosevelt read out the gist of

---

[6] Dinand Library, Walsh Archives, College of the Holy Cross, Worcester Evening Post.

[7] Ibid.

the plan: that when Supreme Court justices did not retire six months after reaching the age of seventy, new judges could be added, up to six. "The leaders had not been consulted or informed. They had been summoned to the White House at 10:00 A.M. to hear a message that would be read to both houses of Congress at noon. The message had already been mimeographed and released to the press — there was no chance for discussion or amendment — it was a fait accompli. Then they were supposed to get out the vote for something they knew nothing about. Rayburn thought FDR was turning into a little tin god."[8]

The executive branch was proposing to take over the judiciary, while completely ignoring the legislative branch. Shortly after FDR's proposal, the Supreme Court reversed itself on a state minimum wage case, and finally started making administration-friendly decisions. The Supreme Court was shaken to its core. However, the battle was completely unnecessary.

Within a year, Roosevelt would have a chance to choose his own justices anyway. Justice Van Devanter resigned in May 1937. Roosevelt had the majority he wanted. But FDR had ignored advice to consider a retirement bill that would have been attractive enough to induce retirement of several justices. All he had to do was talk to Capitol Hill. They were in complete sympathy with the programs FDR was trying to protect. Instead, FDR suffered his greatest domestic legislative disaster, all of his own making. FDR had been humiliated; and messianic personalities don't take humiliation well.

Walsh remained busy on foreign policy issues, and was finally being recognized as an expert on naval affairs. He had been toiling in the vineyard since 1918, and in 1936 was named Chairman of the Senate Naval Affairs Committee. Walsh's work was barely noticed because the vineyard was bearing no fruit. Unlike Great Britain, the United States was inconsequential as a naval power. The "flotilla in Manila" during the Spanish American War was a long time ago, and that was one of the most recent uses of gunboat diplomacy by the US.

Now there was a Democrat in the White House, and this President was a former Assistant Secretary of the Navy — the same gentleman who seemed to be having a grand old time with the ladies on board the naval destroyer at the dedication of the Cape Cod Canal in 1914. Unfortunately, Walsh faced a new challenge. Upon assuming leadership of the committee, he had quickly fallen out of favor with the President. Even more problematic was FDR's preoccupation with domestic problems and legislation. Walsh's personal relationship with the President did not seem to affect naval affairs decisions. Walsh wanted to build up a

---

[8] Morgan, Ted, *FDR: A Biography*, Simon & Schuster, New York, 1985, 470-471.

modern navy to patrol the moat and keep outsiders out; but the Roosevelt family could hardly be branded isolationist. Roosevelt's cousin Teddy had not hesitated to charge up San Juan Hill. While Walsh and Roosevelt would finally get together on naval appropriations, the funds would be used for a different purpose than Walsh had envisioned. FDR, as Commander in Chief, would determine how the navy would be deployed.

The early work of Walsh's chairmanship would set the stage for a struggle between Walsh and FDR. While the Supreme Court battle was intense, the foreign policy battle would be protracted. If Roosevelt had referred to the Supreme Court Justices as "a bunch of tired old men," one wonders what he was saying about Walsh. Walsh's isolationist views remained consistent from 1918 onward. He had hardly changed in domestic policy, either; he was an unreconstructed liberal. Time was on his side regarding domestic programs, as he watched the New Deal legislation take flower. Time was running out on his isolationist views, but no one noticed. Events in Europe were troubling, but rearmament had more to do with the build up of armies than navies. Who could threaten America? There were no armies massed at the borders.

Walsh's isolationist views were firmly rooted on Main Street. He was not out of step with contemporary America. Walsh's views strongly reflected where he came from. He was always deeply distrustful of the capitalists and the royalty that he read about in the history books. He trusted neither the British nor the Germans. After all, when Walsh entered the Senate in 1918, the British Royal Family was at war with its cousin, Kaiser Wilhelm of Germany. In a sense, millions of men perished because of a family feud. Walsh entered the Senate surrounded by giants like Bryan and La Follette, both liberals, and both isolationists. Their views and the views of their conservative contemporaries, kept American boys off the killing fields of Europe, with the US entering the fray only at the very end of the war. British, French, and German losses were staggering.

Because of America's minimal participation in World War I, support for the veteran was lukewarm. Unlike World War II, when every able-bodied male served, World War I was not a generational experience. Even Roosevelt stood against the veterans' bonus (always promised, but never given). When the "Bonus Army" marched on Washington at the end of the Hoover administration, they were branded as malingerers, or worse, "pinkos." Douglas MacArthur, of all people, was sent to get rid of the demonstrators. Even Roosevelt thought the handling of the affair was a disaster. Major General Courtney Whitney charged that a secret document had been captured detailing Communist participation.

William Manchester in *American Caesar* details what really happened.

"There was no secret document; there were only hungry Americans. But as Eisenhower (Major Dwight) observed of his chief, the General 'had an obsession that a high commander must protect his image at all costs and must never admit his wrongs...Eisenhower, a better public relations man than MacArthur, begged the General not to take personal command of the eviction. It would only offend congressmen, he argued, and make approval of military budgets that much harder.'"[9] The veterans had been smeared, not by politicians, but by one of their very own, Major General Courtney Whitney, and then the final blow was administered by MacArthur. This marked the low water point in America's treatment of veterans, and also may explain the very active involvement of veteran organizations in the anti-war movement as World War II approached.

The view of World War I is important to consider. Isolationist views had helped keep America out of the war until the very end, and had also kept American loss of life to a minimum (at least, by European standards). In Walsh's view, that was an overwhelming success. The giants in the senate before him did the right thing on the eve of World War I. He thought they should do the same thing, now.

Back home in Massachusetts, the other senate seat was up for grabs and the race was heating up. As the political carousel turned, new faces but the same old names appeared. Henry Cabot Lodge, Jr., grandson of Senator Henry Cabot Lodge, was about to return the family name to politics. And James Michael Curley, former mayor of Boston, was not going to let this golden opportunity go by. Democrats had rolled up huge majorities across the country. This was the perfect time to run. Walsh had proven a Catholic could win statewide. Curley was convinced that he could do as well as Walsh, outside of Boston. His contempt for Walsh was well known within the party, but in this race it became a very public affair. The press was having great fun with it, and kept the dispute in the news. Curley was counting on the political inexperience of the young Lodge, as well as the Democratic tide. However, the Lodge clan had simply been resting on its oars. Walsh was still close to the Lodge family, and the press knew it.

As election time approached, Walsh's strategy was to stay invisible. In fact, he stayed out of town during election month. The Democrats carried 46 out of 48 states in November, but young Lodge beat Curley by 130,000 votes! This time the dynasty would beat the machine.

Walsh had run his slate against Curley for the delegate seats at the 1932 Democratic National Convention, the convention that nominated Franklin Delano

---

[9] Manchester, William, *American Caesar*, Little, Brown, Boston, Toronto, 1978, 150.

Roosevelt, so their competition was commonplace by now. Curley had thrown his support to Roosevelt early on, while Walsh's slate was pledged to Al Smith. Curley was determined to get to the Democratic National Convention to demonstrate his support for Roosevelt. He dressed up in a Latin American costume, complete with sombrero, and identified himself as Don Jaime of Puerto Rico. Unable to represent Massachusetts at the convention because of Walsh's delegate sweep, he used his political connections with friends from Puerto Rico to go as a delegate from "San Juan Hill." Curley knew how to get headlines. It was a comical routine that Curley could get away with, in sharp contrast to Walsh's dignified manner. The comical Irishman routine was not in Walsh's makeup, and it is doubtful Walsh laughed at all. Walsh's slate controlled the delegates in Massachusetts, while Curley commanded the media attention. Curley could deliver nothing to FDR, while Walsh could deliver every delegate in Massachusetts.

Curley stole the show at the 1932 convention, but Walsh's role was an untold story. Curley tried to take all the credit for being an early FDR supporter, while Walsh was publicly backing Al Smith. Walsh knew that party regulars would not stay with Smith for long. The regulars all wished Smith would bow out gracefully. The Hearst newspapers gave Walsh credit for swinging support to FDR — despite Hearst's own interest in promoting John Nance Garner for Vice President.

"Never in the history of American politics have the services of one man been so valuable to his political party as have been the services of Senator Walsh this week. Assuming leadership for a plank for repeal of Prohibition, when most that was hoped for was eleven votes in committee and four hundred on the floor, Senator Walsh by his able presentation of arguments and his capacity for leadership brought a majority vote from committee and secured an overwhelming vote on the floor. To secure harmony, Senator Walsh accepted a position on the committee to meet Franklin D. Roosevelt. Without this work of Senator Walsh, the Roosevelt-Garner ticket would have gone down to defeat. It is not too much to say that Senator Walsh saved his party." [10]

Many others would claim to have "made the phone call" that influenced Hearst to release the California delegation to Roosevelt, but the Hearst newspapers thought it was Walsh who played a leading role (if not the leading role) in securing Roosevelt's nomination. There is no indication Roosevelt ever thought

---

[10] Wayman, Dorothy G., *David I. Walsh, Citizen-Patriot*, Bruce Publishing, Milwaukee, 1952, 202.

so. No note of thanks survives among Walsh's personal papers. Yet the Hearst newspapers portray a man of significant power. While the Hearst writers would be expected to give the boss credit for playing kingmaker, the veiled references to the power broker on the other end of the deal could only be kept hidden by a source who insisted on anonymity. This added to the mystique. Walsh wasn't necessarily being shy. He apparently believed that his power in the senate was enhanced more by this discretion than by basking in the limelight. Regardless of who made the call to Heart's castle in San Simeon, the most significant issue was who could deliver the votes.

As the political season ended, it would be Walsh's turn to escort a Lodge down the Senate aisle. Curley could not win, despite a landslide of Nixonian proportions. The symbolic scene of a Catholic escorting a Lodge signified how much politics had changed since 1918. The "ethnics" were in the political game for good.

CHAPTER 8. JUST ANOTHER IRISHMAN

During the pre-war years of the 1930s, appeasement politics had been the creed of a long line of British Prime Ministers. Neville Chamberlain simply had the misfortune of being the last; the one the world would remember. Neutrality in the United States was also an article of faith. The Roosevelt-Churchill partnership would take root behind closed doors. David I. Walsh would prove to be a formidable obstacle for both of them, and his historic streak of independence would not portend well for any chance of rapprochement. Walsh's opposition to entry into World War I, and his battles with Woodrow Wilson over the League of Nations (which was primarily a British endeavor), were certainly noted by the British Foreign Office staff.

Churchill was keenly aware of the antipathy of the Irish in Ireland towards Great Britain's incessant wars. His concern over Irish attitudes in the United States was even greater, since US politicians apparently listened to their constituents. Ireland had no standing army, but the war materiel Churchill needed rested in the arsenal of democracy.

Walsh continued his efforts to keep the United States out of war. A letter from the Walsh Archives written back home to the wife of Judge Connelly, perhaps his closest friend back in Massachusetts, reveals Walsh's thoughts on the winds of war in October, 1939.

October 26, 1939

Mrs. Thomas H. Connelly21 Gerald Road Brighton, Massachusetts

My Dear Mrs. Connelly:

This is to acknowledge yours of recent date. I was pleased to hear from you and also to receive the information it contains. I suppose by the time this letter reaches you the Senate will have finished the job, the outcome of which we have known for a long time was inevitable; i.e., repeal of the arms embargo.

However, I think the discussion we had in the Senate has awakened the people throughout the country to a powerful resistance to getting into the European war. Certainly, it has changed the atmosphere here in Washington. A month ago, everywhere you went you heard, "We can't keep out" but at the present time this sentiment has almost disappeared.

However, after the first step is taken we can look for some new and subtle propaganda with view to our involvement.

I was much interested in the peace atmosphere you have observed in the Church. You will be very interested to know that we have received a very large number of letters from ministers of all denominations in support of our position. The National Council for the Prevention of War requested me, a short time ago, to permit them to send out copies of my speech delivered on Boston Common, to clergy of the Catholic faith. They did this themselves, paying all the expenses.

To date I have received about 2,000 letters from Catholic clergymen from all over the country, and not more than two to five percent are on the other side and they are mostly Polish priests. I was amazed at the unanimity of sentiment.

Incidentally, I received a letter from Rev. Mark Keohane, St William's Rectory, 1148 Dorchester Avenue, Boston, who was on the other side. He was, of course, most respectful of my views but his was practically the only letter from a clergyman in Massachusetts (Polish excepted) who happened to be on the other side.

I expect to return to Massachusetts after the Senate acts on the bill for it will not be necessary for me to be here while the House has the bill before it. I will, of course, come back for a few days when the House has taken action on the bill.

Looking forward to seeing you when I return to Massachusetts, I remain, with best wishes.

Sincerely yours,
David I. Walsh

P.S. I wrote to Father Drummond after the Judge had told me about his talk, asking for a copy.
P.P.S. I am enclosing a copy of the speech I delivered in the senate on October 17th.[1]

Walsh's comments remain optimistic even while the arms embargo is being repealed. He apparently pins his hopes on the mood of the country. He certainly seems to think that public opinion as well as the powers of the senate might be enough to check Roosevelt in his path. Churchill had been brought into Chamberlain's government, and it was his job to marshal materiel and ships for an impending confrontation with Hitler. With Roosevelt warming to the cause, Walsh, as Chairman of the Senate Naval Affairs Committee, reminded Roosevelt

---

[1] Dinand Library, Walsh Archives, College of the Holy Cross, letter of October 26, 1939, Mrs. Thomas Connelly.

that he would never approve naval vessels for Great Britain. The Neutrality Act was law, and it forbade the United States to aid any belligerent.

Walsh had many other concerns. The two-ocean navy, talked about in Congress for years, had never been funded. FDR publicly seemed unconcerned about developments in the Pacific, yet he was implementing a very aggressive foreign policy towards Japan. News from Europe still commanded the headlines. Whatever actions FDR took in the Pacific would not get much attention, and Roosevelt refrained from consulting with Walsh.

FDR may not have been seeking Walsh's counsel, but other important people were consulting him on a regular basis. A letter from former President Herbert Hoover dated October 10, 1939, forwards Hoover's ideas on the Neutrality Bill and mentions the numerous inquiries Hoover is receiving from other senators.

> The Waldorf Astoria
> New York City
> October 10, 1939
>
> My dear Senator:
>
>   Apropos our conversation on the Neutrality Bill, I enclose a memo, which sets out the idea in full. As I have had many inquiries from senators and others, I concluded to issue it to the press, where it will appear on Wednesday morning.
>
> Yours faithfully,
Herbert Hoover
>
> Honorable David I. Walsh
> United States Senate
> Washington, D.C.[2]

When FDR proposed trading fifty destroyers to Great Britain in exchange for base leases in the Western Hemisphere in 1940, an action initiated by Churchill, Walsh stood in Churchill's way. Rising to speak in the Senate, on June 21, 1940, Walsh delivered a heated denouncement of those who were dragging the country into war. He spoke with such passion that several colleagues stopped by afterwards to shake his hand.

Speaking after the war, Winston Churchill acknowledged that the transfer of fifty US warships to Great Britain was an unambiguous signal that the US was no longer neutral and it set the stage for the US to enter the war on Britain's side. The

---

[2] Dinand Library, Walsh Archives, College of the Holy Cross, Herbert Hoover letter, December 10, 1939.

US public may not have understood the significance of the decision, but certainly the Senate did. The public did not know that a secret war had been going on for some time now; and the targets at this point were not the "Hun" but loyal citizens who were opposed to FDR's policies.

Walsh continued to speak out in the Senate, and the fight has the ring of Walsh's earlier battles in World War I with Woodrow Wilson. As the debate escalated from a question of strict neutrality to one of possible intervention, Walsh engaged with Senator Claude Pepper (D) from Florida.

> If we are going to attempt to crush the philosophy of the totalitarian states which we hate — in order to be consistent — why not undertake also the extinction of the philosophy of the Soviet Republic? Russia has already taken over part of Poland and Finland and is now threatening Lithuania. Why not undertake the extinction of the Japanese philosophy, which is based on a determination to dominate the whole of the Orient, and which now has China bleeding and prostrate? Ah, gentlemen, if you are preparing to undertake the policing of the world in the name of justice, you are committing your country and future generations to a policy of waging endless wars throughout the world... It would be the slaughter of the manhood of this country to put us into a war today in light of what every member of this body knows about the condition of our Army, insofar as preparedness is concerned. I do not want to do it. I will not do it. I will walk out of this chamber and tender my resignation, if necessary, rather than put my country into a war which is provoked...[3]

While the public may not have remembered the lingering issues of World War I, the Senate did. After the Democratic sweep at the polls in successive elections, the Republican opposition consisted of the "safe-seat" senators who were long tenured, and had grappled with the issues of unpaid war debts throughout the Depression.

It was David I. Walsh's problem to be Irish, as well. While his positions on foreign policy were remarkably similar to those of the WASP members of the Senate, especially conservative Republicans, the British bureaucracy would discredit his isolationist position on the basis of his supposed identification with the Irish cause. British Security Coordination was keenly aware of Ireland's position of neutrality, standing in great contrast to the response of the dominions and British colonies. Since Ireland was now a democracy, public opinion counted. Ireland's Prime Minister, Eamon de Valera, also portrayed as anti-British to the core, would have been drummed out of office immediately if he had proposed support for Great Britain.

Winston Churchill constantly connected the Irish position of neutrality with

---

[3] Dinand Library, Walsh Archives, College of the Holy Cross, Congressional Record, June 19th, 1940.

politics in America, and constantly sparred with de Valera, apparently thinking that if he could change his position, it would help him with Irish support in America as well. Churchill, born of a British father and American mother, was boxing with de Valera, born of a Spanish father from the Bronx and an Irish mother: two outsiders governing two insular races, both being somewhat awkward in the political arena. There, the similarities end. Churchill was ever garrulous; de Valera could be cold, aloof, and introspective. De Valera was a master of details; Churchill was a master speechwriter. Churchill's personality would have been better suited for ruling Ireland, where speaking is prized and details secondary.

Churchill asked FDR on numerous occasions to assist him. Usually pragmatic but sometimes erratic, Churchill displayed anti-Irish sentiment that embarrassed Great Britain. He was hated in Ireland, despite the fact that his father, Randolph Churchill, was much beloved. Winston's ministers constantly had to apologize for his anti-Irish comments. His service as Home Secretary may have worn this Victorian leader down. Churchill had had to negotiate peace with Ireland. Michael Collins, the leader of Ireland's military forces, was the first military leader to beat Great Britain at its own game in modern times. His guerrilla tactics would result in the loss of the first colony since those pesky Americans bolted. While some historians, and Churchill's own writings, suggest that the negotiated peace with Ireland was one of Winston's finest hours, there is nothing in Churchill's makeup to suggest that giving away a piece of the empire had ever been one of Churchill's ambitions. Other colonies were more important than Ireland, particularly the crown jewel, India. Great Britain could sustain the loss of Ireland, since it lacked abundant natural resources, and its proximity to Great Britain meant it would still be dependent on trade with England. But other colonies might copy what Michael Collins achieved, and Churchill hated to lose.

While David Walsh remained the most visible and most powerful politician of Irish heritage in America, it was going to be difficult to reach popular opinion in the Irish American community when its most prominent public office holder was constantly attacking the British position. Additionally, Churchill did not seem to recognize that Walsh was not an Irish national. His isolationist position was American. It reflected the American heartland and simply coincided with Ireland's view of the European war.

Churchill's relationship with Ireland never settled down, and his relationship with de Valera could only be described as bitter. Author Jerrold Packard, in *Neither Friend Nor Foe*, recounts the memorable remark by an unknown Irishman at the outset of the war, who asked, "Who are we neutral against?" While Churchill continued to rant about Ireland's neutrality, Anthony Eden, Dominions

Secretary, counseled that Ireland's neutrality might be the best policy, as their entry into the war would require Great Britain to stretch her defenses further still. Irish neutrality irritated Churchill deeply and personally.

Churchill even proposed invading Ireland. Given Churchill's attitude, it is little wonder that he wandered the political wilderness for much of his life. Anthony Eden opposed him. Such talk may have played well in the factories of Manchester, but not among responsible political leaders. Eden suggested that the neutrality of the United States was a far more significant worry. Eden's wise counsel would win the day, and he displays a more far sighted approach as he casts his eyes on a much bigger prize across the Atlantic, the United States; an approach Churchill would take when he put his emotions aside, emotions that would erupt again in the future.

Churchill, despite having no support in his own cabinet for raising the issue of Irish neutrality, would ask FDR to intercede. In correspondence between the two in 1940, Churchill asked Roosevelt to work on the issue of convincing Irish Americans that it was in their interests to pressure Ireland to become a co-belligerent. In a letter dated December 8, 1940, Churchill proposed selling out the Protestants in Northern Ireland, and giving away another piece of the British Empire at the same time, if only Eire could be persuaded to join the war effort.

Had this letter leaked to the Irish press, there would have been blood running in the streets of Northern Ireland. FDR could not convince America to go to war. It was hardly realistic to ask him to convince the Irish in America that their mother country, with 5,000 troops, should join in. This reveals Churchill the writer; moody, melancholic, dramatic, irrational; not the astute statesman of statecraft. This is the Churchill known on the home front as the most unlikely politician in the history of the British Empire.

Roosevelt did not take Churchill's bait in 1940, but inexplicably, years later in the war, he did. FDR had appointed his cousin, David Gray, as Ambassador to Ireland. Gray would prove a worse fit in Ireland than Joseph Kennedy was in England. In 1944, Gray would pressure Ireland to close the German legation in Dublin. He agitated for both Washington and London to put more pressure on Eire, and recommended harsh economic sanctions. Even the *London Observer* noted that the acrimony "is probably to be regretted from our point of view. We in Britain respected Eire's neutrality in 1940-41 when it was an acute menace to us. To become party to its breach now when it is no longer more than a serious nuisance might undo what history may well regard as one of our more unselfish and far reaching acts in this war."[4]

The British press and public were dumbfounded at the proposal. Roosevelt looked foolish, but perhaps his ill health by this time had something to do with his judgment. Ambassador Gray drew the brunt of the criticism. It was speculated that the policy was aimed more at influencing opinion among Irish Americans than anything else. As for Churchill, his behavior and strategy in regard to Ireland did not seem to change from the early stages of the war right to the end. Logic might dictate this approach as sound strategy in 1940, but certainly did not in 1944. Churchill seemed bent on making the connection of US foreign policy and public opinion to British foreign policy towards Ireland; a connection he had failed to make in 1940.

Churchill, at the conclusion of the war, should have been rejoicing in what should have been his finest hour, but could not stop obsessing about Ireland. In his world wide victory broadcast of May 13, 1945, as the world waited in great anticipation, Churchill attacked Ireland as if it had been a major player in the war. Anglo-Irish relations not being at the head of anyone else's agenda, it is doubtful the listening audience had a clue what Churchill was talking about.

> Owing to the action of Mr. de Valera, so much at variance with the temper and instinct of thousands of southern Irishmen who hastened to the battlefront to prove their ancient valor, the approaches which the southern Irish ports and airfields could have so easily guarded were closed by the hostile aircraft and U-boats. This was indeed a deadly moment in our life, and, if were not for the loyalty and friendship of Northern Ireland, we would have been forced to come close quarters with Mr. de Valera or perish forever from the earth. However, with a restraint and poise to which, I say, history will find few parallels, His Majesty's Government never laid a violent hand, although at times it would have been easy and quite natural, and we left the de Val-era government to frolic with the Germans and later with the Japanese representatives to their heart's content.
>
> When I think of these days, I think also of other episodes and certain personali-ties. I think of ... Irish heroes ... and I must confess that the bitterness by Britain against the Irish race dies in my heart. I can only pray that in years which I shall not see the shame will be forgotten and the glories will endure....[5]

Churchill's attack and his timing stunned both England and Ireland. Churchill wrote his own speeches. Surely any speechwriter would have counseled a head of state against the tenor and the timing. Instead, Churchill used the grand stage to talk about old, festering wounds in Anglo-Irish history. While he thanked Northern Ireland for its loyalty, he failed to mention that he had tried to trade

---

[4] Packard, Jerrold, *Neither Friend Nor Foe*, Charles Scribner's Sons, New York, 1992, 329-331.

[5] Ibid., 334-335.

Northern Ireland for an Irish declaration of war. Churchill would soon be turned out of office. It is doubtful that he received many votes from Irish voters in London and Liverpool. The public was stunned at his defeat, and US newspapers would chalk it up to an ungrateful British public. However, the British public was well aware of the real Winston, not the Churchill of British propaganda, prepared for American consumption.

Unfortunately for Senator Walsh, he faced an army of British bureaucrats whose attitudes towards the Irish were worse than Churchill's. After all, less than twenty years had passed since Great Britain and Ireland had stopped fighting, and most of the senior foreign office people had spent much of their professional career dealing with the thorny issues that were a by-product Ireland's struggle for freedom, which included the assassination of British diplomatic personnel. Lord Lothian, the British Ambassador to Washington, was one of the British old guard that was enamored of Nazism in the 1930s. While he seemed an unlikely fit in the United States, Lord Lothian was needed for a very messy job. Lothian and Churchill did share one thing in common; they were both true Victorians.

De Valera would have to respond to Churchill's speech, and all of Ireland was waiting for his response. "Mr. Churchill is proud of Britain's stand alone after France had fallen and before America had entered the war. Could he not find in his heart the generosity to acknowledge that there is a small nation that stood alone not for one year or two but for several hundred years against aggression, but endured spoilation, famines, massacres, in endless succession, that was clubbed many times into insensibility, but that each time on returning to consciousness took up the fight anew, a small nation that could never accept defeat and has never surrendered her soul?"[6]

This recent colony had been bled dry of the few assets it possessed in World War I, and its loss of life, for a small country, was staggering. It was quite familiar with the colonial game, and was determined not to join in. The Irish losses in excess of 400,000 killed or maimed dwarfed United States totals of less than 60,000; the loss of so many men devastated the Irish farming economy. It was a loss that would reverberate for decades.

Senator David Walsh could not escape being treated as just another Irishman despite his family's long journey to America. While he had traveled far, British-Irish relations had not. The battle was too recent; the bitterness and bile had not subsided. The memories of 50,000 Irish filling Fenway Park to raise money for Irish freedom would not have gone unnoticed by His Majesty's secret service.

---

[6] Ibid., 368-369.

Walsh's role as the highest ranking Irish politician in Boston (the fund-raising capital for Irish independence) made it a sure bet that the British secret service collected a substantial file on Walsh; a far bigger file than the two pages that existed at FBI headquarters. London would never consider Walsh, first and foremost, as a United States Senator. He would always be an Irishman.

CHAPTER 9. THE 1940 ELECTION

David Walsh may have felt on safe ground in his attempts to keep America out of another European war during the election season of 1940. Just one year earlier, Roosevelt had embarrassed himself in his attempts to play a role in European politics, a game America historically had kept out of. FDR's attempts at being a world diplomat would be rebuffed by all the major players, including Great Britain.

In The Last Lion: Alone, Vol. II, 1932-1940, William Manchester writes: "Moreover, Roosevelt had interceded. The president's concern over Europe's murky future had been crystallized by the Italian landing in Albania. The week after the invasion the president sent a personal message to Mussolini and Hitler, asking them to pledge not to undertake further aggression for ten "or even twenty-five years, if we are to look that far ahead." Both dictators ridiculed it. Il Duce called it "a result of infantile paralysis." Goering suggested that Roosevelt was "im Anfangsstadium einer Geisteskranheit"("In the early stages of a mental disease") and on April 28 Hitler cruelly mocked the president before the Reichstag — and then renounced both the Anglo-German Naval Agreement of 1935 and the German-Polish Agreement of 1934, charging that Poland and Britain were conspiring to encircle the Reich. Chamberlain's response was to denounce "Yankee meddling."[1]

While it appeared that Roosevelt's interventionist efforts were feeble, Senator Walsh would see a change of seasons in 1940. A change in office would

---

[1] From THE LAST LION:WINSTON CHURCHILL ALONE 1932-1940 – VOLUME 2 by WILLIAM MANCHESTER. Copyright © 1988 by William Manchester. By permission of Little, Brown, and Co., Inc.

bring in Churchill to replace Chamberlain, and the new Prime Minister would assemble a team to assist FDR. The 1940 US elections presented a formidable challenge to Churchill. The Democratic Party plank for 1940 stated the party's leadership opposition to entering a European war, and if FDR chose to run, he would be expected to take the oath. The Republican Party was similarly opposed. There seemed little daylight for either Roosevelt or Churchill to maneuver, since public opinion was as high as 70 – 80% opposed, according to frequent polling done by the Gallup Poll.

America First was a veritable blueblood organization with members of the nation's most prominent families on its board — from generals and statesmen to industrialists. David Walsh was a frequent speaker at events. The national board consisted of liberal New Dealers Hugh Johnson, FDR's former head of the NRA, and Kathryn Lewis, daughter of labor boss John L. Lewis, as well as war hero Eddie Rickenbacker, *New Republic* columnist John Flynn, Teddy Roosevelt's niece, Alice Roosevelt Longworth, whose husband was the former Speaker of the House, as well as Chairman of the Board of Sears, Roebuck, General Robert Wood, and ex-Navy Secretary Charles Francis Adams. They opposed the war and the group was riding high, packing in full houses wherever a rally was held.

Roosevelt was up against a distinguished group, one that contrasts to the anti-war groups of the 1960s, and certainly more clean shaven. It held its demonstrations not in the streets, but in the major arenas of the country. However, its rallies would grow so large, they would eventually spill out into the streets, and public places would have to be considered for future events.

It is hard to imagine that this group would soon be headed for the dust bin of history. When this group was targeted by the arrival of the "British Invasion," America First would be associated with weakness, with reactionary ideas, and backwardness. Its adversaries, FDR and others would be associated with strength, virtue, and forward looking approaches.

The 1940 election started with suspense involving whether Roosevelt would run for a third term. He played coy, but belief that he would not run was strong enough to sow confusion in the party. On the Republican side, it was assumed that Senator Robert Taft of Ohio, an icon of the conservative wing of the party and a staunch isolationist, would square off with Thomas Dewey, from the Eastern, more liberal wing of the party. Both were opposed to United States entry into the European war.

There was almost no debate regarding United States intervention in the war because Roosevelt took the pledge in a very firm manner, assuring American mothers that their sons would not be sent overseas to fight. Since both candidates in the Republican Party were strongly opposed to intervention, there would be no debate.

Wendell Willkie, who had been a Democrat as recently as 1938, announced his candidacy as a Republican. It was generally described as a grass-roots candidacy, but author Norman Moss, in *Nineteen Weeks*, describes where the seeds came from. "Davenport [Managing Editor of *Fortune Magazine*] took a leave of absence from *Fortune* to become his campaign manager. Henry Luce and John and Gardner Cowles, powerful newspaper and magazine publishers, supported him....People like Henry Luce and Ogden Reid, publisher of the *Herald Tribune*, may have been charmed by Willkie as Marcia Davenport was, but their support was more likely to stem from his views on the war. Stimson would have campaigned for him if he had not joined Roosevelt's cabinet."[2]

Moss describes how Willkie's support started at 3% and jumped quickly based on great press coverage. "On the eve of the convention there was an outburst of press support. Henry Luce's *Time* magazine carried a three-page convention preview hailing Willkie. The *Saturday Evening Post*, published in Philadelphia, devoted much of its issue that week to Willkie. The Herald-Tribune carried a front page editorial in support."[3] It was Henry Luce's *Time* that revealed, in as nasty a piece of journalism as one could find in any era, an aspect of Walsh's personal life that he had managed discreetly. Walsh's support for social programs, such as the minimum wage, made Walsh an inviting target.

As the convention opened, FDR had announced the appointment of two prominent Republicans to his cabinet; Henry Stimson as Secretary of War, and newspaper publisher Frank Knox as Secretary of Navy. There seemed to be an inordinate amount of interest on Roosevelt's part in insuring media support, and the media was showing an inordinate amount of interest, not in the Republican Convention itself but simply one candidate.

The convention got off to a difficult start on June 21, competing for attention with the fact that France had just capitulated. The decision by Stimson and Knox to join Roosevelt's cabinet, announced the day before, threw the party off balance. Dewey denounced the appointments, saying, "It's not a coalition cabinet, it's a war cabinet." The Republican Party leadership resisted Willkie's candidature, as his change of party raised many questions. Willkie won on the sixth ballot, and was paired with Charles McNary as the VP candidate; according

---

[2] Moss, Norman. *Nineteen Weeks*, America, Britain, and the Fateful Summer of 1940, Houghton Mifflin Company, Boston, New York, 2003, 228.

[3] Ibid., 229.

to author Norman Moss, the two had never even met. More importantly, other observers, including FDR's supporters, were dumbfounded.

"Interior Secretary Harold Ickes wrote in his diary: "Willkie nominated. Nothing so extraordinary has ever happened in American politics.".... Willkie's nomination meant that Roosevelt could continue to aid Britain without fearing that every move exposed him to attack by his Republican opponent. Morgenthau commented in private, "The fact that Willkie is running will make it possible for me to continue for the next four months just the same as the last four months to help the Allies, and within the next four months the thing will be settled one way or another."[4]

The reaction to what happened at the Republican Convention in 1940 reverberated in the convention hall, and party stalwarts were furious. Two major powers in the Republican Party, Senator Robert Taft, representing the old guard, and the dashing young crime fighter from New York, Thomas Dewey, had been shoved aside for an unknown candidate who had not joined the Republican Party until 1938. Even outsiders were charging that it was fixed. Senator Robert La Follette decried the manipulation as a move toward war.

William Randolph Hearst had attempted to play kingmaker in virtually every Democratic convention since the turn of the century, perhaps none more so than the 1932 convention that nominated FDR. Now Republican newspaper publishers were playing an extraordinary role in the Republican Convention, primarily the White, Anglo-Saxon Protestant owners of the Eastern press; but their interest in truly Republican candidates was minimal.

The Eastern establishment would attempt to hide their narrowly organized group, and particularly, their connection to Great Britain, by creating front groups that sounded legitimate and broad based. They met over diner at each other's homes, or at their exclusive clubs, particularly the Century Club — forums that David I. Walsh could not be expected to be invited to, and not just because of his anti-war views. He was of the wrong religion, and certainly the wrong class. Yet the group would strive to appear to be broad based, if not on religious or ethnic grounds, then certainly geographic. America's heartland could not be ignored, because it was strongly anti-war. The leadership group was made up of people with strong public relations backgrounds, primarily newspaper and publishing; and they always focused attention on someone from Middle America. William Allen White, the editor of the *Emporia Kansas Gazette*, received an inordinate amount of publicity for an operation that was actually run out of New York's

---

[4] Ibid., 231.

exclusive clubs and boardrooms.

The William Allen White Committee could get as much publicity as they wanted, and it gave every appearance of being a wholesome American group, but in reality it resembled a fifth column of English nationals who had forgotten the American Revolution ever occurred. It was narrowly organized, consisted of predominantly one ethnic or religious group, and had a narrowly focused objective: simply, to aid Great Britain. Thomas Jefferson, when he was ambassador to France, had reminded us that Great Britain was "Europe's least faithful ally."

Roosevelt had warned of fifth column activities, but very little evidence has ever been found concerning German or Italian fifth columns. Author Norman Moss, in *Nineteen Weeks*, indicates that the FBI investigated 20,000-plus cases — and found no sabotage. Rather, there is evidence that British intelligence, operating out of the British passport office in New York City, influenced elections, the media, politicians and public opinion to bring the country around. It was British fifth columns who were spying on America.

David Walsh, in 1940, was speaking to America First rallies on a regular basis. As a person very interested in grassroots politics, he may have assumed that the support that the anti-war movement enjoyed would be more than enough to offset clandestine support from the well-heeled. He may have felt that a free press could not be co-opted. The *New York Post* would eventually ingratiate itself with its friends in British Intelligence by targeting Senator Walsh, but in 1940, the *New York Post* was working on the election campaign of Wendell Willkie. Its connections with British Intelligence were widely known by political insiders, but not to the rest of the country. Willkie was Great Britain's pick since he was the only non-isolationist to choose from.

Author Norman Moss, in *Nineteen Weeks*, links the *New York Post* to the suspicious activities in the 1940 election, their connection to British intelligence in Rockefeller Center, and the British funds that ended up in the pockets of Congressman Pryor, who had organized the Willkie rallies at the Republican Convention.

The *New York Post* would be the instrument used to destroy David I. Walsh's distinguished career as a United States Senator. United States Senator Robert Taft would be sidelined at the Republican Convention by activities of the *New York Post*, and they also failed to support Thomas Dewey, a 'favorite son' candidate from their own state of New York. The *New York Post* would sell a lot of newspapers based on headlines generated by the activities of crime-buster Dewey, but the paper's loyalties were not in New York City; they were in London.

The 1940 election was the occasion for the first attempt at a political assassination of Walsh. Up for reelection back in Massachusetts, Henry Parkman announced against Walsh. It appeared that his candidacy was being orchestrated by the White House. Parkman launched a vitriolic attack against his opponent; he accused him of being an appeaser of dictators. Despite the gutter campaign orchestrated by FDR to unseat a member of his own party, Walsh crushed Parkman. But the big news was that when the votes were counted, Walsh recorded more votes than FDR himself: 12,316 more. FDR fancied himself as having a mandate from the people. Not in Massachusetts. Walsh had that.

Walsh's suspicions of a stealth campaign were confirmed when the defeated Henry Parkman was offered a job by Henry Stimson. Walsh had voted against Stimson's confirmation as Secretary of War earlier that summer. Walsh was opposed to his hawkish war views. Twenty-eight senators voted in opposition. Senator Harry Truman refused to vote at all. "Stimson's diary records:....Consequently when I got back to the Department yesterday I was met with a terrific telegram from Walsh...claiming that Parkman had conducted a very low campaign against him; stating that he was personally obnoxious to himself [Walsh]; and demanding I reconsider the appointment...I called him on the long distance telephone at Clinton, Massachusetts, and he nearly blew me off the end of the telephone, he was so angry and bitter."[5]

It must have been a blow to FDR's ego when he was out-polled by Walsh. In 1940, David I. Walsh was an immovable granite monument — and not only because of his ponderous size. He was far more in touch with the voter than Roosevelt was.

When Lend-Lease was proposed by FDR, with the patriotic number H.R. 1776, Walsh appeared ready for battle, but he committed a blunder with lasting repercussions. The administration had gotten around the Neutrality Act by getting Walsh's approval on a seemingly innocuous transaction that in fact opened the door for the destroyer deal that he had fought to scuttle. Admiral Harold R. Stark, Chief of Naval Operations, told the Senate Naval Affairs Committee that outdated statutes were preventing the Navy from selling off its outdated equipment, and Walsh, seeing this as a navy request, drafted an amendment providing that the Chief of Naval Operations or the Chief of Staff of the Army, respectively, could certify material "not essential to the defense of the United States." Later, it became apparent that the initiative had come from the White House. Walsh inadvertently gave Roosevelt the opportunity of trading what many historians have described as

---

[5] Wayman, Dorothy G., *David I. Walsh, Citizen-Patriot*, Bruce Publishing, Milwaukee, 1952, 288.

"fifty leaking destroyers" for base leases supposedly for hemispheric defense.

The summer of 1940 would represent a sea change in attitudes on Main Street. Just one year earlier, the *Worcester Evening Gazette* had run an article on September 1, 1939 entitled, "VFW Asks Call for Congress, drafts Neutrality resolutions on Foreign Policy." The article states, "The motion for the request was offered by US Representative James Van Zandt (R-Penn)...former commander of the organization. He declared, 'Congress truly represents the American people who don't want war.'"[6] There was no jingoist talk from these veterans. The VFW position was strongly mirrored on Main Street. The thought of sending American boys to Europe to fight a foreign war was a "foreign" idea entirely.

The most important story of the summer of 1940 headlined in the *Worcester Telegram*, "Germans enter Paris." One week later, the same paper reported on events at Harvard University. The article was headlined "Seniors Boo and Hiss Plea to Fight."

> Harvard seniors booed and hissed a Class Day speaker today when he declared that since men of the class of 1915 were "not afraid to fight then you should not be afraid to fight now." Three times, David Sigourney, ivy day orator, of the class of 1915, and later a World War I captain, appealed for quiet so he could continue. There was slight applause, but it was drowned out by jeering as Sigourney, a Boston investment broker, spoke.[7]

The jeers at Harvard were precursors of the Vietnam-era chant of "Hell No! We Won't Go!" The difference was that most veteran's organizations shared the sentiments of Harvard students that day. They had a deep distrust of "European wars," and certainly were wary of a Commander in Chief who had done nothing to support the veteran returning from World War I.

Life in Worcester would change quickly. On July 3rd, 1940, the local and sports pages seemed the same as ever. The *Worcester Telegram* advertised a 1940 Chevrolet for $649, an Oldsmobile for $807, and a DeSoto Deluxe Coupe for $845. The Eden Restaurant featured a lobster special for 50 cents. *Gone with the Wind* had not been released yet, but *Mr. Smith Goes to Washington* had been released a year earlier.

Young males that morning may have anxiously picked up the *Telegram & Gazette* sports page to read Sid Feder's column on the heavyweight championship fought the night before, which indicated that nothing had changed with the fight game. "Unpredictable Maxie Baer, still no more consistent than the

---

6 *Worcester Evening Gazette*, September 1, 1939, p. 1, "The Way We Were," Worcester, Massachusetts, Historical Briefs, Verplanck, NY, 1992.

7 *Worcester Telegram*, June 20, 1940, Page 1, ibid.

weather, got "hot" tonight and chilled Tony Galento in eight rounds, thereby defying any and all comers to challenge his right to the championship of the screwballs. With an assist from Tony's brother, who bounced a beer glass off the Galento chin in a bar room row two nights ago, the former heavyweight boss cut the walking beer keg's mouth so badly that Referee Joe Mangold halted the fight just as the bell sounded to start the eighth round, giving Maxie a technical knockout. Up to that point, the playboy pounder of the Pacific had banged up Tony's face with such damaging effect, that at the finish, blood dripped from Galento's chin like a leaky faucet." A picture worth a thousand pounds shows "Two Ton" Tony hanging on for dear life. The young male sports fan should have turned to Hugh Johnson's column that day, for it would foretell their future. They would soon be heading off to war, but they would have little opportunity to debate the merits of it.

At the same time, on page 7, Hugh Johnson's column is aptly named "People Entitled to Full Publicity on Defense Program":

> According to press reports, future congressional hearings on the defense program are to be in secret to prevent military information from reaching some potential enemy. It will certainly keep information about something that is costing them billions and affects them vitally from reaching the American people."
>
> They are the only interested group that is going to be fooled or mystified. There are some things a government can keep concealed from foreign military intelligence units — but not progress of a ten billion dollar manufacturing program. It would be easier to cover the track of a herd of elephants in ten feet of snow.[8]

Columnist Hugh Johnson explains the only real reason for such hearings to be held behind closed doors: to exclude the public. This retired army general was just one of the former military leaders on the national board of the anti-war movement America First; which British propaganda made out to be irresponsible right-wing extremists. This was the same Hugh S. Johnson that FDR had appointed as the Director of the National Recovery Administration (NRA) in 1933. A liberal New Dealer, Johnson had serious qualms about FDR's foreign policy choices. His column was syndicated nationally by the Scripps-Howard chain.

While Hugh Johnson was trying to uncover the truth that day for the readers of the *Worcester Telegram*, Louella Parsons, the nationally syndicated entertainment columnist, was also writing about politics, albeit on the enter-tainment page. Wittingly or unwittingly, she was working as a British agent. She

---

[8] Ibid.

gave a plug for Robert Sherwood, the producer whose pictures the public would never have guessed were produced by British Information Services, BIS, the propaganda office of Great Britain, using British tax dollars. While Sherwood wrote FDR's speeches, his biggest paychecks came from a foreign power. Just a few pages away, Johnson was making a chillingly accurate prediction about the lack of preparedness of US defenses. "If our people are not candidly informed of that fact, they may some day have their minds shocked, their hearts broken, and their confidence forever destroyed by as great a disaster as the battle of France."[9]

While members of the house and senate were working feverishly to keep Roosevelt bottled up, they knew he was engaging in secret diplomacy with Churchill. Only an avid reader of the daily newspaper could follow the rather mundane descriptions of friction between FDR and Congress. Pearl Harbor was on the horizon, but the public would not see it. Not even a liberal New Dealer like Johnson could catch America's attention.

---

[9] Ibid.

CHAPTER 10. THE MADISON AVENUE PITCH

Like any huckster selling pots and pans, or Encyclopedia Britannica, British Security Coordination would do the job that J. Edgar Hoover refused to do. They would use a propaganda pitch that Joseph Goebbels would have been proud of. They would sell a gullible America a bill of goods.

Professor Nicholas John Cull, from the University of Birmingham in England, hardly anti-British, details the propaganda efforts with the clinical detachment of the academician he is. Cull does drop a few bombshells, however: he details the German Embassy observation of the isolationist movement in America, and the America First Committee in particular.

> The German Embassy watched the growth of organized isolationism with interest. Unbeknown to most of the movement's adherents, the embassy secretly began to provide monetary support for it. Funds flowed, and the German Embassy established a camouflaged literary agent to commission suitable books and articles. German representatives bribed Republican and Democratic Congressmen alike to influence their Presidential conventions toward "no foreign war" platforms, and they continued to promote tired denunciations of British propaganda.....

Cull on the other hand observes Lord Lothian, the British Ambassador to Washington commenting on British efforts at propaganda.

> It is a total misrepresentation to say there is no British propaganda in the United States, if by that it is meant that we are allowing the situation here to drift without doing anything about it. [1]

The statement that Capitol Hill was bribed is unsupported by the evidence despite 2,900 pages of FBI files. Hoover did his best to please FDR, to get him off his back. If there were anything there, Hoover would have found it. And Intrepid? He could find nothing. There is not even a sniff of gossip in this regard. Intrepid

---

[1] Cull, Nicholas John, *Selling War*, Oxford University Press, 1995, New York, Oxford, 75.

would have passed it on even if it were rumor. If it were true in even a single case, it is logical to conclude that Intrepid would have provided the details in his 1976 memoir, in an effort to provide some justification for his admissions of murder and blackmail of citizens and politicians. While he provides detail about his own transgressions, Intrepid only provides broadsides about Germany. The reason? His enemy in the United States was not German agents. His assignment from London was to destroy the anti-war movement in America. They were far more numerous, and far more influential than any supposed German agents.

This unsubstantiated charge seems to be a common thread running through British statements whenever they are getting ready to unleash the dogs of war. It appears to be simply a justification for the propaganda campaign against the American people. The British wanted to believe that the Germans were duping this "nation of sheep," so England would have to do whatever necessary to wake them up. Lothian assured the British press that he was not letting the propaganda situation in America "drift," but his cryptic comment would take years to divine.

Cull quoted Churchill as stating that nothing would stir public opinion "like fighting in England" and that depictions of the "heroic struggle" offered the best chance of bringing them in. Indeed, pictures of the Battle of Britain, with Churchill wandering through bombed out buildings, were powerful. The Battle of Britain only lasted six weeks but Churchill made sure it was a huge propaganda victory. The initial opposition to support of Great Britain was in fact opposition to the thought of sending American boys to fight Europe's war. In other words, the message now was: England needs destroyers, not American boys.

With the destroyers delivered to Great Britain in 1940, both FDR and Churchill trumpeted the close cooperation of the English-speaking peoples. In return for the destroyers, the United States received ninety-nine year leases on naval bases in empire territory. While the base leases were nothing that the United States Senate was interested in, the proposal by FDR would serve two purposes: It would help sell the deal by showing that the US got something in return, and perhaps, more importantly, provide staging areas for the United States Navy in support of Great Britain's war effort. In August, FDR named Nelson Rockefeller to head up the new Office of the Coordinator of Inter-American Affairs. Meanwhile, propaganda efforts went into overdrive. Nelson Rockefeller was in a key position. He knew the oil business and the key "Inter-American" objective was to make sure that Germany did not have access to oil in Central and South America. He was there to shut off the oil spigot. Rockefeller shared a closeness to his tenant in Rockefeller Center, Intrepid. (Also leasing space from Rockefeller was a competitor in the oil business, William Rhodes Davis, who would later be murdered.) Some researchers say the British propagandists in the US outnumbered the Germans 4 to 1. A member of FDR's New Deal brain trust, Assistant Secretary of State Adolf Berle moved to shut down both operations. That touched off an effort to blackmail Berle by secret agent, Intrepid. Berle was viewed as a threat because he was old enough to remember that Britain had stiffed the United States on World War I loans, and regularly reminded his British counterparts of that fact. Berle would soon be the target of a "tail" operation by British Security Coordination. J Edgar Hoover would inform Berle that he was being tailed.

Berle's position, in actuality, had broad support. The idea of throwing both the Germans and British out fit with America's isolationist mood; it just did not enjoy FDR's support. Berle was one of FDR's boys, and he had Hoover's strong support. Whether Hoover's support was territorial, or otherwise (Hoover had responsibility for intelligence matters in the US and Latin America), it was support nonetheless. British Intelligence had crossed the line in its attempts to smear Berle; David Walsh would receive no such protection.

In the autumn of 1941, the propaganda machine was turned up full bore. Sir Gerald Campbell knew that American public opinion counted. London had shown impatience with FDR when he was slow to take up the British position. Public opinion was usually FDR's excuse. At each stage, Roosevelt had had to garner support through "carefully mobilized public opinion." Campbell proposed to settle the matter for good.

British author Nicholas Cull quotes Campbell in a chilling analysis of British propaganda objectives.

> It is essential that our machinery should be able to bring into play all the instruments of modern propaganda….action must be taken through news….the film, radio, the sermon, the photograph, the whispered rumour, the Ambassador's press conference, the special interview, the declaration at home, the repercussion of articles in the English press, the voices of our allies — all these must be used and harmonized in our orchestra. Though the score may be written at home, it must be interpreted by the conductor in this country. And the orchestra must be numerous, disciplined and efficient.[2]

It's a British tradition. No wonder so many knives flash in Shakespeare productions.

Campbell went on to direct an extensive propaganda effort developed by Britons (or Americans whose loyalty was to Great Britain), but he insisted that Americans deliver the message. This served to make propaganda more potent while hiding British involvement. Great Britain would use American newspapers,

---

[2] Ibid., 155-156.

radio networks, American film, books, and false fronts to deliver a propaganda product paid for by the British and, most likely, American taxpayers.

Sir Gerald Campbell stressed the need to use "American instruments" to deliver the propaganda. This brings to mind the shameless use of Edward R. Murrow, an icon of American journalism, in the frontal assault to have Joseph Kennedy removed as Ambassador to Great Britain. Very seldom did British Intelligence step out from the shadows, and if it did so, it was usually by mistake. American faces and voices would bring the ceaseless propaganda drumbeat to the American people.

British propaganda specialists targeted America's heartland, the prairie Midwest, a strongly isolationist region. Few ethnics there; some prairie liberals. No Jews, Communists, Socialists, labor agitators, Japanese, or Irish. All right, a few Irish. Graham Hutton was sent to Chicago to open a British Press Service office. One of his first visits was to pay a call on Colonel Robert McCormick, a staunch isolationist, and owner of the *Chicago Tribune*. McCormick was on the board of America First. However, Hutton managed to develop a friendship with him, and tried to convince McCormick that his coverage of the war effort was biased, and persuaded McCormick to correct "factual errors" (that he attributed to his Irish writers) in *Tribune* coverage of the British case. While his beat writers affectionately called him 'Mick', it is doubtful they thought his position on the war was based on an inordinate interest in Irish affairs or his blind faith acceptance of their work. McCormick was a much bigger danger to the British Foreign Office than any Irish writer because his opposition to the war ran deep, and he could not be blackmailed or bought off. The British were obsessed with the number of Irish journalists whose work they felt must be biased. Graham Hutton's visit to Chicago was by no means unique. While the British agents were convinced that McCormick was being misled by his Irish writers, the visit did little to change his views. Irish journalists were viewed as a far bigger threat than German agents, because Great Britain knew this was a battle of the press to control the news, and shape public opinion. Irish writers were far closer to the presses than German agents.

Other newspapers would simply become propaganda machines for British Security Coordination. Material that was damaging to the Axis powers or to the isolationist position could be leaked to either the press or the US government; most people were happy to believe the worst and such stories got good mileage. On the East coast, the *New York Herald Tribune* was running titillating headlines of Nazi agents and secret missions. The *New York Post* had recently converted to tabloid style, and they, too, were willing to join in the game. BSC was constantly feeding them stories of Nazi penetration. At the same time, actual Nazi penetrations did occur after America's entry into the war, but the events were hushed up by the White House and the press. Circumstances had changed. Now, British Intelligence needed US naval vessels on convoying duty to London. To publicize the events might bring demands to call those ships home to protect US shores.

Also hushed up was the proximity of German submarines to the Eastern Seaboard. David I. Walsh had pressured FDR to keep naval vessels closer to US shores rather than to patrol the North Atlantic; as Chairman of the Senate Naval Affairs Committee, FDR could not brush him off lightly. Neither could BSC. Walsh had developed a lifelong friendship with many admirals, and he was hearing things the White House would prefer he did not know.

BSC and the rest of British Intelligence were clearly anti-Irish, anti-Jewish, anti-French, and anti- anyone who could not be trusted to take their word for it: anyone who was not WASP. And, their American counterparts, FDR's appointments to the OSS (other than Donovan), were clearly Anglophile. While much has been written about friction between American and British Intelligence, cooperation was actually quite close, with the exception of J. Edgar Hoover. The bigger problem was that it was not coordinated. The family connections to the American ruling class were at the highest level. These were clearly FDR's spies, and they knew it. They did not report to Congress.

In *Honorable Treachery*, G.J. A. O'Toole writes, "Notwithstanding the distaste for British Imperialism felt by many of the liberal and leftist elements within the agency, the OSS was possessed with a powerful spirit of Anglophilia. The eastern establishment caste that held so many important OSS posts was partial toward all things English. Many of the most important OSS intelligence officers — for example Allen Dulles, Whitney Shepardson, and David Bruce — had been pre-war members of the Anglophilic ROOM/CLUB or the equally pro-British Council on Foreign Relations (recall that the latter organization had been originally conceived as the Anglo-American Institute of International Affairs). OSS Anglophilia was not simply a reflection of class prejudices, however; after all, Donovan, one of Britain's best friends within the agency, was the son of an Irish-American railroad worker and the grandson of a member of the Fenian Brotherhood."[3]

The extremely pro-British views of many of these American intelligence

---

[3] O'Toole, G.J.A., *"Honorable Treachery,"* Atlantic Monthly Press, New York, 1991, p. 423.

operatives would result in the prosecution of policies that were simply an extension of British foreign policy. American foreign policy either ceased to exist, or was comprised of the one-sided flow of intelligence information to the British. If the same operatives had followed the interests of German or Italian nationalities, they would have been prosecuted for treason.

"To conclude that the Anglo-American intelligence partnership, which became a permanent institution with the creation of the OSS, was the work of a conspiracy between British intelligence and some American Anglophiles would be to confuse cause and effect. The OSS was drawn to the British by necessity. Despite its praise of certain OSS accomplishments, the American military establishment viewed the agency with suspicion and hostility throughout the war, and kept it at arm's length. The British secret services, however, which had taken a major hand in the creation of the OSS, clasped it to their bosom, and played the parts of both mentor and comrade. Donovan exaggerated only slightly when he told a post-war interviewer, 'Bill Stephenson taught us everything we ever knew about foreign intelligence operations.'"[4]

The disconnect between the American military and the OSS is disturbing. Whom was the OSS was working for? If the American military had no confidence in it, where was OSS intelligence information going? It appears that American taxpayer dollars were used to fund an extension of British intelligence.

American citizens were now being spied on from every possible angle, and immersed in a propaganda campaign of unprecedented scope. While propaganda campaigns in Germany and the Soviet Union were beamed at citizens of essentially closed societies, the massive propaganda campaign of the British was being conducted in what was touted as the most open society in the world. Therefore, it had to be subtle. Unfortunately, there were too many willing Americans who forgot where their loyalties lay.

While "Wild Bill" Donovan received poor marks as an administrator, the freewheeling conduct of his agents should not be surprising. The contrast with Hoover's FBI agents is stark. Hoover had his agents firmly under control and the agents clearly knew where their loyalties belonged. Donovan's people had just gotten into the spy business. The British Empire had been around for a long time. Thus, Intrepid's reach went well beyond his own people, and it became impossible to distinguish what was an American operation and what was British. This was particularly so in the targeting of Senator Walsh.

Most Anglophile American agents had bought into the myth that Britain was

---

[4] Ibid., 423.

doing the fighting for us. As a result, Intrepid got his intelligence information without really trying. The truth was that Great Britain was barely fighting at all. Churchill was taking the hits but refusing to go on the offensive. The bombs that rained down on London added tremendously to his propaganda material. The bombing of London was far briefer than most Americans realize, measured in weeks, not months.

Louis C. Kilzer, author of *Churchill's Deception*, and two-time Pulitzer Prize winner, masterfully captures Churchill's strategies from the secret war to the phony war to the real thing. Kilzer's account focuses on the Rudolph Hess mission. Like Richard Nixon, Hess had a "secret plan" to end the war. Whether or not one accepts the thesis of the Hess Affair, Kilzer's documentation is masterly; Churchill, indeed, had a plan. The Hess affair remains an enigma. It is hard to imagine an FBI case without clear command and clear documentation; but, like Shakespeare's works, each case handled by the British seems to have multiple fingerprints or no fingerprints at all.

When Churchill became Prime Minister, his son asked him if there was a way Britain could win the war. He outlined his strategy succinctly. "I shall drag the United States in."[5] That he managed to do just that is perhaps what makes him a hero in England; it is less clear why Americans admire him.

Churchill's motives may have been sound, from a British perspective, but his methods were certainly questionable. If Senators were still upset about false British propaganda in World War I, they hadn't seen anything yet. While the Gestapo operated against its perceived enemies, Churchill would target an ally: the ally that Churchill was counting on to provide the men, materiel, and money to fight the war. Capitol Hill was still balking and FDR had not been bold enough, at least with his public positions, to suit Winston Churchill. Churchill was London's agent in America. Churchill, with an American mother, was having trouble with his cousins. He was not going to return empty handed.

Churchill had asked William Stephenson to use every trick in his arsenal to sway public officials or public opinion, and he was given a blank check accomplish it. With the resistance on Capitol Hill, progress had been slow and somewhat messy. Operating as Intrepid, the Canadian businessman had the blessing of LaGuardia and his landlord Rockefeller, as well as FDR, but FDR's own base had been a problem. The Anglophile conservatives in the senate could not be swayed and FDR was unable to sway his liberal supporters. The black-

[5] Kilzer, Louis, *Churchill's Deception*, Simon & Schuster, New York, London, Toronto, Sydney, Tokyo, Singapore, 1994, 20.

mailing of politicians, the slander, and the phony political fronts all contributed to London's lack of credibility. Spies had been planted in the White House, US government officials had been tailed, and US citizens had even been murdered. The danger, of course, is that rumors of unspeakable horrors coming out of the occupied countries would be assumed to be exaggerated because none of the political leadership in Washington, even those pro-British, placed much stock in what the British said about Germany. Churchill was growing impatient. The public was still quite credulous, but Churchill's foreign office staff had to deal with public policy makers.

It is not that the President was unconvinced; the public was. Churchill had Roosevelt firmly in hand. The money spent to deliver propaganda in the United States was stepped up. The budgets of British Security Coordination, MI5, and the propaganda arms (i.e., various BLI, British Library Information offices, British press offices), the co-opting of American intelligence services for British purposes, as well as the considerable volunteer time from self-sufficient anglophiles, the total expenditure was formidable — yet hidden from public view. Great Britain did not have to worry about that becoming public information through the Official Secrets Act.

An assignment overseas had to be handled directly from London. Propaganda assignments were usually handled by one of the British Press Service offices. In 1940, when Churchill wanted Ambassador Joseph Kennedy sacked, BBC handled the propaganda mission by using an American instrument. They received an assist from an icon of American journalism, Edward R. Murrow. In his broadcasts from London, Murrow presented the British people as affectionate, kind, and patient; putting up with the strains of war. The British lion was not roaring again. This was contrary to the image that many Britons cherished, but it was an American stereotype of them that was very believable. The American image of the British shopkeeper fit perfectly with the image that Murrow's host in London wanted to project back to New York, and then the rest of America. On March 10, 1940, Murrow quoted Harold Nicolson's stinging attack on Ambassador Joseph Kennedy. This was the same Harold Nicolson who had felt guilty about British falsehoods in World War I, and had admitted that Great Britain had lied, in his own words, "damnably." His momentary pangs of conscience were gone.

The American instruments that Sir Gerald Campbell had insisted upon were available in the person of Edward R. Murrow. The American radio audience would have no idea that Murrow had spent Christmas in 1939 in the home of Iveson MacAdam, head of British Intelligence, MoI. (Television audiences would have found it difficult to accept Walter Cronkite's broadcasts from Vietnam if they learned he had stayed in the home of General Thieu, or his head of the secret police.) British author Cull described it as "propaganda of the most potent kind…placing them far beyond the reach of Goebbels."

But journalism was conducted that way in London, and it did not take a wartime situation to produce such an arrangement. Churchill himself had been in perpetual conflict, given his own role as journalist for the many years he was out of office; and Lord Beaverbrook served in Churchill's cabinet while he continued to own the largest newspaper conglomerate in Great Britain. There was no arms-length relationship or blind trust arrangement in place. In that culture, where government and business were intertwined on a regular basis, with charters from the King, it simply wasn't an issue. The Murrow broadcasts from London were memorable for an entire generation, perhaps as graphic as any memory of World War II. Most Americans have no idea that they were coordinated examples of British propaganda.

As has been mentioned, FDR's appointment of the garrulous Irishman, Kennedy, to the Court of Saint James ranks as one of the worst fits in State Department history. However, Kennedy's appeasement views reflected the exact views of the previous Prime Minister, Chamberlain; they were distorted by British propaganda. He may have been out of step with Churchill, but he was not out of step with the previous British government or with American public opinion.

Joseph Kennedy and his tenure in London were indirectly linked to the destroyer deal. The public had no idea that FDR's move to recall Kennedy had been orchestrated. FDR wanted a cheerleader in London, not a realist. When Kennedy was recalled, Congress immediately invited him to Capitol Hill and asked him to testify on the situation in England. His famous line was that he saw no way 1,500,000 Britons could beat 6,000,000 Germans.

David I. Walsh's worst fear was that if England collapsed, and signed a peace treaty with Germany, the fifty American destroyers would fall into German hands. Congress shared those concerns, thus Kennedy's testimony. As far as Walsh, was concerned, Great Britain could not be trusted; it's renouncement of appeasement was simply too recent. Its flirtation with high Nazi officials as recently as 1939 was still fresh in Walsh's mind.

But Great Britain had lied to the American public and congress before, and everyone knew it. It was important not to show their hand. Walsh had supported Woodrow Wilson in 1918 based on his pledge to "Keep America out of War." When Wilson reversed course immediately after the election, Walsh knew that a deal had been made with Great Britain before the election. For Walsh, and all the other isolationists, still angered by British propaganda in World War I, there would be no repeat this time.

The British Council for Cultural Relations Abroad, founded in 1934, could have inaugurated an overt public relations campaign, but they would be marching up hill. The "Speaker's Bureau" approach would only have worked on decision makers, and London realized they had worn out their welcome mat with this audience. Intrepid thus set to work at changing the public mood, and Congress would be influenced covertly.

The fact that some viewed World War I as a spat between British and German royalty, cousins, did not help the matter. The laboring classes especially viewed this as a family feud. Liberals, Socialists, and Communists subscribed to the same view. While often viewed as propaganda, particularly by left-leaning groups, it was believed by a wide stratum of the electorate. Conservatives were almost universally drawn to a "no foreign entanglements" point of view. They believed in the Monroe Doctrine and free trade, but as far as foreign policy was concerned, not much else.

Hollywood was soon enrolled. Michael Powell devised a script about a U-boat crew shipwrecked in northern Canada and portrayed them as escaping across the border into the neutral United States. Escaping Germans encounter a succession of Canadian innocents, each bent on personal neutrality; the story shows how wrong they were. *Forty-Ninth Parallel* played in Canada and after Pearl Harbor (retitled The Invaders) in the United States. It was awarded an Oscar in 1942. A propaganda film won an Oscar!

Louis B. Mayer, of Metro Goldwyn Mayer fame, approached British intelligence regarding a film project in 1941. Mayer had been accused of being the only one not cooperating (with British Intelligence). David I. Walsh and Louis B. Mayer had crossed paths early in their respective careers. Mayer, a Haverhill, Massachusetts theater owner, ended up earning in excess of half a million dollars from the movie *Birth of a Nation*. The film would have been "banned in Boston," if Walsh had his way, because of its characterization of Black Americans.

Walsh filed legislation in Massachusetts, which created a three-person censor board with the intent of stopping the movie. It was passed into law too late to stop distribution of the movie, but it did become a point of contention between Walsh and Mayor James Michael Curley. Curley, always a strong vote getter in the Black community, had promised to stop the movie. He didn't. Walsh made a real effort, despite his liberal credentials which would make him an unlikely supporter of censorship; but he was too late. The Black community viewed Walsh favorably, but it would be several years before Curley would recover his reputation there. Curley finally restored his credibility by making some very significant black appointments in high-ranking professional jobs.

Mayer had proposed to British Intelligence to turn the novel *Mrs. Miniver* into a movie. "When *Mrs. Miniver* finally appeared in 1942, it became an instant classic, sweeping seven Academy Awards. Roosevelt and Churchill are both to have told Struther of their admiration for her creation; but the picturesque England depicted in the film infuriated the British Embassy and many old fighters of the British cause, including Dorothy Thompson. Eager to defend his contribution to the film, Sidney Bernstein commissioned George Gallup to investigate American moviegoers' responses to *Mrs. Miniver*, *Eagle Squadron*, and This Above All. In October of 1942, Gallup polled large samples of residents in New York and Boston who had seen these films and other large samples of residents who had not, to determine their attitudes toward Britain. He found that 86.7% of those who had seen the films were favorably disposed to Britain, versus only 59.2% of those who had not seen the film. Even given the element of self selection (Bund fascists were unlikely to pay to see *Mrs. Miniver*) the result was a testament to the power of film propaganda."[6]

British Intelligence was not running second-rate showings at a back alley cinema. Sir Laurence Olivier was a loyal subject and the film was promoted by winning seven academy awards. Propaganda films had been used before, but usually were easily identified as such. Averill Harriman had created films starring figure skater Sonja Henie to help promote his winter resort at Sun Valley. This public relations masterstroke used British actors but an American icon in Hollywood, Mayer, was the "conductor".

The British public resented the stereotypes in the film, because they had no idea that it was made for American consumption. Indeed, British tax dollars helped pay for it. They got good value for their investment.

Readers also had something to chew on. Harcourt, Brace & Co. published a book in 1941, telling of the travails of a twelve-year-old Dutch boy, entitled *My Sister and I*. The book, written for children, told of the suffering of the Netherlands and their British allies. The book was presented as a diary but it was a complete fabrication. Harcourt, Brace never identified it as fiction.

For the adult movie-going audience, the thriller *Above Suspicion* was released in 1941. The unsuspecting public did not realize that the book it was based on was another fraud, written by the wife of a BSC agent. In other words,

---

[6] Cull, Nicholas John, *Selling War*, Oxford University Press, New York, Oxford, 1995, 183.

one of Intrepid's employees wrote the book using an alias. *Above Suspicion* was actually written by Helen Highet, wife of BSC agent and Columbia classicist, Gilbert Highet.

The use of New York tabloid newspapers to promote propaganda books and movies is also well documented. The movie *That Hamilton Woman* was touted by the New York *Herald Tribune* and the New York papers continue to pop up in Intrepid's operations. They were used to promote British propaganda in New York City. If a movie made it in New York City, it would be coming to a theatre near you soon.

The British propaganda did not stop at films and books. The writer Isaiah Berlin recounts British influence in comic books. Berlin worked for the British Embassy in Washington; he admits to British influence on Ham Fisher, the creator of the comic strip, Joe Palooka. Fisher mixed in factual characters with his strip. After a negative column, the British Embassy got to him and after that they had only positive coverage. One can assume this was a relatively benign operation, despite the insidious nature of the propaganda, since Fisher was a supporter of FDR.

There remains much to investigate about Fiorello LaGuardia, too, who was supposed to be serving as mayor of New York City all this time. His involvement with British Intelligence was extensive, and his involvement with Intrepid went back to their flying days in World War I.

With a flood of movies aimed at shaping the mood on Main Street, most of them financed by British Security Coordination, the stage was set. The propaganda took hold and by mid 1941 Anglophilia and anti-Germanism were replacing isolationism. Late that summer Senator Nye and other leaders in the Senate spoke out against the machinations in Hollywood and Senator D. Worth Clark of Idaho announced his intention to conduct a formal investigation of the film industry. But it was too late.

According to British author Nicholas Cull, on September 9, 1941, Senator Nye noted that Warner Brothers seemed particularly intent on intervention, and questioned whether the producers' interests as Jews outweighed their allegiance to the interests of US foreign policy. Was Nye actually blatantly anti-Semitic, or is Cull's remark another slander of anyone who dared to question British foreign policy? Other news outlets attacked Nye as well, but in each instance the attacks can be traced back to a British source. Nye was as liberal as they come, and as a prairie liberal, his usual targets were Eastern, WASP bankers, who were often blamed for the ills of the farmer. Nye's political leanings hardly suggest someone who would engage in anti-Semitic rhetoric. "Born in Hortonville, Wisconsin, in

1892, young Nye had absorbed the values of Fighting Bob La Follette's progressivism in that state. After graduating from Wittenburg High School in 1911, Nye followed his father's footsteps into the newspaper business, editing small town newspapers in the farming states of Wisconsin, Iowa, and North Dakota for nearly fifteen years. He supported President's domestic reforms and foreign policies and became increasingly active in the Nonpartisan League in North Dakota. The agrarian radical organization's hostility to eastern big business interests influenced both his domestic and foreign policy views....Though a Republican, Nye battled against the conservative, probusiness policies of the Coolidge and Hoover administrations. He supported much of Roosevelt's new deal."[7] What Cull claimed Senator Nye was doing to Warner Brothers is exactly what Senator John Sharp Williams did to Walsh in the 1930s when he questioned Walsh's patriotism for supporting issues from an Irish perspective. There was a strongly held belief that if anyone advocated for causes that were (perhaps, even, coincidentally) favorable for his ethnic nationality, he was not being "American." As America entered the war, the mother countries of all its major ethnic groups were either neutral or were fighting against the US. Ireland, Spain, Sweden, Denmark, Switzerland, and most of the South American countries were neutral, and Japan, Germany, and Italy were against the US; the French were out of the war, and were termed "quitters" by an Anglophile press. It was an uncomfortable time for many Americans.

Senator Nye would have a hard time shaking off the anti-Semitic label because the campaign to discredit Nye was led by Wendell Willkie, counsel for the movie industry. It was Willkie, not the American Jewish community that was charging anti-Semitism. Willkie had charged that Charles Lindbergh was injecting racial hate into the debate, yet it was Willkie who constantly stirred racial discord. Willkie had easy access to the media, earning his living off it, and his repetition of the charges were printed frequently. Both Nye's and Lindbergh's responses always appeared defensive and their coverage in the media was minimal.

Unfortunately, FDR's foreign policy was exactly the same as Nye's position; it refused to accommodate Jews (refusing to recognize that they had no homeland), and Polish Catholics, the other ethnic group in desperate straights that had ties to America. The bitterness of Polish Catholics at the Catholic Church (American) was significant, because the church was dominated by Irish, Italian, and French priests who often seemed uninterested in their plight or were

---

[7] Cole, Wayne S., *Roosevelt & the Isolationists, 1932-45*, University of Nebraska Press, Lincoln and London, 1983, 143-144

preoccupied with what was happening in their own homeland.

Nye's record produces nothing to suggest anti-Semitism, but he did lead the Munitions Investigation in the 1930s and blamed the Morgan investment bank, as well as the DuPont family for the munitions trade. His vitriol was always aimed at the Yankee bankers' influence and the connections they had with the royal families in England and Germany. J.P. Morgan had been the subject of a Nye Committee investigation, the so-called Munitions Committee investigation, focusing on the international arms trade during the mid-1930s. Morgan was the biggest player in financing the arms trade, and Nye had uncovered the intervention of the King of England in the granting of a Polish arms contract in which the King had persuaded the Poles to award the contract to a British firm rather than an American one. In later years, Nye paid with his political life for taking on the eastern WASP establishment as his campaign in the senate primaries was derailed by a carefully timed barrage of innuendo in the press.

Attorney General Biddle had disposed of one more enemy of FDR, another anti-war activist, as Nye went down to defeat. Biddle's actions had connected Nye's name to a sedition trial once again, reminding the voter of the earlier smear job of Pearson. The destruction of Nye was begun a year earlier, in a column written by FDR's relative, Drew Pearson, linking Nye's name with the trial. Biddle managed to bring the trial to a head just five days before the election. Biddle had authorized a subpoena of United States Senator Nye, even though he knew he had no significant testimony to offer. This served to insure that Nye's name would be interspersed with tales of spies just five days before the voters would go to the polls.

At this point, Britain's foreign policy and America's were indistinguishable. Great Britain had completely captured the media, frozen the US Senate out of any foreign policy formulation, and blackmailed any senator who dared oppose them. There was no open debate on whether the United States should go to war, or when.

The secret war for American opinion was over. The British government made ample use of Americans whose loyalties seem to have been confused. A decision had been made to destroy members of Congress who opposed British foreign policy. Congress had been neutralized, and civil rights had been suspended, all without an announcement. Representative government had ceased to function at the most critical hour. Instead, FDR was using Ministers without Portfolio, figures whose positions did not show up on any organizational chart. FDR was operating without the advice and consent of the Senate, and was deciding foreign policy without his Secretary of State, was running his intelligence operation behind the backs of his federal agencies; and facing Churchill, with his army of colonial bureaucrats, alone.

The country was unprepared for war, and FDR was woefully unprepared to prosecute it. FDR had driven away from his inner circle any talent in the foreign policy arena. When the war began, he would have to rely on men like George Marshall, Douglas MacArthur, Mark Clark, Omar Bradley, Dwight Eisenhower, and George Patton by default. Unlike their military counterparts in Great Britain, with the exception of Montgomery, they were not of the landed gentry. These were men who excelled at West Point. The British refer to this as that "meritocracy" in America.

CHAPTER 11. LEND-LEASE AND THE HOT WAR

The summer of 1940 had set the stage for FDR to approach Congress with his proposal for Lend-Lease with the patriotic number H.R. 1776. Perhaps it did not occur to the public relations people that a moniker like that might remind the voter whom it was America fought in 1776. It did not matter. FDR had counted the votes beforehand. He was not about to consult Congress at all unless he had the votes.

When the debate started, the usually staid members of Congress would make some startling charges usually reserved for conspiracy theorists. The Congressional Record would come alive with language seldom seen in Congress, as if it was Mark Lane's *Rush to Judgment*. Members of Congress were warning the public of a British propaganda campaign that had been aimed over the heads of Congress, directly to the American people. They sensed the changing attitude on Main Street, and felt powerless to stop it, but they did cry out. Representative H. Carl Anderson, Republican from Minnesota, speaking on the floor of the House, noted that the job of Congressmen was to prevent a recurrence of our troops again being used abroad. From the liberal side of the aisle, Representative Vito Marcantonio from New York said much the same thing.

Senator David Walsh, speaking in the Senate, derided the claim by FDR that this was a "peace bill."

> Indeed, in my judgment, this bill when viewed in the perspective of all the attendant circumstances is an absolute committal of the United States to war as Britain's ally in her life and death struggle with Nazi Germany and Hitler's associated partners and pawns. I say this fully conscious that the proponents of this legislation, when it was first presented to Congress and to the country...loudly
> proclaimed it a measure to keep the United States out of war. Such a claim is entirely specious. Such a belief is a delusion. The proponents of this legislation, it seems to me, refuse to face the realities of the course which they advocate. If they do face them and perceive them, they have not acquainted the country with the implications....But

it is only fair to say, as the public debate and consideration of this legislation has advanced, less is heard of the claim that this is a peace measure. There is now a tacit admission even from the many proponents that this bill does in fact take us down the road to war.[1]

Walsh seems to be simply asking for someone to tell the truth. As Chairman of the Naval Affairs Committee, he had been fighting FDR in closed-door hearings for some time. He now appeared less shocked than many of his peers, perhaps because of his committee assignment.

Meanwhile, President Roosevelt downplayed any suggestion that the Navy might convoy ships into British waters. Still, Congress decided to pin him down on the matter. The debate had been raging for several weeks. The White House had received thousands of letters and telegrams in opposition. Then, Senator Tobey would spring a surprise on Congress and FDR: he publicly declared that FDR was already convoying ships. He had a letter from a constituent back home in New Hampshire.

My Dear Senator Tobey:

I know you are against convoying by our Navy. Some information has come to me which has shocked me. I think I should pass it on to you. A young relative is in the Navy. He has been at sea on service. He was taken ill and put ashore in order to go to a hospital.. I cannot tell you the name or the port. In fact, I should not be writing this letter at all, but I think you should know.

He tells me that the Navy has been convoying for about one month. His ship was one of the convoys. If I tell you the name of the ship or the lad's name I would perhaps get him in trouble. He has been worried and thinks someone should know'...There Mr. President, is a sincere, fair, frank statement through a close relative, the testimony of a United States naval man...Yet the President of the United States calls the suggestion that convoys are being used as absurd, and laughs it off; and the American public asking for information, are turned down cold. What price democracy? What has become of this country?[2]

Roosevelt had been caught lying to Congress. His Secretary of the Navy, Frank Knox, looked foolish, yet Roosevelt would not admit that he lied. His personal secretary, Stephen Early looked foolish, for he had been repeatedly telling the press that there was no convoying. FDR's next strategy was to continue to lie, saying there was no substance to Tobey's charges, suggesting that this anonymous letter writer was hiding in the shadows.

FDR was constantly invoking national security and keeping the hearings

---

[1] Beard, Charles, *President Roosevelt and the Coming of the War, 1941*, Yale University Press, 1948, 65.

[2] Ibid., 89

behind closed doors. Walsh's searing investigations would not be leaked to the press. Or was it the press that was refusing to print the leaks? FDR was counting on a shooting war in the Atlantic as a justification for entering World War II, and he assumed that, with the sinking of the first American ship, he would have the incident he needed.

FDR made his first attempt to enter the hot war by giving shooting orders in the Atlantic, after the *USS Greer* was attacked off Greenland. FDR had recently promised that there would be no war — except "in case of attack." Members of Congress were talking amongst themselves and did not believe FDR's version of the events. Walsh began to prepare for hearings of his Senate Naval Affairs Committee. On September 20, 1941, Admiral Stark delivered to Walsh "a good picture of what happened" and answers to some questions from Walsh. This information spurred greater Congressional opposition. "Indeed, after the President on October 9, 1941, called upon Congress for another step in the legislation — an act to permit the arming of American merchant ships — Admiral Stark's papers on the Greer were inserted in the Congressional Record and thus made public before the next "case of attack."[3] Stark had admitted that it was the sub that was attacked.

Walsh's very aggressive actions in the *USS Greer* case prevented war from breaking out in the Atlantic. FDR had finally been out maneuvered. The real problem was that Congress could only react. With little ability to anticipate FDR's every move, time would not be on Walsh's side.

Charles Beard, the most prominent historian on the American Presidency during the first half of the 20th century, witnessed firsthand many of the hearings on Capitol Hill, and was frequently asked to testify before Congress. By Beard's own account, the *USS Greer* had chased the German submarine for over three hours, and this was duly noted by Walsh's committee. The naval command staff felt very uncomfortable about lying before Congress. Other naval officers could be counted on to tell Walsh the truth. With Walsh's long tenure on the Senate Naval Affairs Committee, he knew what questions to ask, and he knew that the honor of the naval officers would compel them to answer truthfully. FDR quickly learned that Congressional hearings were not an arena he could control, especially with naval officers who had watched newly commissioned ships sent directly to Churchill.

The *USS Kearny* incident would be the next attempt to start war in the Atlantic. Again, Admiral Stark was asked to provide details, and Senator Walsh's Naval Affairs Committee met in secret session on October 27, 1941. As soon as

---

[3] Ibid., 140-141.

Stark's report was given to the committee, it was reported that she was on convoy duty. FDR was again confronted over his statements that there would be no convoying of ships. Walsh again prevented an escalation of the incident, and FDR had no choice to back off, since prolonging the debate would only be embarrassing for the administration.

Walsh had come to realize that the incidents must be publicized or there would be no way to stop the secret diplomacy between Roosevelt and Churchill. Admiral Stark was now on notice that future hearings, in all probability, would be made public. He could no longer count on invoking national security issues before Walsh's committee. Although they had enjoyed a long and cordial friendship, the incidents of 1941 had worn out the welcome mat. Instead of showing some leadership with Congress, FDR was placing the admirals in the embarrassing position of carrying out the orders of the Commander-in-Chief, and then being sent to Capitol Hill to hedge.

When the *USS Reuben James* was sunk on October 30, 1941, FDR was expected to make his case for war. This was the first actual sinking, with loss of life involved. Congress vainly attempted to get details of the incident; United States sailors had lost their lives, and consequently members of the House and Senate expected an eruption. Yet, even Roosevelt downplayed the event. Something was peculiar.

The British diplomatic corps led by Lord Lothian were learning a lesson in American democracy. They were learning that committee chairmen in the Senate were very powerful. Walsh's role in America First was significant, but in his position as Chairman of the Senate Naval Affairs Committee he was immovable. Enough of the true story was getting out (via those media outlets that were willing to pass it along) to prevent FDR from controlling the information flow. The media focus was now on Capitol Hill, and Walsh was in command of the facts.

> After the attack on the Kearny, General Wood issued a statement urging Americans to withhold judgment on the incident 'until all the facts have been fully and frankly disclosed.' John T. Flynn, chairman of the New York America First chapter, asked whether Americans thought their war ships could 'hunt the ships of any other nation and escape attack.' He charged that the United States was 'asking for these attacks.' He urged Americans to realize that they were victims of a conspiracy to hurry them into this war.' Senator Nye told an America First audience in New Jersey that' these incidents involving the Greer and the Kearny are incidents very largely of our own making and our own inviting. We cannot order our ships to shoot and destroy the vessels of certain belligerent nations and hope at the same time that the ships of those nations are not going to seek to destroy our ships.'...They urged an investigation by the Senate Naval Affairs Committee of the circumstances

surrounding the sinking of the Reuben James.[4]

Roosevelt surprised Capitol Hill and the press by soft peddling the issue. Coming so quickly on the heels of the *USS Kearny* and *USS Greer* incidents, FDR knew that the admirals were not going to perjure themselves before Congress. If FDR wanted to make this an issue, he would have to divulge to the Senate Naval Affairs Committee what had actually happened. If this were another case of a United States Navy ship attacking a German ship, it would be impossible to get it past Walsh's committee. Further, Walsh made it clear that all future hearings would either be open, or its findings made public. The power of committee chairmen was made obvious when Walsh gaveled his committee proceedings to a close in the Kearny case, when he announced 'the Kearney incident is closed.'

The path to war in the Atlantic, through the Senate Naval Affairs Committee, had been blocked. The whole world was watching Walsh and Roosevelt square off in October, 1941. Hitler had given strict orders to his U-Boat commanders that no American naval ships would be fired upon. If they did, they had better be fighting for their life. In the case of the *Reuben James*, what little information the press in America received came from the German Embassy, and the information was that, indeed, the U-boat was fighting for its life. The public would not get the basic message that the United States was attacking German ships. Senator La Follette had raised similar issues in World War I, pointing out that US actions had violated international law; when he did so, he was threatened with impeachment. Yet, in World War II, the Roosevelt administration chose silence as its response. Perhaps, FDR was well aware that the Eastern press would sit on the story.

Overseas governments were watching the Walsh-FDR match closely. Intrepid was watching from Rockefeller Center. The fact that some American politicians actually listened to their constituencies was looked upon with fascination by most overseas governments, as that sort of thing was quite an anomaly. Other countries could make their plans behind closed doors. Japan was trying to make peace with the United States, but they knew that FDR was distracted by public opinion. At least that was the excuse FDR offered, and it was a plausible one. Not even Great Britain seemed to believe that involving the citizen's representatives in decision making is important.

Prince Konoye, the moderate Prime Minister of Japan and a man with many friends in the United States, was under great pressure by Japanese militarists to

---

[4] Cole, Wayne S., *Roosevelt & the Isolationists, 1932-45*, University of Nebraska Press, Lincoln and London,1983, 446

reach a peace agreement with the United States. Japanese generals had plans to invade Siberia. This would fulfill their obligations under the Tripartite Pact, particularly since Hitler had commenced the invasion of Russia in June, 1940. Japan's other interest was to seize French Indochina, since France was already out of the war and could do little to protect its imperial interest halfway around the globe. Konoye expected that war would break out in the Atlantic on the excuse of a convoying incident between the United States and Germany. Konoye's memoirs show a surprising preoccupation with convoying, not as a side show but as the main event. There is no sign of concern over a possible "Pearl Harbor." Given his moderate reputation, perhaps it was unthinkable to him. It would not have been so unimaginable for Japanese hard liners.

Since May of 1941, Konoye had been working feverishly to get FDR to commit to a written peace agreement. His memoirs were recorded for posterity by the United States War Department in 1946. In May, 1941, Prime Minister Konoye had instructed Ambassador Nomura in Washington to propose just two main points: America's non-participation in the European War; and (2) America's agreeing at an early date to advise Chiang Kai-shek to open peace negotiations with Japan.

Secretary of State Cordell Hull was noncommittal. "He remarked significantly that concerning this matter America would have to consult Britain. Further, his explanation that American domestic conditions were not at all such as to make conversations with Japan easy showed he was proceeding with the utmost caution. More than this, the President's speech which had been scheduled for May 14 was postponed to the 29th, and American public opinion was excited about convoys. It was apparent that, pressed by international and domestic issues, America was finding it difficult to determine its attitude. At any rate, contrary to Japanese expectations, the American answer was slow in coming."[5]

Konoye's memoirs raise the issue of convoys in numerous instances, and they were an integral part of discussions regarding an overall peace settlement. Japan had signed the Tripartite Pact, and Hitler was opposed to any peace agreement with the United States unless convoying was stopped. Japan had promised to consult Germany before proceeding further. On May 12, Germany made its position clear. "The gist of the reply was that, since America's underlying motive in planning reconciliation with Japan apparently was that she wished to enter the war against Germany, it was desirable that the Japanese government

---

[5] Konoye, Prince, *Prince Konoye Memoirs*, courtesy of University of San Francisco Library, 11.

make it clear to the American government that: (1) the patrolling and convoying being carried on by America was an act deliberately provocative of war, and one which would inevitably cause Japan to enter the war, and that; (2) if America refrained from such actions, Japan would be ready to study the proposal." Cordell Hull's response to Konoye indicated that he had to consult Great Britain, but he did not mention consulting Congress.

Japan's Foreign Minister even speculated that Army and Navy officials were trying to sell out Germany. "On the other hand, the Foreign Minister had an interview with me on the 23rd, in which he argued strongly that "although it appeared that Army and Navy leaders were trying to have the Japanese-American understanding put through, even at a cost, more or less of disloyalty to Germany and Italy, —what could be accomplished by such a weak-kneed attitude? Concerning the interpretation of Article III of the Tripartite Pact, the Foreign Minister yielded not an inch in his stand that even if American convoys were attacked by the Germans, Japan would be obliged to enter the war and help the Germans, convoying itself being regarded as an attack. In fact, the Foreign Minister frequently, in a half threatening manner stressed this point upon [US] Ambassador Grew, thinking this might just possibly prevent America's entry into the war. However, the American President was apparently determined to enter the war, and if that should happen, the Japanese-American understanding would be useless. Under such circumstances the nation would never be satisfied with an attitude such as the Army and Navy's present one, and a national uprising might ensue. At all events, Japan would have to clarify its stand, and come out for England or America, or for Germany and Italy...."[6]

In May, 1941, Japan's military was upbeat about the possibility of reconciliation with the United States, even at the risk of undermining the Tripartite Pact. Ambassador Joseph Grew had been stationed in Tokyo for almost a decade, and was highly respected in Japan as well as in Washington. Konoye knew that if they could not make headway with Grew, it was because he was only representing FDR. Convoying in the Atlantic was as big a part of discussions as Japan's occupation of China. The United States had little position from which to lecture Japan regarding the treatment of Indochina, since it was a European free-for-all, including the British, French, and Dutch. FDR wasted very little time hectoring the allies over the occupation of Indochina. Ironically, David Walsh had pressed for China's freedom from foreign domination since the debate on the League of Nations at the conclusion of World War I, and would have insisted on Japanese

---

[6] Ibid., 13.

troop withdrawal. At the same time, he would have stopped the convoying immediately, because it was a violation of international law and could only lead to the US joining in a European war.

Ambassador Nomura thought that he was making some headway in Washington regarding a peace agreement; he assured Washington that everyone in Japan was in favor of peace except Foreign Minister Matsuoka. These comments were immediately made known to Lord Halifax, who cabled the news to London. Unfortunately for Nomura, Japan had intercepted the message, and the contents were made known to Foreign Minister Matsuoka, who exploded.

Konoye's Memoirs do not indicate whether Japan had broken the British codes, or if they had a spy in the British Embassy. However, there appear to have been no secrets at the outbreak of the war. All parties "were reading other people's mail." Since Konoye's Memoirs specifically mention Lord Lothian, the message was not intercepted on the American end. There is a whole cottage industry in books on code breaking in World War II, many of which trumpet the achievements of Great Britain; but, very little information is provided on the failure to protect our own allied codes.

Both Washington and London had solid information of Japan's readiness to make peace with America, and certainly London had every reason to believe it. London had had excellent relations with Japan, right through the 1920s, and had a formal treaty alliance. The two countries may have collaborated for colonial reasons, but it was a longstanding business relationship, certainly not one based on democratic ideals. London had a much closer relationship with Japan in the 1920s than it did with the United States. The Stimson Doctrine would be a sore point that strained US-British relations; it was the present Secretary of War, Henry Stimson, who had first proposed the policy when he was Secretary of State under Herbert Hoover. Even before Stimson, United States foreign policy was driving a wedge between the London-Tokyo alliance, and London was furious. Winston Churchill did not rule out war with America. Washington and London had been arguing about naval strength all through the 1920s.

> The British, concerned about the protection of their global trade, claimed the right to seventy cruisers. Winston Churchill, then Chancellor of the Exchequer, told the cabinet that no doubt it was right in the interest of peace to go on talking about war with the United States as "unthinkable." But he added, "every one knows this is not true. However, foolish and disastrous such a war would be...we do not wish to put ourselves in the power of the United States. We cannot know what they might do if at some future date they were in a position to give us orders about our policy, say in India, or Egypt, or Canada, or on any other great matter behind which their

electioneering forces were marshalled.[7]

Churchill, himself, continued to raise the question of why America would listen to its citizens. Not much had changed in the British Empire since 1776. Churchill had plenty of company in the British ruling class. The recurring theme throughout much of the correspondence from the diplomatic service is the notion of responding to voters, as if it were a strange aberration.

Great Britain was apparently not used to listening to its constituents, and certainly was not going to tolerate the "preachiness" of United States diplomats. They certainly did not want to hear any talk about indigenous peoples from the United States. The public may not have realized how bad relations were between Great Britain and the United States in the years leading up to World War II, even if they had their own reasons for distrusting Great Britain, and much of the opposition to entering the war came from the fact that in 1940, most Americans did not see much difference between Germany and Great Britain. Hitler, at this point, was still an unknown quantity; Great Britain was a known quantity.

Prince Konoye's Memoirs provide excellent insight from the Japanese perspective, which dispels any possibility that the war happened by accident, as a result of language or cultural barriers. Assistant Secretary of State Adolf Berle's diary supports the same position. Berle describes secret meetings across the street from the White House, and an active participant was Lt. Commander Arthur McCollum, Director of Far East Intelligence for the Office of Naval Intelligence. McCollum's expertise on Japan was second to none. "McCollum had a unique background for formulating American tactics and strategy against Japan. Born to Baptist missionary parents in Nagasaki in 1898, McCollum spent his youth in various Japanese cities. He understood the Japanese culture, and spoke the language before learning English. After the death of his father in Japan, the McCollum family returned to Alabama...[as a young naval attaché]. In 1923, as the fads of the Roaring Twenties swept the world, members of the Imperial household were anxious to learn the Charleston. McCollum knew the latest dance routines, so the embassy assigned him to instruct Crown Prince Hirohito, the future Emperor, in slapping his knees to those jazz-age rhythms."[8]

Secret meetings were regularly attended by McCollum' boss, Admiral

---

[7] Renwick, Sir Robin, *Fighting with Allies, America and Britain in Peace and War*, Times Books, Random House, New York, 1996, 20

[8] Reprinted and edited with the permission of the Free Press, a Division of Simon & Schuster Adult Publishing Group, from DAY OF DECEIT: Truth Abouth FDR and Pearl Harbor by Robert B. Stinnett. Copywright © 1999 by Robert B. Stinnett. All rights reserved.

Walter Anderson, Director of the Office of Naval Intelligence. Instead of spying on Japan, ONI was again used to spy on American civilians, and the presence of Attorney General Biddle is so noted. The main agenda item was to spy on America First.

Robert Stinnett observes,

> During his ONI tenure, Anderson developed very close friendships with FBI Director J. Edgar Hoover and Adolf Berle, Jr., FDR's Assistant Secretary of State. Three days before McCollum put his eight action provocations in writing, Anderson met with a group of Roosevelt's staff in the Hay-Adams Hotel, across Lafayette Park from the White House. The group included Berle, Attorney General Francis Biddle, FCC Commissioner James Fly, and Lowell Mellett, a presidential political advisor.

> The group, according to Berle's diary entry, discussed the isolationist movement and ways to form an integral mechanism to combat the kind of propaganda spreading across the country. Their concerns echoed those enunciated by Roosevelt on the secret recordings but, Berle wrote, "the group was unable to agree on policy. Three days later, in his proposal to Anderson, McCollum advocated uniting the country by creating 'ado' with its eight provocations. Throughout 1940 and 1941, Anderson lent McCollum to Hoover for consultation and advice."[9]

The presence of both Biddle and FCC Commissioner Fly in a meeting whose main agenda item was to stop anti-war activists provides a chilling nexus of Orwellian police state tactics. Walsh, Wheeler and others charged that the national radio networks at previous America First rallies had refused to cover the anti-war events, and Berle's diary documents the active participation of the FCC Commissioner, combined with the military (ONI), to spy on civilians. At this point, Japan was seen as less of an enemy than the US citizens who were opposed to war. Japan appears to have been viewed more as an opportunity. McCollum's eight-point memorandum was an action plan to deliberately provoke Japan. The author knew Japan intimately, and knew all the hot buttons to push. War in the Pacific was not something that the United States blundered into. While FDR marshaled his cabinet and other high officials to spy on the anti-war movement, there seems to be little preparation to spy on Japan, a country that FDR was trying to provoke into war; a country FDR knew would have little choice but to attack soon.

---

[9] Ibid., 35.

CHAPTER 12. ANOTHER SENATOR FROM MASSACHUSETTS

David Walsh enraged the British Empire with his obsession with citizen participation, and his heartfelt belief that he was obliged to represent his constituents views; his behavior was chalked up to "that Irish thing." Yet Great Britain could find no such excuse when it came to targeting a "Yankee from the West," Senator Burton Wheeler. In his autobiography, Wheeler describes his firebrand image representing the State of Montana. A liberal democrat, Wheeler had a freewheeling style. Wheeler was a big supporter of organized labor in mining towns shared by the likes of Anaconda Copper and the IWW (International Workers of the World), otherwise known as the Wobblys. He was used to a tough fight. Born just two towns removed from Walsh's hometown of Clinton, in the town of Marlboro, he was quite far removed from the likes of the Duke of Marlborough, Winston Churchill's ancestor. Wheeler moved to Montana at a young age, bringing with him the contrariness of a Massachusetts Yankee, combined with a law degree; a volatile combination. Wheeler built his law career representing mine workers.

Wheeler had never met Sir William Stephenson, whose code name was Intrepid; but with war ready to break out, he was about to. Wheeler could speak at the drop of a dime, and spoke at America First rallies even more frequently than Walsh did. To give a sense of how tough Montana was, when Pearl Harbor was attacked, only one Congressman voted against the war resolution: it was a woman, Jeanette Rankin, D-Montana.

Stephenson, in *A Man Called Intrepid*, recounts a conversation he had with FDR's speechwriter, who was working as a double agent for Intrepid. This was the same Robert Sherwood whom columnist Louella Parsons was shamelessly plugging in the *Worcester Telegram* in the summer of 1940. Sherwood, with his frequent work in the White House, had a conversation with Harry Hopkins. Sherwood was stunned by the isolationist tone of one of FDR's closest advisors.

"What are you war-mongers plotting now?" Hopkins demanded. Sherwood replied that he was helping Stephenson get fifty old American destroyers. Hopkins protested that, with an election coming up, such public demands embarrassed Roosevelt. The playwright shrugged and said some of his colleagues were persuading Roosevelt's rivals to adopt the proposal, too. Anyway, it was in line with the President's general policy.

"What do you know about his policy?" snapped Hopkins. "You know this country is neutral."

Sherwood told Stephenson he was shaken by evidence that someone so close to the President should be a narrow minded isolationist. Hopkins remarked further, in curt terms, "The whole country's isolationist except for a few pro-British fanatics like you. If the President gave up fifty destroyers, how d'you suppose he'd keep up the confidence of the American people?"

Sherwood answered hotly: "You don't give the people credit for sense. They're a damn-sight more anti-Nazi than you think. It's time Roosevelt plucked up courage to speak frankly the way he has before."

A sudden grin broke over Hopkins face. "Then why waste your breath shouting at me? Say these things to the people yourself."[1]

This is Intrepid's own account of the beginning of the propaganda campaign that he would manage, to target the American public. FDR would finally trade fifty destroyers for base leases in the Western Hemisphere, and a trade did not involve Congressional approval.

Intrepid would play an active role in the propaganda campaign, planting stories in newspapers. By Intrepid's own account, he targeted Senator Burton Wheeler and labor leader John L. Lewis. Lewis' daughter served on the board of America First. Intrepid claims that Lewis's name was in German intelligence files, but the probable reason he was targeted was his fervent opposition to the war. "Goering, by promising to get rid of the fanatical elements in the Nazi leadership, hoped to confuse and divide the British and the Americans. He readily believed that the American presidency was at the mercy of John L. Lewis, who was in effect the boss of the Confederation of Mexico workers, and that Lewis had pressured the Mexican government into guaranteeing oil supplies for the German Luftwaffe.....the covert war against John L. Lewis began in early 1940 and was

---

[1] Stevenson, William, *A Man Called Intrepid, The Secret War*, Harcourt, Brace, Jovanovich, New York, London, 1976, 133.

waged by the British on US soil. The danger was that it might seem to be a campaign against the workers of America."[2]

Sir William Stephenson's remarkable candor is accompanied by an excuse for targeting Lewis. It seems hardly plausible that Stephenson really believed his own story. Lewis' daughter's participation in the anti-war movement was all the excuse Intrepid needed. However, because of Lewis' prominence in the labor movement, Intrepid describes a change in strategy to destroy Lewis. A direct attack, an overt campaign, was too risky and might backfire; but they could discredit less prominent men who were linked to Lewis and opposed the President, and bring him down indirectly. One such figure was Senator Burton K. Wheeler.

The top British secret agent in America published his best-selling memoir, *A Man Called Intrepid*, in 1976, and finally admitted to destroying the career of a United States senator and attempting to destroy the most visible labor leader of the day. America First had made those charges in 1940. Lewis had plenty of preparation for blackmail and intimidation after battling mine owners for decades, and it would have little effect on him; but Wheeler, as an elected official, needed his good name to remain a powerful force. A man who was expected to be a serious presidential candidate in the 1940 elections would find his campaign tampered with by an invisible outside force — not Germany, but a supposed ally, England.

As a direct report to Winston Churchill, who had a direct pipeline to FDR, Intrepid's admission is disturbing. Before smearing Wheeler in a propaganda campaign, Intrepid would first shut off the Mexican oil connection that he alleged Lewis was connected to. William Rhodes Davis was an "oil man" working out of Rockefeller Center in New York. As a citizen of a neutral country, America, he had the right under US law to sell oil to Germany. Intrepid made the decision to be judge, jury, and executioner.

William Rhodes Davis died suddenly while he was visiting his oil interests in Mexico, at the age of fifty-two. Intrepid's version of his death was "a sudden seizure of the heart" but in the same breath he admits that Davis was "removed from the scene." Since killing the largest contributor to FDR's reelection campaign might cause an uproar, Intrepid made sure it did not happen on US soil. US agencies had no jurisdiction, and newspaper coverage was minimal. The BSC papers note that Davis had agreed to many business deals with Nazi Germany. Mexico, at that time, was governed by Socialists who were working with John L. Lewis. They had no interest in helping Nazi Germany but also had no market for their oil. Intrepid fails to mention that US oil companies had used their political

---

[2] Ibid., 290.

influence to boycott Mexican oil in retaliation for expropriation of their properties. Because of British trade barriers they could not trade on competitive terms with England or her colonies. The Mexican government and economy was the victim of economic encirclement, and had no other significant market to sell their oil.

More than likely, Davis was simply selling oil to the Germans and refused to stop. British officials would have considered him a traitor. Thus, while America was still neutral, its prominent business citizens were being murdered for how they conducted business.

Intrepid admitted creating fictitious labor groups to do combat with John L. Lewis in the newspapers. He admitted that the American Labor Committee to Aid British Labor, the Fight for Freedom Committee, and other subcommittees within the American Federation of Labor were phony. They now shared the headlines with America First. These phantom war groups were given generous press coverage by newspapers friendly to Great Britain, including the *New York Post* and the New York *Herald Tribune*, which fed these stories to other dailies. Historians today still reference these groups, even though Intrepid admitted in 1976 that they were frauds.

Intrepid's people at British Security Coordination prepared a "white paper" that described the young factory workers that would soon be headed for Europe to save the British Empire. The report was part of the effort to undermine John L Lewis, and Intrepid intended it to educate the White House staffers; a copy was also sent to J. Edgar Hoover. Intrepid's staff wrote:

> The American working class is uninformed and politically disorganised. Many workers come from the uneducated foreign born population, which have no political tradition (and often a good deal of language difficulty) is confused and easily swayed by mass emotional appeals of the crudest character......As the majority of unions in the vital defense industries are affiliated with the CIO, Lewis' prejudices are a menace to Great Britain.[3]

Apparently, Intrepid did not realize that Lewis was a registered Republican. He had raised large sums of money for Herbert Hoover, and, feeling that Hoover had let Labor down, switched his support to FDR.

However, at least one member of the White House staff apparently shared Intrepid's bias. Leo T. Crowley described a meeting with FDR and Treasury Secretary Henry Morgenthau. Crowley, an economist in FDR's administration, was shocked to see his Catholicism brought up by FDR himself. For no apparent reason, FDR started giving the following lecture: "Leo, you know this is a Prot-

---

[3] Ibid., 288-289.

estant country, and the Catholics and Jews are here on sufferance. It is up to both of you (Crowley and Morgenthau) to go along with anything that I want at this time." Crowley told Morgenthau he had never been so shocked in his life. "Something has happened to the President," he said. "He has lost touch with the people." "What am I killing myself for at this desk if we are just here by sufferance?" Morgenthau asked.[4]

Morgenthau used his personal wealth in operations to rescue Jewish refugees, but there are no indications that FDR offered to contribute his own funds; not even an offer to go 'Dutch Treat'. He certainly must have been frustrated with his friend and wealthy Hyde Park neighbor, Roosevelt. The Neutrality Act forbade the use of government funds for purposes such as aiding Jewish refugees. While Rabbi Stephen Wise was a frequent guest at the White House, and considered himself a personal friend of the President, he was surprised at Roosevelt's reaction when Wise first informed him of the beginning of the holocaust. FDR informed him that he already knew about it, having been briefed one month earlier. FDR never bothered to inform Wise.

The Congressional Franking Case embroiled Senator Burton Wheeler in scandal; this was a propaganda operation, but the public never found out until Intrepid's memoirs were published. Congressional franking had been a long standing perk on Capitol Hill, which allowed any organization to use postage from a Senator's office. Naturally, a member of the House or Senate would only approve mailings for advocacy groups that supported issues the member supported. America First distributed its mailings through Wheeler's office, and its mailings were enormous. America First could have distributed its mailings throughout the House and Senate offices because of its popularity, but it was more convenient to use Wheeler's good offices.

To cut off their postage, Intrepid used the New York newspapers to spread the word that Congress had been converted into a "distributing house for enemy propaganda." The free press, with a helping hand from London, finished Wheeler off. The Congressional Franking Case would appear in high school history books throughout the 1950s and 1960s as if it were a real event, not something manufactured out of a propaganda campaign. Intrepid mentioned that FDR had ordered the closing of the German consulates just a month after the Congressional Franking Case. If there was a connection between Roosevelt's executive order and Intrepid's dirty work, then FDR was providing the soft smear that would leave in the public's mind a connection between the liberal Wheeler and Germany.

---

[4] Morgan, Ted, *FDR: A Biography*, Simon & Schuster, New York, 1985, 553.

FDR was by now making executive decisions in the White House with little talent around to guide him. The New Deal brain trust was a distant memory. Secretary of State Cordell Hull was still plodding along. Ted Morgan, in *FDR, A Biography*, says: "Hull liked to illustrate stories, like the one about the man who came to a little town and asked directions to another town, and was told to take a short cut over the mountains. At nightfall, he found himself back in the first town. 'At least,' he said, 'I am holding my own.' That about summed up his career at the State Department. He was slow, plodding, but he held his own. When someone asked FDR why he kept Hull in the cabinet, he replied: 'You must realize that Cordell Hull is the only member of the Cabinet who brings me any political strength that I don't have in my own right.' The unavowed reason was that he wanted to be his own secretary of state."[5]

While Tennessee has produced some colorful congressmen, Hull was not one of them. Hull had no foreign policy experience, and by some accounts, had never left the United States in his life. He was Chairman of the Democratic Party, and his reward for supporting FDR was his appointment at State. Certainly few observers of the Washington scene thought he would survive eleven years.

William Donovan, the head of the Office of Strategic Services, another in a long list of direct reports to the President, was playing a far more important role than Hull, and since his was not a Cabinet position, he did not have to go up to Capitol Hill to testify. While he was operating behind the scenes, it would be difficult for a man of his personality to keep a low profile. He was known on Capitol Hill as a controversial character, and his service in Washington actually went back many years. Both Burton Wheeler and David Walsh were well acquainted with the man.

Senator Burton Wheeler had been set up once before during the scandals of the Harding administration. The Teapot Dome Scandal had surfaced due to Wheeler's committee work in the Senate. The United States Justice Department, rather than investigate its own administration, decided to turn the tables on Wheeler and he was indicted in 1923. The investigation was conducted by J. Edgar Hoover. Hoover despised Wheeler. Wheeler obtained a prominent attorney for his defense: the other Senator from Montana, Senator Thomas Walsh. Wheeler and Walsh were not the most restrained personalities; the case was sure to generate some headlines.

The corruption in the Harding administration was revealed in bits and pieces, few

---

[5] Ibid., 371.

of which seemed significant in themselves....Walsh discussed the matter with his friend, Burton K. Wheeler, Montana's newly elected junior senator, who agreed something smelled bad. Wheeler was itching for a fight of his own. What if he took on Attorney General Daugherty and his Department of Easy Virtue? It would be, they agreed, be a hell of a fight, a pair of "Montana Boys" against more or less the entire administration, the odds didn't bother them — both would have been uncomfortable if they hadn't been the underdogs — and they'd fought and won just such a battle before, breaking the Anaconda Mining Company's domination of their state......Back in Washington, Bureau agents placed the two senators, their families, and friends under surveillance....(BI chief) Burns tried to frame Wheeler with the standard props, a woman and a hotel room. That he failed proved only that Wheeler had been forewarned. That he tried proved that Burns knew his man. He knew Walsh, too, and didn't bother trying.[6]

Wheeler and Walsh fit the category of colorful characters of Montana history. Wheeler may have been a Yankee from Massachusetts, but he had long since gone native. The other Walsh, David I. Walsh, back in Massachusetts, with his serious demeanor, still reflected the farmers of Western Massachusetts — a pretty serious lot. When Wheeler was accused of being a "Commie" for recommending grain sales to Russia, strangely enough by the weekly newspaper in a town called Red Lodge, Montana, he came out with his favorite line, "Where would you deport me — back to Massachusetts?"[7] Wheeler was upset that the grain farmer in the West was kept out of an important market, while Great Britain was doing a brisk business with Russia.

Despite their vivid personalities, they would meet their match with "Wild Bill" Donovan. Wheeler would be introduced to him shortly. Wheeler was indicted on April 8, 1924. "I was bucked up at that point from an inspiring source — Supreme Court Justice Louis Brandeis. The justice was a new and valued friend. After my election to the Senate in November 1922 he had written me suggesting we get acquainted when I came to Washington. I was flattered that I had attracted the attention of the eminent liberal jurist. On the night of my indictment, Justice and Mrs. Brandeis invited Mrs. Wheeler and me to dinner at their apartment."[8]

Perhaps Brandeis knew something about the prosecution. The Hearst newspapers were doing a brisk business, writing about the Teapot Dome Scandal. Wheeler's committee was getting plenty of press coverage. A reporter asked Wheeler if he would proceed with the hearings even if there was no press

---

[6] Gentry, Curt, *J. Edgar Hoover, The Man and the Secrets*, W. W. Norton, New York, London, 1991, 119.

[7] Wheeler, Burton, *Yankee from the West*, Doubleday & Co., Garden City, NY, 1962, 202.

[8] Ibid., 235.

coverage; he had heard that William Randolph Hearst was being threatened with prosecution for taking actress Marion Davies across state lines — unless he stopped covering the investigation. Wheeler assured him that he was not in it for the news story.

When the prosecution completely fell apart, Wheeler learned that Assistant Attorney General William Donovan, who was prosecuting the case, was not above fabricating information for political purposes or blackmailing people as a way of ending the investigation. "Wild Bill" had earned his nickname.

Senator Wheeler was told in later years that Chief Justice Harlan Stone would not have prosecuted the case except that he had been given false information.

Wheeler may have thought that he never had anything to do with Donovan again, but surely he meant it in a personal sense. Wheeler played a role in blocking the nomination of Donovan as Attorney General during the Hoover Administration, and it is doubtful Donovan would ever forget. Donovan would soon be fabricating events again, and use the press to carry the false stories.

In the spring of 1940, Wheeler had taken center stage in the race to replace FDR. It was widely assumed that FDR would not run for a third term. Wheeler was "Man of the Week" on the cover of *Time Magazine* on April 15, 1940, and pundits were suggesting that if Roosevelt did not run, Wheeler would be the Democratic nominee. While this may have made Wheeler euphoric in April 1940, there was little chance that the British Empire would allow an anti-war leader take center stage. George Gallup would measure a sea change in public opinion in the summer of 1940, and by September the fires of belligerence were well stoked.

"Wild Bill" Donovan and Intrepid both had a direct channel to FDR. Even the Director of Naval Intelligence had direct access to the President. Admiral Anderson was not necessarily highly regarded in the Navy, but FDR had put in place a man who had strong connections to London yet whom he felt could be trusted.

> Anderson's reign in naval intelligence was marked by poor morale in the agency. "ONI was the haven for the ignorant and the well connected," according to Marine Corps Colonel John W. Thomason, Jr., at the time head of the ONI Latin Desk. At least three times a week, Anderson met with FDR, Major General "Pa" Watson, the military aide, and Colonel John Magruder, then the Army intelligence chief would join them, ... according to Berle's diary entry to discuss the isolationist movement....[9]

---

[9] Stinnett, Robert B., *Day of Deceit*, The Free Press, New York, 2000, 35

It is an unusual arrangement for the Director of Naval Intelligence to directly report to the President three days a week. FDR was collecting intelligence directly from many different people, and in this instance FDR was using ONI to spy on domestic political activities. ONI would soon be actively involved in slandering both Wheeler and David Walsh, but for the time being they are simply spying on them. The agencies that would soon destroy David Walsh were all reporting directly to FDR. The unusual arrangement of a relatively low level naval official having direct access to the President appears once again.

Intrepid had earlier promised that he was not done with Senator Burton Wheeler, and he made good on the claim. A young military officer provided Senator Wheeler with a lengthy report indicating that the United States had plans to attack Germany. The officer indicated that he thought it was his patriotic duty to inform this anti-war senator; Wheeler did not suspect a ruse. The plan looked legitimate, and it was.

> Determined to denounce the undercover operations by a foreign power, Wheeler seized upon a War Department report, some 350 pages in length and clearly stamped TOP SECRET, which came his way in circumstances that should have aroused his suspicions. It was called Victory Program and purported to forecast US government plans to enter the war. The "Germany First" thesis was set forth, with an estimate of the numbers of troops and equipment required to launch offensives in Europe and Africa. Wheeler passed this report to the *Chicago Tribune* (whose publisher was on the board of America First), which splashed it under banner headlines and a lead paragraph: "A confidential report prepared by the joint Army and Navy high command by direction of President Roosevelt.....is a blueprint for total war."

> The leak reached the anti-Roosevelt press in the final days of peace. By December 3, 1941, a copy had reached the German Embassy. A summary was dispatched by radio to Berlin and was duly decoded in England. The German High Command celebrated "this fantastic intelligence coup." The fact was, the Victory Program was a plant.[10]

The head of British intelligence in the United States admitted that he planted the story in the press, by duping an anti-war senator. The military plan threatening an attack on Germany was leaked simply to antagonize Germany, just days prior to Pearl Harbor; since it was purportedly discovered and leaked by an anti-war senator, Germany would believe it to be true. It looked authentic, yet Roosevelt had not given any orders to implement such a plan.

Intrepid's behavior, while treacherous to the United States at the most sensitive hour, is wholly consistent with Intrepid's mission: to get American into

---

[10] Stevenson, William, *A Man Called Intrepid, The Secret War*, Harcourt, Brace, Jovanovich, New York, London, 1976, 298.

the war. Intrepid's actions may have convinced Hitler that war with America was inevitable; Germany declared war on the United States immediately after Pearl Harbor. Many observers of World War II were puzzled by Hitler's declaration of war, particularly since he had spent so much effort to avoid confrontation with America, and also because in declaring war he was doing FDR a big favor. FDR no longer had to worry about asking Congress for a declaration of war on Germany. It is doubtful that Congress would have declared war on Germany, when all eyes were focused on Japan. Germany's declaration of war got FDR out of a tight situation.

Intrepid's actions to destroy Burton Wheeler, while aided by William Donovan's long standing animosity towards Wheeler, makes Richard Nixon's enemies list seem tame. Intrepid claims a double hit. At America's most vulnerable hour, he destroyed a Presidential contender, thus tampering with US elections, while goading Germany to either attack us or declare war. And he used an anti-war senator in the ruse. British critics of Intrepid's memoir seemed more concerned that he admitted to such actions, even though the admissions came 35 years after the transgressions.

CHAPTER 13. J. EDGAR & SIR WILLIAM

With British Intelligence undermining the US government, American public officials and citizenry did not have much protection. However, the fact that Hoover and Intrepid could not tolerate one another created countervailing forces that provided for a safety net of sorts. J. Edgar was spending an inordinate amount of time watching Intrepid's agents, perhaps for turf reasons more than anything else. The 2900 pages of FBI files on America First, while representing the most massive political surveillance ever conducted in the United States, also served to protect many Americans. Most of the FBI field agents gave the organization glowing reports, as a wholesome, home grown movement. Reading the FBI agent's reports gives the reader the impression that the boy next door was writing them. Donovan, on the other hand, was hiring a different breed, perhaps because his organization was receiving training from Intrepid. Hoover's field agents were writing far more damaging reports about Intrepid and British Security Coordination than they were about America First.

Hoover was working endlessly to damage Donovan, and tried to discredit his hiring practices. He went to Attorney General Biddle in an attempt to quash some of Wild Bill's appointments. Ernest Cuneo, who was the liaison between Donovan, Intrepid, and Fiorello LaGuardia, had tried to run interference for Donovan on new hires. Hoover stopped him cold on one occasion. Donovan was trying to get Justice Department approval for a visa for an overseas hire. US Department of Labor regulations allow work visas only in occupations where the US lacked skilled candidates. Hoover eagerly provided a rap sheet that indicated the man was guilty of a few homicides and manslaughters. Hoover certainly enjoyed embarrassing Donovan, but he must have realized that FDR knew, and approved of, Donovan's mission and behavior. Perhaps his goal at this point was to show Donovan that the FBI was well aware of his activity.

What job was Donovan hiring the agent for? The OSS, which the public may have assumed was spying abroad, was importing killers to the United States. Maybe, Donovan could not find anyone in the United States to do the job — maybe there really was a skills shortage in that field. But Donovan's sloppy hiring practices would have devastating results for the United States later on, when he hired a Soviet spy to be one of his top assistants. Hoover, despite his oddities, had standards. His written opposition to Japanese internment puts him in sharp contrast to his nominal boss, Attorney General Biddle, who was also opposed but lacked the backbone to stand up to FDR.

Adolf Berle, Assistant Secretary of State, and an ally of Hoover in the intelligence game, was openly opposed to the presence of British spies on US soil. He confided in his diary, "No one has given us any effective reason why there should be a British espionage system in the United States." In an attempt to sever the link between OSS and the BSC, Berle proposed that the BSC deal exclusively with the FBI. Learning of this, British intelligence assigned an agent named Paine to "get the dirt" on Berle. Alerted to the plot, Ed Tamm (an Asst. FBI Director) warned the Assistant Secretary of State. Hoover and Tamm called on Stephenson and told him they wanted Paine out of the country by six o'clock, "or else." Professing "surprise and horror that any of his men should do such a thing," Stephenson had Paine on a plane to Montreal that same night."[1]

Berle's proposal that Intrepid's organization, if it was permitted at all, report to Hoover was considered so onerous by British intelligence that it started an immediate blackmail operation against Berle. BSC was not going to have any reporting relationship to an American. Given the infancy of Donovan's OSS, they were in no position to supervise BSC and by Donovan's own admission, they were learning from British intelligence. More importantly, Donovan had no interest in supervising British intelligence.

While Ernest Cuneo was serving as White House liaison to British Security Coordination, he also served as the personal attorney for columnists Walter Winchell, and Drew Pearson, both of whom had willingly planted BSC propaganda in the media. Cuneo also was the former legal counsel for Mayor Fiorello LaGuardia, who was protecting BSC operations at Rockefeller Center in New York City. Very soon, Intrepid, Donovan, and LaGuardia would come together in New York City to destroy David Walsh. Burton Wheeler had been eliminated, and the man who had stopped war in the Atlantic, Walsh, would have

---

[1] Gentry, Curt, *J. Edgar Hoover, The Man and the Secrets*, W. W. Norton, New York, London, 1991, 268.

his career in the Senate left in tatters.

Meanwhile, Hoover had been working with the State Department to close down Intrepid's organization. At least, he saw to it that cooperation was minimal and the welcome given to British visitors to FBI headquarters was correct but cool. Great Britain did not send any military commander to the United States, only people armed with literary weapons like the future writer, Ian Fleming. They fully understood the battle with American opposition was a propaganda war. and that the instrument to be used was the English language. Commander Ian Fleming was sent to meet Hoover in an attempt to forge a relationship. Fleming himself would admit to a less than cordial greeting by Hoover, and he would return to London empty handed.

Despite David Walsh's attempts to prevent war in the Atlantic in October of 1941, it was about to break out. Hoover had worked feverishly to stop Intrepid. Hoover was now warned about the imminent outbreak of war, but the warning came from a very suspicious source, Intrepid himself. Intrepid sent a double agent, Popov, a German, to see Hoover. Popov claimed he had been given an assignment to help Germany's Japanese friends who needed information on Hawaii: specifically, the layout of Pearl Harbor. At the same time, a second German agent, von der Osten, was ostensibly given the same assignment. When Intrepid sent Popov to Hoover, Hoover kept him waiting in order to check out his story. He had FBI agents tailing him throughout New York City, detailing his playboy lifestyle. In the end, Hoover scarcely gave him the time of day, especially given the general low regard enjoyed by double agents.

Hoover did send a report to FDR, but it was incomplete, and he did not pass along the alarming information that perhaps two German agents had been assigned to study the defenses of Pearl Harbor. There was also a partial translation of a Japanese document that indicated a suspicious degree of interest in Hawaii, most particularly Pearl Harbor.

Intrepid studied Hoover the way he studied all his targets. Hoover was suspicious by nature, and he would be doubly suspicious of anything Intrepid sent him. The long delay in getting the information to FDR, and the down-playing of its significance, is exactly what Intrepid expected. Hoover would be in no rush because he knew that Intrepid had direct access to FDR through Donovan or James Roosevelt. If Intrepid was interested in warning FDR, he certainly would not allow Hoover to take any credit for it.

Intrepid's actions served two other purposes, as well. They covered Great Britain's tracks, because Intrepid could always claim that he had warned his nemesis, J. Edgar Hoover. Given Intrepid's admission of his own attempts to goad

Germany to attack the United States through his leak of the Victory Program at the most sensitive time of US-German relations, through Senator Wheeler, this might serve to goad FDR to attack Japan before the United States was herself attacked. Either way, Intrepid could not lose. Leaking the attack plans through another party (Hoover), as he did with Wheeler, would give Intrepid the cover he desired.

The other spy, von der Osten, is said to have been killed by a New York City cab driver; a plausible enough scenario. However, Intrepid explains in his memoirs that, "Someone had disposed of von der Osten, a native born American traitor who had become an officer and secret agent for a foreign government. In this period of neutrality, however, deeper probing by the FBI would have led to acute embarrassment. The case, coming early in FBI-BSC collaboration, became a textbook example of manipulative techniques. The British knew more than they dared to tell about the German consulate's internal business. There was a limit to what they could do about a spy ring themselves. They neither wished to compromise their sources inside German organizations nor could they afford to be caught trespassing on American tolerance to the point where it might lead to a public outcry."[2]

A public outcry would have been problematic, since America was still neutral. His concern seemed to be that Americans usually prefer a trial by jury before citizens are executed. The murder remains a mystery today, since von der Osten had been tailed for a long time by the FBI and posed no dramatic threat to the United States. Was Intrepid fearful that Hoover might get his hands on von der Osten and learn something inconvenient?

FDR was operating in the White House with Harry Hopkins, a former social worker who was in ill health, as his close advisor. FDR, a former governor of New York, with no foreign policy experience himself, was keeping his Secretary of State at a distance. He kept his Attorney General, Biddle, from exercising any power. His Secretary of Treasury, Morgenthau, who had no experience in finance, was dabbling in foreign affairs., Harry Dexter White, his Assistant Secretary and close confidant, was confirmed as a Soviet spy when the Soviet Union collapsed. FDR had a brand new Secretary of the Navy, Frank Knox, whom he had brought into his Cabinet in 1940, and a new Secretary of War, Henry Stimson, who was also new to the Cabinet in 1940. He kept away from the lions in the Senate. He was locked in a deadly embrace with Churchill, who was a first rate mind and who was surrounded by a cadre of advisors who had kept the British Empire together

---

[2] Stevenson, William, *A Man Called Intrepid*, The Secret War, Harcourt, Brace, Jovanovich, New York, London, 1976, 176-177.

for centuries. It was Roosevelt, not Churchill, who was the emperor with no clothes.

Intrepid's operation from Rockefeller Center also had a cadre of able actors. New York artist Clayton Rhight was a big assist to Sir William, having flown with him in World War I. Rhight would help organize young Americans who wanted to fight, and funnel them to Canada to enlist, which was the opposite of what happened in Vietnam, where Americans headed for Canada to avoid the draft. One of Rhight's comrades in World War I was a young captain by the name of Fiorello LaGuardia, the current Mayor of New York. LaGuardia's former legal aide, Ernest Cuneo, was now FDR's aid on intelligence matters. This could best be described as an "All in the Family" operation.

Intrepid was equally well protected in Washington. He had planted a spy in the White House. Now he was spying directly on FDR. Eleanor Roosevelt was a big fan of Roald Dahl, whose books she read to her grandchildren. When she was aware that Dahl was in Washington, she invited him to dinner at the White House; later, he became a frequent visitor at Hyde Park. Dahl was working for Bill Stephenson, smoothing relations between London and Washington. As an innocuous writer of children's books, Dahl was assumed to be safe company; in fact, he was a paid British spy.

J. Edgar Hoover did not enjoy the access that Intrepid or Bill Donovan did. He could do an end run around Attorney General Biddle at any time, particularly if he had some information that would be useful to FDR. Hoover did have his circle of advisors. Walter Winchell, Drew Pearson, Hoover and his deputy, Clyde Tolson were very close. The FBI files in Washington contain so many letters from Walter Winchell to Hoover that the question of a very unhealthy relationship between the most prominent investigative agency in America and an investigative reporter cannot be avoided. In any case, Hoover did have an informal circle of very experienced advisors. Congressman Vito Marcantonio had labeled Hoover "the Stork Club Cop" for a reason. Every Friday night, Hoover would take the train to New York to party at the Stork Club. David Walsh made the same social scene, but was not close to Hoover, as most of the committees he served on had little to do with the FBI.

Arriving by train Friday night, the pair [Hoover and Tolson] usually breakfasted in their complimentary Waldorf suite Saturday morning, usually playing host to one or two friends, who then accompanied them to a nearby racetrack, wherever the ponies were running. Although Saturday nights invariably ended at Winchell's table at the Stork, they were usually preceded by dinner at Soule or Maxim's or Gallagher's and a brief visit to "21" or Toots Shor's. Shor, who had been a speakeasy operator during Prohibition, recalled, "When Hoover put his stamp of friendship on you, somehow you felt like a clean, decent guy."[3]

Hoover operated openly with the fourth estate; they aided him in his objectives, counseled him, and gave him generous publicity in his exploits. Intrepid collaborated with his friends in the fourth estate, operating behind a London fog, and wanted no credit for anything.

While Hoover's access to FDR usually depended on his ability to provide Roosevelt with useful information, quite often it had nothing to do with national security matters. In 1940, Hoover was coming under increasing attack by Congress, and there was even some speculation that FDR might replace him. However, FDR praised Hoover at the House Correspondents Dinner on March 16, 1940.

> As usual, the President was the guest of honor. Spotting Hoover among the attendees, Roosevelt called to him, "Edgar, what are they trying to do to you on the Hill?"
>
> Hoover replied, "I don't know, Mr. President." Roosevelt grinned and made a thumbs down gesture, at the same time remarking, loud enough for those at a nearby table to hear, "That's for them."
>
> A master of time and place, Roosevelt, with a single gesture, killed the rumor that Hoover no longer had his support. There was — as there always was with FDR — a quid pro quo. A few days later the president started calling in some of his due bills.[4]

FDR had Hoover on a string and kept him jumping throughout the war. When liberals started attacking Hoover, liberal columnist John Flynn, who sat on the board of America First, defended him. People wanted to think that Roosevelt was against the snooping and spying, but a clear-minded person could not overlook the fact that J. Edgar Hoover could not have been engaging in wiretapping and similar practices if Roosevelt was actually opposed to these activities. John Flynn made the point forcefully, writing in *The New Republic* that Hoover could not have acted on his own without direction from FDR. Flynn would later have his career destroyed, as the *New Republic* would fire him because of his anti-war views. He would be blacklisted by all the major magazines headquartered in New York, and never again would find full time employment in his field. He would be later painted as a "right wing nut" when he supported the McCarthy Hearings in the 1950's. The Communists may have gotten lucky that the messenger was crude, ethnic, and a drunk. The two key staffers of that committee,

---

[3] Gentry, Curt, *J. Edgar Hoover, The Man and the Secrets*, W. W. Norton, New York, London, 1991, 217

[4] Ibid., 224.

Roy Cohn, of "Angels in America" fame, and Bobby Kennedy, would prove to have done excellent staff work. One liberal, one conservative, their staff work would be vindicated when the KGB files were opened, with the dissolution of the Soviet Empire.

William Donovan also reported directly to the president, but it is difficult to discern which of them had the other on a string. Donovan's murky responsibilities led him to propose all sorts of outlandish schemes with little thought of coordinating with other intelligence agencies. In *Roosevelt's Secret War*, author Joseph Persico describes a proposed swap of spy missions with the Soviets, a plan that virtually all other agencies opposed. Based on nearly universal sentiment, FDR shot it down. The Soviets knew the minute it happened.

> One man who knew immediately of the President's decision to kill off the spy swap was Duncan Lee, another lawyer protégé' of Bill Donovan's who had become the Director's executive assistant. Almost immediately upon the formation of the OSS, Moscow had made the fledgling intelligence service a priority target. The Soviet intelligence strategy for 1942 specifically stated: '[O]ur task is to insert there our people and carry out cultivation with their help." The NKVD found a wedge in Lee, who epitomized the establishment figures inhabiting the upper reaches of the OSS. Thirty years old in 1944, he had been born to missionary parents in Nanking, China. He had returned home and graduated from the Woodbury Forrest School in Virginia, took a B.A. from Yale, became a Rhodes Scholar at Oxford, then received a law degree from Yale. A Communist intermediary described Lee as "[a]verage height, medium brown hair and light eyes, glasses, rather studious looking.' Though Lee was not a Communist, he would prove a profitably placed NKVD source. Immediately after graduating from law school, Lee had been snapped up by Wild Bill's Manhattan law firm, Donovan & Leisure, and subsequently followed his boss to Washington. By the time the COI had become the OSS, Lee had received a direct Army commission, risen to the rank of captain, and worked in the Donovan front office secretariat. Essentially, whatever happened in the OSS was known to Duncan Lee.[5]

Again, the same pattern is repeated: a spy so close to the President that he is able to see documents coming from or going directly to the President. The Rube Goldberg contraption that was FDR's intelligence network ill-served the President and had devastating results for the country. Neither the intelligence nor the intelligence gatherers were vetted. One of the most oft quoted lines from FDR was "that he never let the right hand know what the left hand was doing." His compartmentalization of intelligence, with so many access points to the White House, created a sieve over which he had no control.

---

[5] Persico, Joseph E., *Roosevelt's Secret War*, Random House, New York, 2001, 293

CHAPTER 14. FDR'S SEX LIFE AND THE NEWPORT SEX SCANDAL

To understand FDR's antagonism towards David Walsh, it may be important to understand FDR's own sex life. His curious interest in homosexual sex would get him in trouble in 1920, and like Walsh's, his conduct would be the subject of an investigation by the United States Senate. Both would end up in the usually staid Congressional Record. While the record of Walsh's conduct was fabricated, FDR's was real. With the publication of *Closest Companion*, in 1995, historians were treated to a trove of information concerning the small social circle surrounding FDR. It introduces the dysfunctional coterie of women surrounding FDR and brings new meaning to the term "kissing cousins." This is a straightforward publication of hitherto unknown love letters between Margaret Daisy Suckley, a Roosevelt distant cousin, and FDR himself. The letters provide remarkable insight from within the Roosevelt White House regarding important events, as well as firsthand observations of the characters in the White House, most of whom were social friends or family of FDR. While the public was made aware of FDR's affair with Lucy Mercer after the war, and there had been speculation over his relationship with the Crown Princess of Norway, no one had ever heard of Daisy Suckley. Given the fact that Daisy Suckley virtually lived with FDR, it is hard to comprehend how she escaped the attention of historians. FDR and Daisy worked hard at being discreet, and were rewarded for it with anonymity; however, Eleanor Roosevelt had to face the humiliation on a daily basis. As Eleanor Roosevelt walked into one room, Daisy was whisked into the next.

If Eleanor Roosevelt had only had to contend with Daisy, life would have been simpler. On any given day, it could have been Lucy Mercer Rutherford, Daisy, or "Missy" LeHand, with whom the president had a strange relationship.

Historians have generally treated FDR's relations with each of these women as asexual. This approach, whether taken out of deference to a dead president, or because historians felt they lacked a "smoking gun," simply adds to the intrigue. The fact that he was in a wheelchair did not stop FDR; wheelchair-bound people may have more romantic relations than historians.

Elliott Roosevelt, FDR's son, was far more forthcoming about his father's relationship with Missy Lehand, Roosevelt's long time personal secretary, and criticizes historians for treating his parents as cardboard characters. He admitted his father's flaws. Elliott explains.

> Missy was, as Father put it, his conscience. Most evenings after dinner, she would leave the table when he did, her blue eyes sparkling, with her innocent wise smile. They would make their way together to his upstairs study, as they used to in Albany when he was governor, to go over the events of tomorrow and the days ahead. He used her as a sounding board for a host of his ideas. He employed her once in a telling gesture to humble Joe Kennedy, whom he had recalled from London as Ambassador to the Court of St. James for his frequently stated opinion early in World War II that Hitler was likely to defeat the Allies.

> Prior to that occasion, Father had urged the founding father of the Kennedy clan to end his long term relationship with Gloria Swanson, with whom Joe had been close since his days as a motion-picture czar. Joe replied that he would be willing only "if you give up Missy Lehand." Father looked on that as a score to be settled. When Kennedy arrived back in disgrace, his President refrained from sending any ranking member of the Cabinet to meet him, as custom required. Instead, at Washington Airport stood Missy, all smiles.[1]

In the summer of 1940, Missy Lehand suffered a debilitating stroke. FDR made remarkably generous provisions for her in his will, leaving over half his estate to her; and although she predeceased him, he did not change his will. Elliott surmises that his father wanted to show history how important Missy was to his life. Eleanor would have to undergo one more round of humiliation at the hands of FDR, who left half of his estate to one of his employees.

Historians have long glossed over FDR's lifelong infidelity to Eleanor, and frequently blamed her for FDR's conduct. Describing her as cold and frumpy, historians come close to suggesting that Eleanor was incapable of providing the affection that FDR craved and that Daisy's position was justified. It is unlikely that any woman could have provided FDR with the constant affection he craved.

While David Walsh's sex life would explode on the national scene in the summer of '42, FDR's would stay out of sight. FDR was protected from scrutiny by all the president's men, while being surrounded by all the president's women.

---

[1] Roosevelt, Elliott and Brough, James, *The Roosevelts of Hyde Park, An Untold Story*, G.P. Putnam & Sons, New York, 1973, 297-298.

Senator Walsh enjoyed no such protection, and a fictionalized version of his personal life appeared in the headlines while FDR's truly bizarre habits remained where most people thought they should remain: behind closed doors. FDR had the entire federal bureaucracy working for him; Walsh had one personal secretary.

Daisy Suckley's relationship with FDR was discreet, but it is surprising that such an exhaustive written record remains. FDR must have felt confident it would remain hidden. Houghton Mifflin chose a dignified subtitle to *Closest Companion*, "The Unknown Story of the Intimate Friendship between Franklin Roosevelt and Mar-garet Suckley." Yet they quickly launch into the bare facts. In a diary entry in 1935, Daisy posted the poem "Eros" by Leslie Grant Scott as a reminder to an afternoon spent with FDR. Geoffrey Ward, editor of her letters, says,

> Later that day, FDR took Daisy for another long drive, following winding back roads through the beautiful Hudson River country, then stopping to park again on the crest of the forested ridge that he and Daisy had named Our Hill.
>
> Something happened in that place on that afternoon that neither of them ever forgot. Three years later, FDR was still calling it the beginning of "a voyage." Perhaps they simply kissed. A poem clipped from the newspaper and carefully pasted by Daisy into their diary suggests that they did. [2]

The Suckley letters, written to Eleanor's husband, hardly sound like a platonic relationship. Ward makes further reference to Roosevelt's efforts that very night to persuade Daisy to come along on a trip to dedicate Boulder Dam, then a fishing voyage off Baja California. "Mrs. Roosevelt was to travel with her husband as far as the Pacific Coast, but she was not going aboard his ship." The letters and Roosevelt's reactions to them appear almost childlike, as if FDR was a teenager cheating on his girlfriend. His effort to lure Daisy on board the ship, after dumping Eleanor on the Pacific Coast, is a theme that is repeated over many years.

FDR and Daisy were able to hide their relationship thanks to the help of his former law partner, Harry Hooker. He would often act as Daisy's escort so that she could attend presidential occasions without causing gossip; and he might retire early, leaving the two lovers to enjoy the rest of the evening. Given his peculiarly appropriate name, his function should not be surprising.

A letter of March 24, 1935 from FDR indicates that Daisy had the honor of naming the presidential yacht Sequoia — "she awaits your inspection next month — very necessary because you are responsible for her name." In a later letter, FDR credits Daisy with naming his dog, Fala. Apparently, Eleanor Roosevelt was First Lady in name only.

[2] Ward, Geoffrey C. *Closest Companion*, Houghton Mifflin, Boston, New York, 1995, 34.

In later years, FDR arranged the appointment of Daisy as a junior archivist at the FDR library in Hyde Park. Geoffrey Ward cites this as perfect cover for their relationship. "On September 6, [1941], he [FDR] came to tea at Wilderstein," she noted, and "announced to the family that I am to have a job in the F.D.R. Library in Hyde Park half-time, — beginning October 1st. Just what I want!" She was to be made a junior archivist assigned to sorting the President's personal and family papers, at a salary of $1,000 a year." [3]

The new position at least legitimized her frequent presence at his side; she and FDR no longer had to come up with pretexts for her visits to Washington or Hyde Park. There were always papers to pore over together.

It is unclear whom FDR is hiding the relationship from at this point, because they had been an item since 1935 and certainly, at this point, Eleanor Roosevelt was aware of the relationship. Perhaps this was FDR's way of making Daisy feel more important. Or was she simply replacing Missy LeHand in FDR's daily routine? LeHand had suffered a stroke, and it was obvious that she would not be returning to the White House. There have been characterizations of FDR's relationship with Missy LeHand that would certainly suggest a sexual relationship, but the obtuse references leave the reader with more questions than answers. At a minimum, it provides another "strange relationship" to ponder. Elliott Roosevelt would shed some light on that.

Daisy Suckley witnessed firsthand Churchill's visits to the White House, and had more of an insider's view than Eleanor Roosevelt herself. On September 11, 1944, Daisy joined the President and Mrs. Roosevelt for dinner with Mr. and Mrs. Churchill and the Duke of Windsor. This was not Daisy's first dinner with Winston Churchill. During Churchill's visits to Washington in search of arms and money, Daisy attended most White House functions. One wonders what Churchill thought in regard to FDR's dinner list. When Winston held an event at Chequers, no one was invited without a purpose; Churchill's dinner list contained the best and the brightest. FDR's list included many people who did not seem to have a specific diplomatic role to play. Churchill's dinner list contained luminaries from all walks of life, but they were there to conduct business; Churchill was all business, and the British Empire was certainly big business.

One visit from the Churchills came following the Quebec Conference, where, for the first time, Winston did not get his way. He found out that he would have to deal from now on with George Marshall. He obviously expected to be socializing with decision makers, and thought that by turning his charms on the

---

[3] Ibid., 143.

White House he could reverse Marshall's decisions. Furthermore, Churchill's spy in the White House, Roald Dahl had been spending weekends at Hyde Park, where FDR carried on most of his affair with Daisy Suckley. In all probability, a spy with Dahl's brains could figure out what was going on. Churchill was probably thinking the same thing about Daisy that Daisy was thinking about Wallis Simpson, the Duke of Windsor's wife: "Why is this wench sitting next to me?" Daisy could not be expected to debate the pros and cons of a cross-Channel invasion strategy with Winston. The "ill-mannered" Mr. Churchill had every right to be patronizing. He assumed that he would be able to "wheel and deal" with decisionmakers; something that British social occasions allowed for.

Daisy's diary entry of September 2, 1943, gives further insight regarding FDR's relationship with his Secretary of State. "Speaking of Mr. Hull the other day, he said Mr. H. was so upset over being criticized in the papers during the past year; also the differences over Sumner Welles, etc. Finally the P. just reminded him that for the past 10 yrs. the P. himself has been attacked constantly & has been able to survive it & still smile, whereas Mr. Hull received no word of criticism for the first nine years and can't stand it! This kind of thing is more wearing on FDR than the real big problems of the war & the future peace

— The 'little foxes' that gnaw at the roots of the vine."[4]

Daisy Suckley had found Churchill in a better mood in an earlier visit in 1942, when he was still getting his way with FDR. FDR's mistress noted that Churchill dutifully called his wife while away from home. Her written observations certainly reflect the official version of events, as this was perhaps the high water mark of their relationship, at least from Churchill's point of view. From an American viewpoint, it might be considered the low water mark, as the relationship at this point was so decisively one-sided in Great Britain's favor. While the tug of war went on, the civilian corpses in Europe were beginning to pile up, with US military leadership pushing to join the fight now, and British leadership pushing for later.

On July 19, 1942, the Roosevelt coterie retired to Rhinebeck, presidential cousin Laura Delano's home, for afternoon cocktails. Some historians have described Laura Delano's idea of fashion as something that would stand out in a red light district. In any event, she was a rather odd character. Knowing that Churchill only drank scotch, she handed him a sweet Tom Collins, the kind the President preferred. He spat it out.

It certainly must have grated Churchill to attend this stultifying affair. The

---

[4] Ibid., 234.

social scene at the White House was no mirror to the kind of reception that Averill Harriman, FDR's personal envoy, would receive in London. There, festivities would revolve around the business of the British Empire. Harriman was treated royally, but it was all business. When Churchill came to the United States, he was coming to a backwater country with a shopping list. In essence, he was begging. This was certainly a novel experience for Great Britain. Usually, most important meetings were held in London, the hub of trade and politics. Great Britain was used to dictating terms to other countries.

It could be excused if some in the US did not know how to provide hospitality of an international caliber. But the Roosevelts? The Hudson Valley scene had been an insular society, wealthy, but not necessarily worldly. While Churchill was a throwback to the Victorian Age, he was surrounded by thinkers like George Bernard Shaw, Bertrand Russell, Isaiah Berlin, and Roald Dahl. An aging British Empire was being led by first-rate minds harnessed to an old idea, colonialism. A robust America was being led by an aging, fragile President whose ability to find consensus had always been sorely lacking. His messianic tendencies drove away the members of an inner circle that became frighteningly small as entrance into World War II became inevitable.

Given FDR's penchant for appointing freelancers who reported directly to him (Donovan, Harriman, Murphy, Welles, Hoover, his son James, the entire Cabinet, etc.), coupled with his poor health and his personal coterie, one wonders how FDR focused on the prosecution of the war effort at all. And his time and attention were further diverted when Lucy Mercer Rutherford came back to him after her husband's death. Lucy would be with FDR at Warm Springs, Georgia, when he died.

Daisy's diary entry of April 2, 1943 provides a fascinating insight into British maneuvering towards the peace table, which historically had been a British euphemism for "dividing the spoils." She portrays Anthony Eden, in a visit to the White House, as undercutting Churchill, saying that Winston Churchill would not ever see beyond the British Empire. The British had long since figured FDR out; they knew flattery went a long way. Eden is shown praising FDR's progressive image, which one might reasonably assume, given the context of the discussion, is FDR's anti-colonial rhetoric.

Suckley's diary provides some insights to the evolution of relations between FDR and other world leaders. She shows the Brits flattering FDR by encouraging him to run for a fourth term, and she records how Stalin came to realize that he was paralyzed. Apparently, his intelligence men managed to get him information on the atom bomb from Los Alamos but overlooked this aspect of the situation.

155

Daisy Suckley's diary on May 16, 1944 records the following:

> When I was at the W.H. last week, I asked the P. if he thought Stalin might per-
> haps come to see him nearer home next time. The P. said, "I think he may."
>
> I asked on what he based the thought & he answered about in the following
> words: "When I first got to Teheran, Stalin came to call on me. Of course, I did not
> get up when he came into the room. We shook hands & he sat down, and I caught
> him curiously looking at my legs and ankles. Later, I entertained him at dinner, and
> was sitting at the table when he & others came in. When Stalin was seated, on my
> right, he turned to the interpreter & said: 'Tell the President that I now understand
> what it has meant to him to make the effort to come on such a long journey — Tell
> him that the next time I will go to him.'" Stalin evidently had no idea that the P.
> couldn't walk.[5]

Even at the Casablanca Conference, FDR was writing to Daisy on an almost daily basis, sharing his joy at seeing his son Elliott and complaining about de Gaulle's reticence.

Daisy's letters and diary confirm, in many instances, on many issues, an insider's view in the White House which can be compared with the external view. Much of the external view of the White House cast the New Dealers as sympathetic to the cause of the Soviet Union, and blindly idealistic. For example, in a diary entry in June 1944, Daisy mentions a D-Day prayer written by Anna and John (FDR's daughter and son-in-law). "'It is wonderful, in these days, to find the head of this huge nation leading the people in prayer. Imagine Hitler and Stalin doing it! And yet I wonder if Stalin may not go back to his priest's training and, under the personal influence of FDR, regain something of the spiritual, which he has cast aside these many years. This may be a fantastic thought, but it is not an impossible one.'"[6] Given Daisy's hero worship, one can deduce that her thinking mirrors Roosevelt's thinking. If so, the ultimate New Dealer himself is guilty of fantastic thinking. It again gives rise to the messianic traits of FDR, thinking he can personally charm Stalin. These observations give credence to the belief of Roosevelt's critics who have long charged he was soft on Communism. FDR's failure to take a realistic approach to Stalin during the war years would leave Harry Truman, and the United States, with a postwar problem that would resonate for the remainder of the 20th century.

FDR's original plan was to serve two terms and then retire. When that happened, Daisy had assumed they would live and work together at Top Cottage, near Poughkeepsie. It never came to pass. Roosevelt's plans to retire from the

---

[5] Ibid., 299.
[6] Ibid., 310.

presidency changed when the war broke out, and it soon became clear that Daisy's dream would not be fulfilled.

For a reader to fully understand FDR's attitude towards gays, it is important to understand the facts in the Newport Sex Scandal, a bizarre chapter in FDR's life. His lifelong infidelity to Eleanor Roosevelt, his dalliances with Lucy Mercer Rutherford and Daisy Suckley, the alleged affairs with the Princess of Norway and, possibly, his "strange" relationship with Missy LeHand raise sufficient questions about his integrity. But, if Bill Clinton perjured himself concerning private affairs, FDR perjured himself over serious government matters. At least, that was the finding of the Senate Naval Affairs Committee in 1921.

When Franklin D. Roosevelt was Assistant Secretary of the Navy, in 1919, he commenced an investigation of a group of homosexuals known as the "Ladies of Newport." He attached the investigators to his own office, with a direct report to him as the Assistant Secretary of the Navy. This reporting arrangement certainly seemed strange in 1919, but this was typical of reporting relationships in the White House during World War II. FDR never showed any penchant for following a chain of command.

In the ensuing investigation, navy investigators allowed homosexual acts to be performed on them, in order to obtain evidence. More amazing yet, the Court of Inquiry under Lieutenant Commander Foster recommended citations for the investigators. "In its report, the Foster court of inquiry named the Arnold squad operatives upon whom completed homosexual acts had been performed, and recommended that a notation be entered in their service records "in recognition of their interest and zeal in their work in assisting the Judge Advocate, and in the best interests of the naval service."[7] As the committee investigation unfolded, the direct reporting relationship would become a problem for FDR. The committee was troubled by the unusual reporting relationship in a hierarchical military structure, and this further prevented FDR from escaping responsibility (although he would try).

In the ensuing investigation, the military chaplain, Episcopalian Minister Samuel Kent, was arrested but his case was thrown out because it was based on entrapment. The Episcopal Bishop of Rhode Island, James De Wolf Perry went to Washington to protest the bizarre behavior of the investigators. On January 17, 1920, a Court of Inquiry was appointed, headed by Admiral Herbert Dunn. On January 22, the Senate Naval Affairs Committee launched a separate investigation. Pandemonium broke out, just as FDR was being mentioned as a possible vice

---

[7] Morgan, Ted, *FDR: A Biography*, Simon & Schuster, New York, 1985, 235-236.

presidential candidate.

> The Dunn court of inquiry convened in Washington on January 26, and met for eighty-six days collecting 4,800 pages of testimony. By the time Franklin was called to testify, on May 20, the Senate Naval Affairs Subcommittee had also launched its investigation. Questioned by Judge Advocate Henry L. Hyneman, Franklin denied all knowledge of the Arnold squad's activities....
>
> Q. "Mr. Secretary, did you know that in nine instances, between the 18th of March and the 14th of April, that certain naval operators had permitted sexual perverts in the naval service to suck their penis for the purpose of obtaining evidence to be used before the Court of Inquiry, which evidence resulted in a recommendation by that court to try by general court-martial sixteen enlisted men and to give two men undesirable discharges?"
>
> A. "The answer is no. I knew absolutely nothing about the court or its methods or its personnel......"
>
> Q. "Who would be responsible for the acts of the men in an organization so constituted?"
>
> A. "The officer in command."
>
> Q. "Did you give them [the men] any instructions or orders as to how the details should be carried out?"
>
> A. "Naturally not."
>
> Q. "Would not that have been your duty, since these men were attached to your office?"
>
> A. "Absolutely not."
>
> Q. "Whose duty would that have been?"
>
> A. "The commanding officer."[8]

Franklin blamed the commanding officer, in unambiguous answers. But virtually no one connected to the Navy saw it that way. FDR had arranged for the investigative unit to report directly to him, the Assistant Secretary of the Navy on the grounds that no other investigative arm of the service was moving fast enough. Having bypassed all other sections of the service, he could not claim to know nothing about his own investigation. It is hard to avoid concluding that FDR's prurient interests played a part in his interest in this case. FDR laid all blame on Lieutenant Hudson and Arnold; the commanding officer, Hudson, became "sick" and was excused from testifying. He surely would have let it be known that he had kept FDR informed of every detail. Author Ted Morgan explains how he got away with this. FDR had just done Commander Dunn a favor, writing a letter to insure that his nephew would receive an appointment to the Naval Academy. FDR

---

[8] Ibid., 240-241.

escaped under the Court of Inquiry, but he would not be so fortunate with the Senate Naval Affairs Committee, who took up the investigation because of their lack of confidence in the performance of the Naval Court of Inquiry.

> [A] strong case was made that Franklin had known about the methods used by Section A from the start, and had lied to the Dunn court under oath, committing perjury.
>
> … The committee….believes that at this time Franklin D. Roosevelt and the others present had knowledge that enlisted personnel had been and were to be used to investigate perversion and must have realized in that in previous investigations under charge of Hudson and Arnold men had allowed lewd and immoral acts to be performed upon them and that a similar plan was being adopted. If, during the conferences of May 1 and June 6 and 7, Assistant Secretary Franklin D. Roosevelt did not inquire and was not informed as to the proposed method theretofore used and to be used by the men attached directly to his offices and under his supervision, then it is of the opinion of this committee that Assistant Secretary Franklin D. Roosevelt was most derelict in the performance of his duty. The committee, however, cannot believe so. Franklin D. Roosevelt was a man of unusual intelligence and attainments, and after three days of conversation on the subject must have known the methods used and to be used to secure evidence.[9]

Furthermore, any claim that FDR did not know what was going on was tantamount to dereliction of duty. The Senate Naval Affairs Committee found that he had perjured himself.

The report could not have been more damning. FDR was devastated. Author Ted Morgan speculates that the distress from this event brought down his immune system, contributing to the vulnerability that led to his contracting polio in the ensuing few weeks.

This incident exposed deep flaws in Roosevelt's character. He perjured himself and was willing to make Lieutenant Hudson walk the plank to save himself. This incident further explains his jaundiced attitude towards the Senate Naval Affairs Committee, of which David Walsh was chairman. While Walsh was not a member of the committee at the time of FDR's humiliation, later in life he insisted on holding FDR accountable before this same committee once again.

FDR showed an inability to work with the committees of Congress throughout his entire presidency. His searing experience with this congressional investigation would not help; and his personal hatred of the Senate Naval Affairs Committee would put Walsh in one of the most uncomfortable seats in Washington.

---

[9] Ibid., 242-243.

CHAPTER 15. THE ATLANTIC CHARTER, BUT THE PACIFIC CONFERENCE

David Walsh had focused most of his energies on preventing Roosevelt from starting war in the Atlantic. At the Atlantic Conference held in August 1941 off the coast of Newfoundland, Churchill and FDR met, virtually alone. Afterward, they issued a vaguely worded document about the outlook for a postwar world: the Atlantic Charter. This ought to have seemed odd, since the Congress had not authorized US entry into the war and therefore the US would have no say in a post-war world. The public was never informed of the actual purpose of the meeting.

Subsequent events would prove that the primary purpose of the meeting was, in fact, to discuss events in the Pacific. In just a matter of months, events would lead to the attack on Pearl Harbor. The US- Great Britain joint oil embargo of Japan had been put in effect earlier in the summer, and Churchill and FDR knew that Japan was desperately short of this war commodity.

The events of Pearl Harbor would result in at least five investigations, all concentrated on the event itself rather than the events leading up to it. The spate of books on Pearl Harbor provide endless fascination, replete with conflicting testimony, probable perjured testimony, and failed memories from people whose whole careers were based on attention to detail and documentation. The memory lapses of men in uniform probably had much to do with their belief that the investigations were not impartial; that there was no intent to pursue the investigation to the end — which would point to civilian leadership in the White House. There was an overwhelming feeling among those called to testify that they, too, might be scapegoated. After all, Admiral Husband Kimmel and General Short, who had been responsible for Pearl Harbor base security, were removed from command — without a hearing. They were not tried and found derelict in their duty; any hearings on the attack on Pearl Harbor were held long after both had been removed, and no military commander was likely to reverse FDR's action. This unprecedented maneuver stifled career officers who might have testified; the long held principles of military justice were clearly in suspense.

The records of other governments, however, provide an understanding of what happened, and why. Great Britain's colonies in the Pacific were concerned by Japan's mounting strength. Churchill's government was fixated on problems in Europe and the Middle East; Australia, Britain's only white colony in the Pacific, had assumed Great Britain would defend her. Earlier in the war, Australia had felt so confident that she had sent two divisions of troops to fight in the Middle East. Australian politicians began feeling the pressure as Japanese encroachment continued southward; only one division remained to protect the small continent.

Australia received assurances immediately after the Atlantic Conference that the United States would come to her aid in the event of any danger; Churchill needed a partner in the Pacific, and apparently FDR had decided to be that partner without consulting Congress.

During the 1920s, US-British relations in the Pacific had been confrontational, with Great Britain feeling threatened by the growing US naval presence. Public opinion in the United States would have been against any colonial expansion by FDR, or his predecessors, but London was wary of losing its hegemony. Apparently, in this hour of need, the view had changed.

Prime Minister Fadden of Australia and his successors failed to get the absolute promise of protection that the Australian public demanded, and Churchill's abandonment of the colony undercut the stability of the government. Australia sought its independence from Great Britain after the war, although it retained its commonwealth status.

Great Britain's control of its colonies meant that Australia was not permitted to trade freely with the United States; she had to buy inferior machine parts from British factories, and at inflated prices. Yet, America was now coming to the rescue.

Indeed, Churchill seems to have brought FDR to the threshold. Washington warned Tokyo against any further encroachment in the southwest Pacific. "According to General Pownall, Vice Chief of the Imperial General Staff, Roosevelt was all for coming into the war, and as soon as possible....but said he would never declare war, he wished to provoke it. He want[ed] to create an incident [to bring] war about, being no doubt sure that he [would] then be fully supported by the people."[1]

It remains a mystery what promises were made by Great Britain at the Atlantic Conference. No aides were present during this meeting.

The high-sounding declarations of the Atlantic Charter, outlining an Anglo-American operation to police Europe, would take on a different meaning for the British than for FDR. "Apart from the immediate necessity to have America as an ally against Germany, there was the growing conviction that the war should be used to cement a permanent Anglo-American alliance to act as the post-war policeman of Europe. This was Churchill's vision and it was also urged on by Eden at the Foreign Office. According to his secretary, Oliver Harvey, 'The British people will be exhausted after the war and will refuse to police Europe alone. But if it is an Anglo-American operation, then you will get what you want, and I am sure we can manage the Americans. They are simple, naif, yet suspicious.' Eden riposted that he would not regard Roosevelt as 'simple or naïf.'"[2]

Eden had proven to be a reasonable man, but this plan was Churchill's. He did consider Roosevelt easy to lead, and he had a lot of company within the British diplomatic class. The Aussies and Americans were lumped together as nations of sheep. Churchill would meet Australia's defense needs by using the United States Navy.

Earlier that summer, in May 1941, Australia had been shocked at the transfer of much of the American fleet from the Pacific to the Atlantic. Churchill had jumped the gun, even promising Australia before the Atlantic Conference that the United States would defend her. Then Prime Minister Menzies, in London at the time of the announcement of the transfer of the American fleet, had been caught off guard by the announcement. He could not return to Australia without a defense commitment, help with aircraft production equipment and other materiel, but he got nowhere with Churchill.

Relations between London and Canberra would further deteriorate when casualty counts started arriving. With Australian troops fighting in the Middle East, it was a sensitive issue. Churchill had promised Australia to abandon the Mediterranean campaign if the Japanese threat became serious. Whether or not that was credible, it became a moot point. The body bags in Canberra became a bigger issue.

Australia's complaints about high casualties were not new in the British Empire. While strategy was directed out of London, colonial troops often made up

---

[1] Day, David, *The Great Betrayal*, W. W. Norton, New York, London, 1988, 168
[2] Ibid., 169.

the majority of the men who did the fighting. Even during the American Revolution, Great Britain had imported Hessian troops to fight.

With the attack on Pearl Harbor, Australia no longer felt alone in the Pacific, but was still determined to pin down London on defense guarantees. Americans were shocked, but British diplomats were not, as they had been actively planning for American participation for some time now: "As Sir Horace Seymour observed with his usual aplomb, the 'Japs went off as expected' and seemed to have started well.' He admitted that 'the little beasts are a serious menace' but remarked how 'that, of course, was inevitable.' Admiral Somerville, soon to be Commander-in-Chief of the Eastern Fleet, had a more down to earth desire to 'give the little sods a real kick' although, the Admiralty's weekly intelligence report was more sympathetic to the plight of Japan, acknowledging that, 'had she not gone to war now, Japan would have seen such a deterioration of her economic situation as to render her ultimately unable to wage war, and to reduce her to the status of a second rate power.'"[3]

While British officials were euphoric, and in a self-congratulatory mode, Australian diplomats were working hard at pinning down specific defense guarantees. There weren't any. The "Germany First" strategy would continue to leave Australia exposed. An American officer would be in charge of the Pacific. The problem for American army and navy leaders, both before and after Pearl Harbor, was that none of FDR's commitments were communicated to them. Far East plans were made without any idea of the scope of defense commitments that Roosevelt had agreed to; and the navy in particular lacked the resources to develop an operational plan for defense of the entire Pacific region. The two-ocean navy that Walsh had fought so long and so hard to build simply did not exist.

The only British priority in the Pacific was to protect the crown jewel — India. There were, in fact, no plans to protect Australia. Churchill planned to use the US army against Germany, and the US navy against Japan. "The "Germany First" strategy ensured a low priority for the Far East, and Australia no priority at all.

Churchill would continue to deceive a succession of Australian diplomats over the "Germany First" strategy, while at the same time delaying George Marshall's efforts to head straight for the democracies of Europe. No effort would be made to use British troops to protect Australia, while at the same time, Churchill's delaying tactics in Europe would result in the greatest refugee crisis Europe had ever witnessed. As relations with Australia deteriorated further, the only thread

---

[3] Ibid., 209.

now linking London and Canberra was racial. Sparsely populated Australia had a deep-seated fear of her prolific yellow-skinned neighbors, and had difficulty believing that the mother country would not provide defense.

Indeed, fear of a united Asia has driven much of the Anglo-American political approach to Pacific relations in the past hundred-plus years. Churchill, unable to sacrifice the resources necessary to defend Australia, suggested some Asian partners — but warned his commander not to get too close to them. In Churchill's mind, it was a temporary arrangement. He cabled Wavell, the Far East Commander, urging him to accept Chinese assistance in defending Burma but he saw it strictly as a temporary alliance based on expediency. Meanwhile, he blamed the Prime Minister Curtin for Australia's jitters; as always, Churchill expressed disbelief that a leader would bother to listen to the electorate.

Churchill did, however, express his views of Australians, which were derived from the pervasive class attitude of aristocratic Englanders to the convicts and working-class Irish who had made up large percentages of the settlers.

The Australian government had stationed troops in Singapore under the assumption that Singapore was the Empire's last line of defense, but when they learned that Churchill was diverting troops to Malaya, they decided to bring the boys home. When they had demanded the return of their divisions in the Middle East, British Chief of Staff Pownall noted that "Winston had little enough use for them before, especially after they demanded to be relieved at Tobruk, to everyone's great inconvenience. He'll be madder now...If the Australians were not so damned well pleased with themselves all the time, and so highly critical of everyone else, it would be a bit better. But they are the most egotistical, conceited people imaginable."[4]

Australia was not the only country in the Pacific that lacked information as to British foreign policy in that area. Prince Konoye, the Prime Minister under Japan's moderate government prior to Pearl Harbor, has left his memoirs for posterity. Konoye was forced to resign twice, forced out by Japanese hard liners. Konoye's representative in Washington, Ambassador Nomura, was even more popular; he had many American friends, including numerous US Navy officials. On the American side, Ambassador Joseph Grew had been in Japan almost a decade when war broke out. He was as popular in Tokyo as Nomura was in Washington.

Konoye's government was forced out only because he failed to reach a peace agreement with the United States. Japan's military had no interest in

---

[4] Ibid., 278.

attacking the United States; they were committed to attack Siberia under the Tripartite Pact, and could not attempt to do that without a peace agreement first with the United States. Furthermore, and perhaps more urgent, was their need to end the oil embargo. Konoye was baffled at Cordell Hull and FDR's continued delaying tactics. Konoye used the good relations with Nomura in Washington and his friendship with Grew in Tokyo as conduits; when both avenues failed, he realized that FDR did not want peace.

Prime Minister Konoye's army and navy leaders were keen to establish peace with the United States. They simply wanted to participate in the colonial game in Asia; there were easy targets everywhere, and the supply lines were shorter. The French, prostrate in Europe, could not defend French Indochina. FDR's warnings to Japan about Indochina rang hollow, given FDR's shabby treatment of de Gaulle and the Free French. Was FDR coveting a colonial claim himself? Siberia had been an easy target before, and perhaps the European powers would not be too upset if Japan took on this Bolshevist country. Both Siberia and Indochina would provide the raw materials Japan needed.

With Konoye's failure to reach a peace agreement with FDR, his second Cabinet submitted their resignations. Japan was desperate for a peace agreement with America, and if Konoye could not achieve it, the honorable thing was to resign. It was becoming clear, however, that if Konoye's government, with its close personal relations with Washington, could not conclude a peace agreement, it was simply that FDR did not want one. Konoye's Memoirs provide the background.

> The resignation en masse of the Konoye Cabinet gave a considerable shock to America. Admiral Turner, Chief of Naval Operations, and a close friend of Ambassador Nomura — he was captain of the ship that brought back Ambassador Saito's remains to Japan — visited Ambassador Nomura. At that time he said that he supposed that the reason for that resignation of the Konoye Cabinet was due to the fact that Premier Konoye considered the success of the Japanese-American negotiations to be hopeless, inasmuch as the President had refused the meeting, which the Premier had proposed. However, the President had not refused flatly; there were merely two or three points that he wished to clear up. If these points had been clarified, he would have been more than willing to see him. It had been decided to send a personal message to that effect from the President to His Imperial Majesty, the Emperor of Japan, and it was understood that steps had already been taken. Two or three days later, the Admiral again visited the Ambassador and told him that the decision referred to on his earlier visit had been cancelled, since opinions had arisen within the American Government that such a procedure would constitute an interference with internal affairs.[5]

---

[5] Konoye, Prince. *Memoirs*, courtesy of University of San Francisco Library, 64.

Peace negotiations were over. Admiral Turner and Ambassador Nomura were powerless in the face of FDR's intransigence. Japan, cut off from the oil that the United States had been freely selling them just months earlier, would have to fight. Was this FDR's policy, or Winston Churchill's? At the Atlantic Conference, Churchill claimed credit for stiffening the message to Japan, and just two months earlier the Japanese talks had been going smoothly.

FDR would succeed in scapegoating the Japanese over the failed negotiations, and when they attacked Pearl Harbor he would scapegoat his Army and Navy command for being unprepared. Even before an investigation was started, FDR would relieve from command Admiral Husband Kimmel and Army General Short, giving the public the impression that they were to blame.

Subsequent investigations regarding Pearl Harbor were essentially shelved for the duration of the war. Even anti-war leaders like David Walsh refused to second-guess the events at Pearl Harbor, in an effort to invoke national unity. Rear Admiral Robert Theobald provides an eyewitness account of FDR's actions, detailing each step FDR took to provoke a Japanese attack. Each step, standing alone, would represent a major provocation from a supposedly neutral country.

> To implement the solution to this problem (how to trigger an action that would get us involved despite public opinion), the President: (1) instituted a successful campaign to correct the nation's military unpreparedness; (2) offered Germany repeated provocations, by violations of neutrality and diplomatic usage; (3) applied ever increasing diplomatic-economic pressure upon Japan which reached its sustained climax on July 25, 1941, when the United States, Great Britain, and the Netherlands stopped trade with Japan subjecting them to complete economic encirclement;(4) made mutual commitments with the British Prime Minister at Newfoundland in August, 1941, which promised mutual support in the event that the United States, Great Britain, or a third country not then at war were attacked by Japan in the Pacific;(5) terminated the Washington Conference with the note of November 26, 1941, which gave Japan no choice but surrender or war; (6) retained a weak Pacific Fleet in Hawaiian waters, despite contrary naval advice, where it served only one diplomatic purpose, an invitation to a Japanese surprise attack; (7) furthered that surprise by causing the Hawaiian Commanders to be denied invaluable information from decoded Japanese dispatches concerning the rapid approach of the war and the strong probability that the attack would be directed at Pearl Harbor.[6]

> ... [O]nly officers of high reputation are chosen to fill the top positions in the Army and the Navy....Unless we accept that their actions were controlled by motivating orders from President Roosevelt, the simultaneous ineffective conduct of affairs of the Army and the Navy in Washington, during the month preceding the

---

[6] Theobald, Robert A., *The Final Secret of Pearl Harbor*, Devin-Adair Company, Old Greenwich, CT, 1954, 4

attack, and especially during the first days of December, is absolutely incomprehensible."[7]

Winston Churchill provided the answers that Admiral Theobald sought, in a speech that was intended for the House of Commons, not for the American audience. On January 27, 1942, Churchill explained to Britons that during the Atlantic Conference it had become clear that the United States would likely join Great Britain in the war, that

> the United States under the leadership of President Roosevelt, from reasons of its own interests and safety, but also out of the chivalrous regard for the cause of freedom and democracy, has drawn ever closer to the confines of the struggle ... that the United States, even if not herself attacked, would come into the war in the Far East, and thus make victory sure...." [8]

As the greatest refugee crisis in modern times was unfolding in Europe, Churchill indicated that FDR was intent on spreading war in the Pacific — even though there was not a democracy to save within three thousand miles — only colonies.

Admiral "Bull" Halsey, a true war hero, who was on the scene in the Pacific at the time of the attack, provides a view that is described with his characteristic clarity.

> Had we known of Japan's minute and continued interest in the exact location and movement of our ships in Pearl Harbor, as indicated in the "Magic Messages," it is only logical that we would have concentrated our thought on meeting the practical certainty of an attack on Pearl Harbor. I am sure I would have protested the movement of my Task Force to Wake Island in late November and early December. I am also sure no protest would have been necessary; because if Kimmel had possessed this intelligence, he would have ordered that movement.
>
> We were sadly deficient in long-distance scouting planes....We were further handicapped by directives requiring the training of large quotas of personnel in these planes for service in the Atlantic. This, together with the transfer of the carrier Yorktown to the East coast of the United States, was a tremendous drain on our already slim resources.
>
> I have always considered Admiral Kimmel and General Short to be splendid officers who were thrown to the wolves as scapegoats for something over which they had no control. They had to work with what they were given, both in equipment and information. They are our outstanding military martyrs.[9]

Just one year before Pearl Harbor, Admiral James Richardson, then commander at Pearl Harbor, had demanded a meeting with the President to protest

---

[7] Ibid., 162.

[8] Ibid., 188.

[9] Ibid., vii-viii.

plans to keep the Pacific Fleet stationed at Pearl rather than at San Diego. Richardson put his concerns on paper and followed up to get answers. "As commander of America's main sea command, Richardson's first duty was to carry out the orders of Roosevelt and his military chiefs. He reluctantly obeyed the orders but stated his objections for the record. He would not sacrifice his ships and men to what he saw as a flawed policy. Richardson listed five objections to basing the fleet in Hawaii: (1) lack of fundamental training facilities, (2) lack of large scale ammunition and fuel supplies, (3) lack of support craft such as tugs and repair ships, (4) morale problems of men kept away from their families, (5) lack of overhaul facilities such as dry docking and machine shops."[10]

Richardson was not satisfied with the answers he got, and pressed further. When he was asked to state his support publicly for basing the fleet in Hawaii, he declined. Richardson tried to dissuade Roosevelt, at a meeting in the White House on July 8, 1940. "I came away with the impression that, despite his spoken word, the President was fully determined to put the United States into the war if Great Britain could hold out until he was reelected."[11]

Richardson resigned.

The Roberts Commission, and at least four other subsequent investigations, would fail to inform the public what really happened. Cordell Hull and Henry Stimson were not available for questioning because of "health issues," and only submitted written responses to a list of questions provided in advance. The two most significant living witnesses who could have shed some light on events leading up to Pearl Harbor could not be cross examined. This confirmed what men in uniform believed; there would be no civilian accountability. Any incentive military commanders had to tell the truth had been removed even before the hearings began.

Historians would find much better luck in getting answers from Henry Stimson's diary. In an entry dated just before Thanksgiving in 1942, Stimson records FDR's plan.

> He (FDR) branched into an analysis of the situation himself as he sat there on his bed saying there were three alternatives and only three that he could see before us. His alternatives were — first, to do nothing; second, to make something in the nature of an ultimatum again, stating a point beyond which we would fight; third, to fight at once. I told him my only two were the last two, because I did not think anyone would do nothing in this situation, and he agreed with me...One problem troubled us very much. If you know your enemy is going to strike you, it is not usually wise to wait

---

[10] Stinnett, Robert B., *Day of Deceit*, The Free Press, New York, 2000, 18.
[11] Ibid.

until he gets the jump on you by taking the initiative. The question was how we should maneuver them into the position of firing the first shot without allowing too much danger to ourselves. It was a difficult proposition...In spite of the risk involved, however, in letting the Japanese fire the first shot, we realized that in order to have the full support of the American people, it was desirable to make sure that the Japanese be the ones to do this, so that there be no doubt in anyone's mind as to who were the aggressors.[12]

Despite five Pearl Harbor investigations that avoided proving it, the commanders at Pearl Harbor bore no responsibility. Only historians seem to have heard that message.

---

[12] Henry Stimson, Diary, quoted in Stinnett, Robert B., 178-179.

CHAPTER 16. "HURRY UP! AND WAIT"

David Walsh would face a formidable array of talent and resources aimed at crushing his career, not the least of which was the bandleader across the chilly Atlantic. As America went to war, Walsh would have to be dealt with. Churchill had been going it alone for some time now, and had not had to coordinate strategy with anyone. With the arrival of United States generals, a protracted tug-of-war would begin and Churchill would learn that American military leaders have an inconvenient way of asking questions all the time instead of simply following orders.

A prolific writer of books and newspaper columns, everyone knew where Churchill stood. He had a pulpit, even out of government. He was awarded the Nobel Prize for Literature for his publication of Great Contemporaries, and published 44 books in his lifetime. Of course, Churchill was not an objective author. He lived a part in almost every book he wrote. He served on the battlefield as a battalion commander. Churchill covered guerrilla warfare in Cuba in 1895. In 1896, he wrote his first book while in India. In 1897, he witnessed heavy fighting in the Khyber Pass. In 1898, he participated in his last cavalry charge in Omdurman. In 1899, he was captured in the Boer War. In 1900, he was recommended for the Victoria Cross. In 1900, he was elected to parliament. In the short span of five years, Churchill had witnessed what few heads of state see in a lifetime. Yet, the 20th century had just begun.

In 1911, Churchill served as First Lord of the Admiralty. For an island country, that is an important position; for the greatest naval power in the history of the world, it was monumental. In 1916, Churchill served in the trenches as a Lieutenant Colonel. In 1919, he became Secretary of War and Air. He had already learned to fly an airplane.

In 1921, Churchill became Colonial Secretary. In this capacity, he had

Lawrence of Arabia as an advisor. He had carved up the Middle East, founding the states of Jordan and Iraq and supporting a Jewish homeland, and had founded the Irish Free State. The preceding is abbreviated from author William Manchester.

His outbursts in the House of Commons were often viewed as coarse and unstatesmanlike. His diatribes usually drew immediate retaliation, and Churchill welcomed that. He knew how to get attention. He outraged Britons for generations, and seemed more famous for his long periods out of office than his many accomplishments in office. His commentary was highly sought after, even though, for much of his career, he was out of step with the public mood in Great Britain.

However, this half-American perpetual outsider was also as British as they come. His commitment to the Victorian Age made him an anachronism, even in Britain, throughout the 1930s. The War to end all Wars had been fought, and it was time to give peace a chance. Yet Churchill would not let go. He argued for a strong national defense. From the Boer War to the Atomic age, no one could have had better preparation for World War II than Churchill.

Despite the foregoing, Churchill was not living in the past. No one was better versed in current events. It was not uncommon to have conservative generals and liberals at the same dinner table at Churchill's Chartwell residence. Philosopher Bertrand Russell was a frequent dinner guest. Churchill was insatiably curious about other people's opinions, but he could just as quickly ignore them.

David Walsh would be facing a formidable foe, a master at government as well as the fourth estate. The two antagonists had some remarkably similar traits. Both men remained consistent in political outlook from the turn of the century to mid-century. Both had entered politics in an era of horse-drawn carriages. One was liberal and the other conservative; neither blew with the political winds. Both spent considerable time standing alone, out of favor with the ruling parties. Walsh fought for the rights of the downtrodden. Churchill, a conservative, had an impressive record of domestic legislation, although labor unions would never give him his due.

They certainly held divergent views on individual rights. In a country that has an Official Secrets Act, little time is spent debating civil rights. Churchill's writings constantly extol the virtues of Great Britain, not its citizens. The individual was expected to give his life for the greater glory of the British Empire. Walsh believed strongly in Jeffersonian Democracy, and felt he was representing the citizens in a watchdog role. He felt his role in the Senate was to keep an eye out for executive abuses.

Churchill, in his memoirs, in 1940, writes,

By the confidence, indulgence, and loyalty by which I was upborne, I was soon able to give an integral direction to almost every aspect of the war. This was really necessary because the times were so very bad. The method was accepted because everyone realized how near were death and ruin. Not only individual death, which is the universal experience, stood near, but incomparably more commanding, the life of Britain, her message, and her glory.[1]

Senator Walsh would face an adversary whose focus was on a Victorian Age empire, not the civil liberties of citizens. Walsh had lost his battle to keep America out of war, and he was in the company of many distinguished people in the anti-war movement. This broad-based volunteer group was no match for the tight network of paid professionals and media moguls who would orchestrate the pro-war campaign. Now that America was in the war, they suggested, "perhaps civilization would be saved." Unbeknownst to most Americans, who were in favor of intervening to save "democracy," civilization would have to wait until the British Empire was saved, first. Much of the anti-war movement had made the charge before the United States entered the war, and the charges were not necessarily coming from the radical fringe. Father James M. Gillis, editor of the *Catholic World*, speaking on September 22, 1941, criticized the foreign policy of the administration. The national defense policy has become in reality one of 'offense,' designed to help preserve the British Empire. Great Britain's preoccupation with marginalizing the Catholic viewpoint was well-founded; mainstream Catholics shared the same position as the Mayflower crowd. No amount of propaganda could move them from their position.

Now that the hot war had begun, the elite of West Point and the Naval Academy arrived at the scene. Roosevelt's clan of civilian counselors would be replaced by military leaders who were used to speaking out, and who surprisingly would show very little tendency to follow orders that were poorly conceived. FDR would now have to turn the war over to military commanders who were used to asking questions before drawing up battle plans. They would quickly pick up on the fact that Winston Churchill was in no hurry to save Europe.

In typically American fashion, General George Marshall would propose invading Europe, in May of 1942, exactly six months after Pearl Harbor. Winston Churchill had other uses for American troops, and worked tirelessly to delay the invasion of Europe. In the meantime, the civilian casualties in Europe from carpet bombing, starvation, and the holocaust would rise to monumental proportions. Americans in favor of early intervention would find that "saving democracy" and

---

[1] Manchester, William, *The Last Lion, Winston Spencer Churchill, Alone, Vol. II, 1932-40*, Dell Publishing, New York, 1988, 682

172

the refugees of Europe would have to wait. When Army Air Force General "Hap" Arnold arrived in London, he was shocked to find that Churchill was not attacking German military bases but was instead carpet bombing cities. Churchill did not want to risk his planes in direct air to air combat, and he chose to fly at night to avoid losses. The corollary was that, due to the difficulties of targeting at night, carpet bombing was employed. Churchill had decided that the destruction of the means of production was the safest way to attack Hitler. Unfortunately, the civilians in occupied countries would pay a terrible price. These were the same civilians who had been abandoned once before, when the Phony War began, as Hitler jawboned Great Britain to abandon its treaty obligations. While Dunkirk was symbolic of Great Britain's failure to honor its treaty obligations, only British propaganda could paint a spectacular retreat as a moral victory. Had any American general ever engaged in such a retreat, no amount of propaganda would have been able to rescue him. While MacArthur would engage in some intelligent retrograde maneuvers in Manila, he was using Filipino troops, and was facing overwhelming Japanese naval and marine forces, with no supply lines.

By the time the United States entered the war, England was not fighting at all. The Battle of Britain was over in six weeks, when the bombs mysteriously stopped coming. Then there is the mysterious Rudolph Hess affair, in which Hitler's top deputy flew to Scotland with what he claimed, all his life, was a proposed peace plan; an event made stranger by Britain's response. Great Britain refused to let anyone talk to him for his entire life; even his family. Having been prisoner for the duration of the war, he could not be held accountable for any war crimes committed after 1940. Instead of receiving the lightest war crime sentence, he received the harshest. The secrecy and the inconsistencies have fueled much speculation as to what was actually behind Hess's mission, and who. One possibility is that Churchill had asked Lothian to participate in a ruse to convince the German high command that a group of plotters, the appeaser group, were working behind Churchill's back to sue for peace (a thesis posited by Pulitzer Prize winning author Louis Kilzer in *Churchill's Deception*). As soon as a peace agreement was reached, then Churchill would be sacked and replaced by the group that had expressed solidarity with the Nazis before the war. (Lothian, in particular, had issued so many pro-Nazi statements before the war that Germany would certainly have reason to believe it.) Another possibility is that indeed there was a plot behind Churchill's back.

David Lloyd George, Prime Minister from 1916 to 1922, was a respected voice in British politics. He, among others, turned to journalism while out of office, and he had written that the leader of the Nazis was "a born leader, a magnetic, dynamic personality with a single minded purpose": to keep the peace. Lloyd George declared that with Hitler at the helm, Germany "would never invade any other land." A year later he wrote to T. Philip Conwell-Evans, another admirer of the Nazis and one of Lothian's closest friends, "of the admiration which I personally feel for (Hitler)....I only wish we had a man of his supreme quality at the head of affairs in our country today."[2]

Pre-war England's infatuation with Nazism may be surprising to readers today. Comments like those above were made before the holocaust was revealed. Indeed, after the war, the world would learn of Britain's active role in discrediting their own diplomats who warned of the danger, and smear them as well. "According to one Wilhelmstrasse document which came into British hands when Berlin fell in May 1945, MacDonald assured Germany's ambassador to Britain, Leopold von Hosch, that he knew there were no atrocities, no beatings, no desecration of synagogues — that everything England's own envoys had reported, was, in short, a lie. Macdonald explained that he understood 'very well the character of and the circumstances attending a revolution.' According to The Times, Baldwin told Hosch that England was 'entirely willing to work closely....with a Germany under a new order....'"[3]

Author William Manchester takes Ramsey MacDonald to task for ignoring the obvious anti-semitism of the Nazi regime. He was, after all, a once and future Prime Minister, not a factory worker from Manchester. His criticism was pointed at the early and mid 1930's, a time when the rest of the world was not watching Anglo-German relations. Rather than sound the alarm, Ramsey MacDonald discredited his own diplomats, thus assuring the German government that their present behavior was acceptable. Worse, MacDonald sent the signal to the diplomatic corps that he did not want to hear any bad news. Foreign policy would be determined by the elite in London.

The Roaring 20's had given way to the economic collapse of the 1930s, and social disruptions were generally attributed to ethnics of all kinds, with Jews being especially targeted. While anti-Semitism was perhaps considered bad form, it was socially acceptable throughout Europe and anti-Semitism was as rooted in England as it was in Germany. Even long after the war, the mutual admiration society between Germany's and England's ruling classes remained in place.

If the Hess Peace plan was a ruse, it certainly got the attention of a lot of high German officials, as well as officials in the United States. FDR was intrigued,

---

[2] Ibid., 80.

[3] Ibid., 101.

and begged Churchill for more information. One day before the killing started on the Russian front, American writer Anne McCormick, observing the rising German-Soviet tensions, wrote:

> In some way his flight is associated with the present crisis. Even if it is completely unreal, another war of nerves, he is somehow involved in the plot to create the impression that Germany must fight Russia or against her."[4]

Over a year afterward, and before the invasion of Russia began, the US press was still fascinated by the Hess mission and directly linked it to an attack on the Bolsheviks. Fear of Bolshevism amongst German and English leaders gave rise to much of the speculation. The bombing of London had stopped over a year ago, and at the point when the United States was entering the war, not much was happening on the English front. The English were sitting in England, and continental Europe was under Hitler.

Pulitzer Prize-winning author Louis Kilzer provides further direct evidence about the Hess affair, from US military intelligence files. On November 5, 1941, the American military attaché at the London Embassy cabled Brigadier General Sherman Miles, head of US military intelligence, with information from "someone whose intimate acquaintance with the affair is unquestionable."

> Hess said he flew to the Duke [of Hamilton] to tell him that Germany was about to fight Russia. Hess said that he "knew the Duke would see immediately that it would be absurd and awful for England to continue to fight Germany any longer. For, if England continued fighting from the west, we should have to destroy England after we have destroyed Russia".....Captain Lee expanded further. Hess, he said, expected the Duke to go right to the head of the British Peace Party: none other than King George himself. Once the King knew "about our plans to fight the Bolsheviks...the King could have made peace with us." [5]

Captain Lee's memo from 1941 confirms the speculations of the worldwide press, and J. Edgar Hoover's independent investigation corroborated Captain Lee. Hoover had sent his own report to FDR. However, Lee provides one more gruesome detail.

> Finally, Lee got a second major revelation, no less shattering than the first. During Hess's early stay, a psychiatrist observed him. The doctor asked about his fears. Hess didn't have any except he did not want to be poisoned. But, asked the psychiatrist, did he not fear the Jews in Germany?

[4] Kilzer, Louis, *Churchill's Deception*, Simon & Schuster, New York, London, Toronto, Sydney, Tokyo, Singapore, 1994, 54
[5] Ibid., 61.

"No," Hess responded, "We are obliterating the Jews." [6]

Captain Lee was writing on November 5, 1941. This was before Bergen Belsen and Auschwitz and Dachau. If Captain Lee had this information, certainly British intelligence had it. Joseph Goebbels had expressed concern in his diary that Hess might reveal the atrocities, and his fears were well founded. Atrocities were revealed to decision makers, but there was no outcry.

While Hess's mission would have a strange ending, leaving much unexplained, it would not be the only peace initiative to have a mysterious ending. William Rhodes Davis, the oilman whom Intrepid admits was murdered, had interceded as a peace emissary with Germany. While historians have generally treated his gesture as a fringe effort by a fringe character, evidence from responsible figures suggest this was not so. Author Dale Harrington contends that Davis was the single biggest contributor to FDR's 1936 reelection campaign, with no one a close second. He did succeed in securing a meeting with FDR in the White House, and FDR was very enthusiastic about his peace effort.

> Secretary of Agriculture Henry A. Wallace was waiting in the White House to see the president. Seated near him was William Rhodes Davis. The two struck up a conversation, and the middle-aged Davis explained that he was an international oil entrepreneur involved in the marketing of Mexican oil abroad. His appointment was before Wallace's, so the Secretary of Agriculture continued to wait while Davis conferred with the president and with Assistant Secretary of State Adolf Berle. When Wallace was finally ushered into the president's office, Roosevelt was excited. 'The man who has just been in here, he told Wallace, brought me the most amazing story about the possibility for peace that you ever heard. Probably nothing will ever come of it but I am going to follow it up just the same.'...As FDR predicted, nothing positive came of it. Wallace did not learn any of the details until he read columnist's versions in the newspapers five months later. But that episode was a part of a succession of futile efforts to prevent or end the war in Europe through mediation or negotiation. The Munich Conference a year before, Congressman Hamilton Fish's abortive peace explorations a month before, the much publicized diplomatic mission by Undersecretary of State Sumner Welles five months later in 1940, and the incredible flight and parachute jump into Scotland by Hitler's Nazi associate Rudolph Hess on May 10, 1941, were all parts of the long trail of fruitless quests for the phantom negotiated peace. Those efforts all failed. They affected evolving patterns in relations between Roosevelt and the isolationists, however, and were parts of the sequence of events that helped the president triumph over the isolationists.[7]

Various peace attempts were made, to the detriment of the initiators. Assistant Secretary of State Berle was blackmailed and William Davis was mur-

---

[6] Ibid., 62.

[7] Cole, Wayne S., *Roosevelt & the Isolationists, 1932-45*, University of Nebraska Press, Lincoln and London, 1983, 331

dered. Hess was imprisoned for life, was allowed no visitors, and after being tried in Nuremberg ,after the war was isolated in Spandau prison until his death in 1987. Congressman Hamilton Fish, the conservative Republican from FDR's home district of Hyde Park, was painted as a rightwing reactionary. Hated by FDR, perhaps his pedigree and leadership qualities helped make him a target.

His background hardly suggests a right wing extremist. Fish was awarded the Silver Star for his leadership of a black infantry unit in World War I, and was an ardent supporter of a Jewish homeland. An All-American football player at Harvard, his only sin (other than beating Columbia in football on Saturday afternoons) may have been his lack of allegiance to the New York Anglo elite. The propaganda campaign that brought down Fish would be as vitriolic as any conducted, as Fish would not bend his views to conform with FDR's vision of world engagement. He had seen war first hand, and was another heroic veteran who had no intention of witnessing the slaughter of so many young men again.

As America had been dragged into war, General George Marshall was called upon to mobilize the country. Marshall would begin sending troops overseas; the fresh faced as well as the not so fresh faced. As he continued to build up force strength, he began asking questions. Why were the troops sitting in England; why was there no fighting going on? British leaders, led by Churchill, argued that a cross-channel invasion would cost too many lives. While Marshall remained focused on Europe, Winston Churchill worked tirelessly to direct the military buildup towards the British colonial empire, instead. George Marshall was in the unenviable position of dealing with FDR, Churchill, and General Douglas MacArthur, who was demanding troops to help him fight the Japanese in the Pacific — if England was not going to start fighting soon.

Marshall battled with Churchill over war plans; his subordinate commanders were frustrated. As Churchill continued to delay, even General Dwight Eisenhower became frustrated and on March 25, 1942, he wrote a memo to Marshall, in which he asked his like-minded boss to abandon Europe if Churchill would not commit immediately, and concentrate forces in the Pacific. The Russians were ready to collapse, and Churchill seemed in no hurry to help them. If that was the case, the US had better go ahead and focus on Japan.

Unfortunately, the conditions for the post-war peace were already being set in stone. An embittered Stalin knew the British strategy since Kim Philby, his spy in British Intelligence, was providing him with all the details. Russia, having sustained frightening losses, was not going to give back Eastern Europe voluntarily. This was not because of any special ideology or "Red menace"; the European powers had been playing the game this way for centuries. The Versailles

177

Treaty had, indeed, declared, "To the victor belong the spoils."

Churchill continued to press for control of strategy, even in the Pacific. While Marshall would increasingly concentrate on the Pacific, Churchill went around his back to FDR. Roosevelt even agreed to divert reinforcements intended for the Philippines to Singapore, to the dismay of Marshall and Eisenhower.

FDR quickly reversed directions, and denied making any commitment to Churchill. Singapore was a British colony, and the Philippines an American possession. Perhaps the point was brought home to FDR that if the Philippines fell, and MacArthur captured, it would be difficult to explain why troops had been diverted to a British colony. Marshall and Eisenhower won that battle — but not the battlefield victories they envisioned. They would have to win many more battles of the boardroom, the war boardroom.

With continued delays in Europe, Harry Hopkins joined Marshall and Eisenhower on a visit to London to pin Churchill down on fighting for Europe.

> When Churchill started emphasizing the defense of India, even Hopkins was dismayed. While the meeting is reported to have ended in a glow of enthusiasm, with Churchill expressing strong support for a cross-Channel invasion, British sources indicate that Churchill simply lied. Sir Charles Wilson told his diary that the "P.M., as an experienced and tenacious campaigner," must have "decided that the time has not come to take the field as an out-and-out opponent of a Second Front in France....We should have come much cleaner than we did."[8]

Churchill's powers of persuasion had worked with FDR during America's undeclared war, but he was having difficulty now dealing with West Point. Roosevelt's band of civilian advisors had been replaced by professionals. The "long, gray line" of military officers was in fact colorful, and smart. England would have to use new tactics to keep control of American foreign policy.

Marshall's aggravation with Churchill was not over. By July, 1942, Marshall was informed that the British Cabinet had canceled plans to invade Europe and wanted the United States to invade North Africa instead. "US Army Chief of Staff ... George Catlett Marshall ... was sick and tired of arrangements made with the British only to be unmade by them shortly thereafter; it had happened over and over again. He was sick and tired of their proposals for risky, costly operations that, even if successful, could have no important effect on the outcome of the war. He was most emphatically sick and tired of the slipperiness, the evident phoniness, of their 'commitment' to the only operations against the Germans that could

---

[8] Davis, Kenneth, FDR: *The War President, 1940-1943*, Random House, New York, 2000, 491.

possibly be truly decisive."[9]

Once again, US troops were being volunteered to defend British colonial areas. Marshall and his commanders were universally opposed to it, even though FDR was won over. When Stalin heard about it, his eruption would be as bad as Marshall's. When the press got wind of the disagreement, some commentators suggested that the President was overstepping the bounds of his office and was ignoring the advice of highly competent military advisors. Roosevelt fought back, strongly intimating that no such suggestion had better reach the media again.

Marshall, however, had no choice but to fight his Commander-in-Chief, because the proposed landings in North Africa were a diversion from the focused strategy of going after "Germany First." And, as the North African landings were being prepared, Charles de Gaulle was not even notified in advance, despite the fact that the site chosen was in French North Africa. As head of the French Committee of National Liberation (FCNL), he was justly indignant. The bitterness of both Stalin and de Gaulle would persist in the war's aftermath.

Americans would get a glimpse of the real Churchill, not the Churchill of war propaganda but the Churchill known back in London, as the invasion of North Africa began.

> Churchill announced, "Let me make one thing clear, in case there should be any mistake about it in any quarter. We mean to hold our own. I have not become the King's First Minister in order to preside over the liquidation of the British Empire."

> This had a shocking effect on American public opinion and was almost universally deplored in the United Kingdom, even by those who shared the Prime Minister's commitments.[10]

Churchill was beginning to see that FDR's military advisors were a less homogenous group than he had advising him regarding the details of the British Empire. They were a group that was difficult to control. They were outspoken, and not likely to care what their superiors thought. West Point was turning out graduates from poor towns in the plains of Kansas (like Eisenhower), kids who grew up on Indian reservations riding horses bareback (MacArthur), as well as loudmouths like "Vinegar Joe" Stillwell (who labeled Chiang Kai-Shek a corrupt dictator, and was almost fired by FDR). West Point even accepted WASPS of the pedigree of George Catlett Marshall. This group had brains; and they were taught to question authority. The invasion of North Africa would mark the beginning of the end of Nazi Germany, and it also marked the end of the influence of Intrepid's

---

[9] Ibid., 537.

[10] Ibid., 641.

friends at Rockefeller Center. West Point would run the show from now on.

FDR tried to make Fiorello LaGuardia a general, and send him to North Africa with the occupying force. "A fantastic and protracted tug of war resulted when Roosevelt proposed to commission Mayor Fiorello LaGuardia a general and send him to Eisenhower's headquarters as an expert in military government.... There was no question of LaGuardia's qualifications for a role in military government or psychological warfare. But the army saw other factors to consider. His waspish tongue and hot temper angered many. As one of the top political figures in the country, he could be difficult to hold in check in an allied military command. In addition, both Stimson and Marshall opposed giving direct general officer rank to civilians."[11]

When Marshall blocked this appointment, LaGuardia may have begun to suspect that his and Intrepid's influence were wearing thin. Now that the nation was at war, there was less need for psychological warfare and less need for spying on Americans. Marshall would take it one step further. He would do the unthinkable and appoint the Chairman of America First, Major General Robert E. Wood, head of Sears and Roebuck, to handle supply problems — and he was certainly good at it. There was little FDR could do, now. He was losing whatever grip he had on the war effort; Marshall was simply moving too fast for FDR to keep up.

---

[11] Pogue, Forrest C., *George C. Marshall, Organizer of Victory*, New York, Viking Press, 1973, 121.

CHAPTER 17. THE "MOB" HELPS OUT

New York City would soon become the center of a different plot — a plot to dispose of an anti-war senator. Other locales would be explored first, but New York was chosen as the site to corner David Walsh. New York provided the most weapons, and it was the epicenter of the pro-British movement bent on achieving the goals of an aging British Empire, even if those goals were not necessarily in the interests of the US. A cast of characters from the publishing centers of the world, New York and London, would be enlisted to remove FDR's antagonist from the political scene. From Rockefeller Center to editorial boardrooms, from LaGuardia to Lansky, from the docks in Brooklyn to the manor at Hyde Park, the troupe would employ a wide array of people to bring down a man who simply wanted to direct America's military dollars to defensive ends, to providing a navy that could guarantee our security — at a time when the US was funding a nation that apparently was not willing to fight the good fight. The unanswered question is how many other senators were silenced as well.

It mattered little to the pro-British movement that they would have to undermine the United States Congress. In Great Britain, democracy operated within a framework that included a king or queen, and a House of Lords, an Official Secrets Act, a Prime Minister, and a House of Commons for the common folk. It operated with Ministers without Portfolio and consorts. It was all very confusing, but one thing was clear. There was no confusion over which class ran Great Britain, and that was the upper class. Great Britain had very specific plans to control the peace table, and Great Britain did not want Walsh around at the conclusion of the war, particularly as Chairman of the Senate Naval Affairs Committee, with his outspoken views on colonialism.

Walsh had proven throughout his long career that he could not be bought off. Even organized crime would be enlisted to take care of him. They would prove the most reputable of the lot, for Meyer Lansky in his memoirs would indicate that he smelled a rat. The conductor at Hyde Park would stay at a safe distance. He had many underlings willing to do his bidding, and the British were happy to go after a homosexual Irishman, especially against the most powerful political leader from Boston. It was Walsh who had introduced Eamon de Valera at Fenway Park before 50,000 people in 1918 for a fundraising event that helped promote Irish freedom. It was Walsh who was the visible leader of the American Irish during the Irish Revolution, and it was Winston Churchill, then Dominions Secretary, who had to negotiate Irish freedom with Michael Collins. It is doubtful he forgot Walsh's role in the period following World War I.

The characterization of Walsh as anti-British was all it took to put him in Intrepid's sights. Walsh was tarnished so badly that even today, historians continue to misrepresent the man. Writing in 2000, author Kenneth Davis, in *FDR, The War President, 1940-43*, describes Walsh in a debate on the release of Liberators to Great Britain. "The great legal obstacle to the release of these and future Liberators to the British was an amendment attached to last summer's navy expansion bill at the behest of Senator David Walsh, a conservative isolationist Democrat, chairman of the Senate Naval Affairs Committee, who had a Boston Irish Catholic's hatred of Perfidious Albion. The Walsh Amendment forbade the sale of any army or navy materiel to a foreign power without the prior certification by the chief of staff or the chief of naval operations that said materiel was not 'essential to the defense of the United States.'"[1]

Thus, even modern day historians have fallen for the propaganda spewed out a half century ago. British propagandists led everyone into believing that the "anti-war types" were right wing reactionaries. The very liberal Walsh had plenty of company in the US Senate. His core constituency in Massachusetts were the WASP farmers from the central and western parts of the state, people who did not trust anyone to the east — not their rich WASP brethren in Boston, and certainly not any of their ancestors in London. Walsh had been unbeatable in Western Massachusetts from the time he entered politics in 1913. If the conservatives in the Senate who supported Walsh's position were "reactionary," it was because their thinking went back two hundred years, to Thomas Jefferson's time.

The British intelligence service knew their prey. Intrepid, while running the Rockefeller Center operation, had done most of the training of the OSS officers under Donovan, with his top assistant, Major Dick Ellis. Churchill had appointed

---

[1] Davis, Kenneth, *FDR—The War President, 1940-1943*, Random House, New York, 2000, 46

Intrepid, and he had a direct channel to the Prime Minister. Sir Stewart Menzies, Intrepid's nominal boss in London, resented this and he directed Ellis, a real agency man, to keep tabs on Intrepid. But Ellis was apparently not so "loyal" after all; he turned out to have sold information to the Russians and to the Germans.

Meanwhile, Roald Dahl was reporting from the White House every Monday morning at Rockefeller Center. As the information passed under Major Ellis' nose, it was forwarded to London to Sir Stewart Menzies (and from there, one of his top deputies, Kim Philby, then sent some of it on to Stalin.) Congress could get little information from the White House. J. Edgar Hoover had to ask for an appointment. Yet the British and the Russians had a direct pipeline.

Stephenson and Ellis set up a curriculum for training sites in the Maryland and Virginia countryside, where OSS recruits were trained. Many American recruits, however, felt uncomfortable with the curriculum:

> Dirty fighting, the sine qua non of special operations, conflicted with the national self image cherished by many Americans and was adopted with reluctance by some OSS trainees who had been raised to believe that only a coward or a sneak fights with his feet or hits below the belt. One OSS veteran recalled many years later, the training in hand-to-hand combat he and the other recruits received at Camp X from Major William Ewart Fairbairn, a former assistant commissioner of the Shanghai police, and the SOE's leading expert on silent killing. Fairbairn taught the OSS recruits there were no rules in staying alive. He taught them to enter a fight with one idea: to kill an opponent quickly and efficiently.... Even in the gentler subversive art of psychological warfare, some OSS novices were shocked by the British methods. Edmond Taylor, an American journalist recruited by Donovan during the COI period, was sent to England to study the methods of the Political Warfare Executive, the principal British black propaganda agency. At PWE's country headquarters in Woburn Abbey, in Bedfordshire, Taylor was introduced to sibs (supposedly from the Latin word whisper), rumors dreamed up by planners at Abbey and intended for unattributable launching by "black" radio, by secret agents, or by the resistance networks in occupied countries and in other ways.[2]

As of 1940, David Walsh's FBI file contained only one page, despite the fact that he had served in public office since 1913. Contrary to public perception,

J. Edgar Hoover had not been having him tailed for the duration of his career. The only item that caught the FBI's attention was that a little, old lady was following Walsh; one Sadie Maple. She wrote letters accusing Walsh of conspiring with *National Geographic* and "delaying clipper ship trips to bird sanctuaries on Wake Island and Midway." If Miss Maple had waited a year, she would have had a lot to say to the Japanese, who did not give a hoot about her bird sanctuaries.

---

[2] O'Toole, G.J.A., "*Honorable Treachery*," Atlantic Monthly Press, New York, 1991, 405

His file suddenly ballooned to approximately 200 pages, when the "whispered rumors" began. FBI agents actually worked feverishly to clear his name. They were forced to file reports because rumors were surfacing against Walsh, and Attorney General Biddle obliged them to investigate.

One item in the FBI file is a Memorandum for the Director, dated May 4, 1942, from P.E. Foxworth, Assistant Director. That was the first slanderous rumor. The source (name deleted) had telephoned from New York concerning a naval contract "believed by him to be fraudulent involving Senator David Walsh. He stated it was a sixteen million dollar contract known as the South Boston Works, which involves work on the docks in Boston. Walsh had boosted a friend, whose identity was unknown to (name deleted) was under indictment in an income tax case. He was not eligible for the contract. The contract was finally given to a corporation which is under the control of the same man."

The source indicated that "there is only one man on the level in the Navy Board [contract board] concerned with the awarding of contracts but he states he is...afraid to talk for fear of getting in bad with the powers that be." That certainly sounds like the whispered rumor. "He further stated that he was fairly well convinced unless the FBI or the ONI [Office of Naval Intelligence] interposed an objection he was going to tell [name deleted], which means the *New York Post*, that they might break the name of Senator Walsh in their story." The source also refers to "their other story"; the memo was dated May 4, 1942. The only other story the source can be referring to is the Nazi Spy Nest Story, also called the Gustave Beekman case. The *New York Post* had already broken the story (without names) on May 1. Public imagination was already being whipped up to a frenzy.

While FBI field agents were working to test the validity of the source for a Boston investigation, there was an implied threat that the story might be leaked in the *New York Post*. The FBI would have to do a cursory investigation, even if they questioned the source, in the event it became public. A hot potato had been tossed into J. Edgar Hoover's lap.

The FBI memo continued. "The source [name deleted] also asked that I relay to you his opinion that this matter, that is, the one pertaining to the homosexual activities of Walsh, be presented to the Grand Jury in the District of Columbia. [Name deleted] stated he did not think the matter should be handled in either New York City or Brooklyn. He further stated that if Biddle did not bring the matter to the Grand Jury he then proposed to get some Senator to insist upon a congressional investigation."

The source ended on a telling note. He "also said he had one special lead which grew out of a remark that [name deleted] a newspaper reporter, had made.

[Name deleted] according to [name deleted] overheard Walsh state at the Twenty-One Club a few days ago that Hitler was going to win the war, and for that reason he was going to do what he could for a negotiated peace" — the coup de grace — another whispered rumor, this one connecting Walsh to Hitler. All the favorite ingredients of British intelligence came together: Hitler, homosexual sex, corruption, and a member of the fourth estate.

On May 12, 1942, J. Edgar Hoover wrote a confidential memo to Attorney General Biddle advising him that the bureau had received a report from a confidential source that Senator Walsh might be involved in the fraudulent awarding of a Naval contract. Hoover's memo reduced it to the bare essentials, and stated, "According to our source, Walsh had boosted a friend for the contract, but because the friend, whose identity is unknown to our source, was under indictment in an income tax case, he was not eligible for the contract. This contract was finally given to a corporation which is under the control of the same man."

Hoover closed the letter by asking Biddle for instructions. "I would appreciate being advised as to what action, if any, you desire this Bureau to take in this matter." Hoover made it clear that he would not proceed further without direction from Biddle. Hoover even suggested not doing anything, with his phrase "if any." Hoover did not mention the implied threats in the letter, and does not seem impressed with the source. Perhaps he felt that Biddle needed no explanation; it was fairly obvious they were only dealing with a blackmail operation.

However, Biddle responded in his own handwriting, "Immediate investigation authorized. Please report to me after preliminary investigation." This prompted an exhaustive review by various field agents, particularly in the Boston, New York, and Chicago field offices. The number of companies involved in the bidding on the South Boston Works project was substantial, and it would require interviews and investigations of officers in six different companies to find out which officer (if any) had a problem with the IRS.

Hoover reported to Biddle on May 27, writing that, "A list of the names of the firms, as well as the officers and directors of the Morton C. Tuttle Company, New England Foundation Company, Roy B. Rendle Company and the Sawyer Company was checked against the Intelligence Unit, Internal Revenue Service at Boston, and it was determined that none of these companies or any officers or directors had ever been indicted for any violation of income tax laws, nor were any of the companies or individuals the subject of an investigation." The field agents have come up with a complete blank, as Hoover had expected.

At the same time, the Gustave Beekman story had already broken in Brooklyn, which the FBI source had already mentioned as a possible venue for crushing Walsh. The mysterious source had originally mentioned Washington as a possible venue, but so far Hoover had been uncooperative, even hostile to the investigation, and it was Hoover who would control any prosecution in Washington.

Hoover continued, in his report to Biddle of May 27, by commenting on an investigation to see if any members of the Navy board believed wrongdoing had occurred. He concluded they did not. "In view of the information developed to date as compared with the allegations of [name deleted], it would be appreciated if you would advise whether you desire any additional investigation in this matter." Hoover clearly thought the investigation should end. And, if it didn't, and if there were a subsequent investigation, Hoover had created a clear paper trail showing who was ordering the investigation. Hoover's field agents had so far found that none of the charges could be substantiated.

The remainder of the FBI report shows an exhaustive background check on each principal in each firm, all in an effort to find the person with the tax problem. The report goes on to characterize each company doing business on the project. One of the bidders is characterized in a memorandum for Mr. Ladd, dated May 18, 1942, as "the cleanest outfit doing Navy work."

In a separate memorandum for Mr. Ladd of the same date, May 18, 1942, a Lieutenant Horan at ONI (Office of Naval Intelligence) reported his findings. He corroborated what the FBI agents had found: nothing.

On June 17, 1942, D.M. Ladd, a senior FBI official in Washington, updated J. Edgar Hoover, but added a new twist. His three-page memorandum shows that an exhaustive review was conducted, and it turned up nothing. Ladd closed with the suggestion, "that arrangements be made to interview [name deleted] with a view of determining from him the source of his information regarding this matter or at least the degree of credibility that he accords to this source. It would also be desirable to have [name deleted] amplify, if possible, his original allegations both as to the identity of the individual who is involved in the income tax violation as well as the [name deleted] on the Contract Award Board, who is said to know the entire story concerning this situation. The possibility exists that if this interview is conducted with the view of drawing [name deleted] we may be able to determine if this information is based on the remarks of a reliable informant or if this is just another 'shot in the dark' in an effort to stir up additional unfavorable publicity on Senator Walsh's behalf to augment the [passage deleted]."

"Just another" attempt to smear Walsh.... The reference was obviously to the Brooklyn grand jury hearing in the Nazi Spy Nest case. Two different smear attempts had been developed, one in Boston and one in Brooklyn. The unidentified source mentions several venues, including New York or Washington.

In a memo to Attorney General Biddle dated July 24, 1942, J. Edgar Hoover gave his report, as promised. His investigation showed that the original allegation of awarding a government contract to someone convicted of tax evasion was false. What was true, Hoover points out, was that the original bidder, Perini and Sons, and C.J. Maney and Company, were disqualified because they had pleaded guilty to tax evasion on June 6, 1940. One of Hoover's field agents identified Perini and Maney as supporters of the former Mayor of Boston, James Michael Curley, Walsh's bitter rival. This shows that the charges could not have arisen in Boston, because anyone connected to the Boston scene would have known that Walsh would not have intervened for supporters of his rival, Curley.

But Hoover's memo to Biddle slammed the door shut on any further investigation. In closing, Hoover indicated the source of the information, without disclosing the name (the identity is never revealed), as is standard procedure in FBI files. The source was identified as a lawyer from "Wild Bill" Donovan's organization, OSS, the agency that was supposed to be dropping spies into France.

Hoover indicates that they "have been endeavoring to have this lawyer personally contact a representative of this bureau in order that more definite information concerning this allegation may be obtained. It would appear, therefore, more desirable to withhold any further investigation until the lawyer mentioned by [name deleted] as the original source of this investigation is interviewed, unless, of course, you desire some specific investigative steps taken at this time." Hoover's paper trail was complete. The investigation was finished, unless Attorney General Biddle spelled out what "specific investigative steps" Hoover should take. His agents had been chasing the source at OSS, who is only identified as "a very able lawyer" in Donovan's organization. After dropping such a bombshell, the lawyer was always unavailable. Given the number of people the FBI had to investigate in the case, it was surprising the case did not leak to the press.

It perhaps did not leak because the OSS had made other plans; and perhaps that is why the OSS lawyer became completely unavailable after suggesting three venues in Boston, New York, and Washington. Mayor Fiorello LaGuardia could, and would certainly be willing to, control a local prosecution in Brooklyn. The OSS had tested Hoover, and he was unwilling to cooperate in bringing Walsh down; therefore a federal prosecution would have to be discarded. They could bring in more firepower, and Meyer Lansky would describe his role. One solitary anti-war senator is drawing the orchestrated attention of an army of shadows.

When the initial raid was made on the homosexual brothel in Brooklyn, the Office of Naval Intelligence led the operation, with the New York City police in tow. The initial press coverage described it as "a Nazi Spy Nest." Walsh's name was not mentioned at all. The case began with sensational headlines, but few facts. After the initial story broke in the *New York Post*, mention was made of a United States Senator. The investigation was immediately turned over to Mayor LaGuardia's New York City Police. The rationale for turning it over to local police was that it would be easier to make arrests and prosecutions on myriad local laws as well as licensing violations. ONI would slip into the background. If the alleged purpose of the raid was to get Nazi spies, it is unlikely a local prosecution would net more than a 30-day jail term.

Intrepid didn't trust J. Edgar Hoover, anyway. He and Donovan used ONI to lead the raid because they knew they could control the outcome. ONI had been working with Meyer Lansky and Lucky Luciano for some time to protect the Brooklyn waterfront. When ONI first showed up there, the dockworkers laughed at them. If they wanted cooperation, they were told to get permission from the boss. The boss, Lucky Luciano, was away at Sing Sing Prison. Crime buster Thomas Dewey had sent him away on a questionable prosecution for running a brothel, the same charge used against Gustave Beekman.

It would take the sinking of a ship in New York Harbor, the *Normandie*, to get ONI to work with the mafia. ONI was under considerable pressure to find out what had happened and Lansky quickly offered to help with his highly organized dockworkers that kept an eye on the waterfront. However, Lansky was never able to solve the ship sinking. It was later said that one of his men, Albert Anastasia, had set a small fire in an attempt at intimidation during a labor dispute. The fire went undetected during the night, and the ship ended up at the bottom of the East River. Luciano certainly did not wish to solve that crime. Anastasia was not known for having a delicate touch. He went on to become head of Murder, Inc, and was gunned down Hollywood style in a barber's chair in the 1950's while getting a 'close shave'.

Thomas Dewey had promised a commutation for Lucky Luciano after the war for his contribution to the war effort; he kept his bargain, with an unexpected twist — he deported him to Italy. Dewey was planning to run for President, and did not want to appear soft on crime. Luciano should have known that politicians could be treacherous.

Meyer Lansky, the brains of the Mob, met on a regular basis with ONI, and they engaged him to help out in the Walsh case. Lansky eventually fled to Israel to avoid prosecution. In an account of his life, he described his role in the Nazi Spy Nest Case, at a time when the German Bund was holding large pro-German rallies at Madison Square Garden, and concern about possible sabotage on the Brooklyn docks remained a worry of the Office of Naval Intelligence.

> My stand against the pro-Nazis also got me involved in what must have been one of the most sensitive problems the intelligence people had to deal with. Right in the middle of the war the Navy was worried — and so were some big shots in Washington — about some senator named Walsh. For some reason, he had gotten in the habit of coming up to New York, and there was a strong suspicion that he was a regular patron of a brothel over near the Brooklyn Navy Yard. It was a homosexual joint but it was not the senator's preference that was upsetting people. Everybody knew it was a hangout for Bundists....That's why [Commander] Haffenden was asked to find out about this particular senator. Was he being blackmailed? It sounded like Walsh was more dangerous than the other politicians who dropped in from time to time. He had a big say in the Naval Affairs Committee and knew as much as anybody in Washington about that branch of the service. If he was being blackmailed, the Navy had no secrets.[3]

According to Lansky, the request to target Walsh came from Washington. Someone in Washington said Senator Walsh was frequenting the place. Lansky put his men to work on it right away.

> Haffenden first asked Polakoff for suggestions about what to do. Polakoff asked me and I got Mikey Lascari into it. I had known Mikey for a long time — he was a childhood buddy of Charlie's — And I knew he was an expert on that part of Brooklyn. By the 1940s he was involved in the rackets in New Jersey, but I knew I could count on him.

It did not take long to confirm the rumors. Twenty-four hours later, we got news from Mikey that, sure enough, there were bona fide spies operating out of that brothel. And in addition, one of the male prostitutes had a customer whom he had to treat very special and who was known as the "Senator."[4]

Lansky began placing Navy ONI personnel within the club, but as soon as he did so, Commander Haffenden suddenly reversed directions.

> Haffenden reported to his bosses and they told him to find out about this man. Some of Mikey's boys showed the Navy team where to hide in the brothel and who to watch out for. They put surveillance on the place around the clock from the outside. Then one day Haffenden told me, "Please take no further action. I don't want any of your associates involved from here on. There's probably going to be a big scandal but it'll be hushed up because it's wartime."[5]

However, Lansky did not trust Haffenden, and while appearing to cooperate, he had is own men keep an eye out.

---

[3] Eisenberg, Dennis, Dan, Uri, Meyer Lansky, *The Mogul and the Mob*, Paddington Press, 1979, 199.

[4] Ibid., 200.

[5] Ibid.

I was curious. I didn't want the Navy doing something without my knowing what they were up to. They weren't always efficient, as Cockeye said, and it's always worthwhile knowing what is going on.

Well, they pulled in the owner of the place and threatened him until he told them who the spies in his brothel were. The authorities arrested five men and three of them proved to be enemy agents. The other two were released. I was surprised — I knew from our own network they were spying, too. A couple of days later these two men were found dead. Nobody had seen anything and nobody ever got charged. We knew these men were spies, and if the authorities weren't going to handle them, then Charlie's men probably settled the matter themselves

The brothel owner went to prison to protect him from a revenge killing. He had talked a great deal, and the police or the Navy or somebody handled the information in a rather ham-fisted way. Haffenden did not want to discuss the case at all. I got the impression he was gagged by his superiors. Mikey's boys and I heard some of the Washington press corps knew the story, but it was pretty much hushed up, just as Haffenden predicted. Once he tried to tell me that the senator was not Senator David Walsh but actually another Walsh who had been a New York State senator. I looked Haffenden straight in the eye and said, "That's funny. I know the guy you're asking me to believe is the guilty party and he's exactly 87 years old. Are you kidding, he's going to a brothel four times a week?[6]

Lansky, with his years of experience in the Mob, did not trust ONI and did not believe Haffenden's version of events. His instincts were correct. What is remarkable about Lansky's account is not so much the details themselves but his overall impression of the operation. He never indicated that his men actually confirmed that Senator Walsh was there; but he knew that Haffenden's story that it was a state senator was false. Lansky's description of Haffenden, whom he seems to like, is best summed up in the line that he "was gagged by his superiors." Lansky's impression is that Haffenden could not level with him because of Washington; perhaps Haffenden did not know the real story himself.

Lansky's story confirms that the targeting of the brothel came from Washington. Usually, intelligence flows the other way, from the field to headquarters. Now, everyone was waiting for Senator Walsh to show up and despite massive surveillance, he still had not arrived. Walsh never did show up at the scene; and Meyer Lansky was perhaps unaware that someone else was also watching the brothel in New York — J. Edgar Hoover. This was the most watched brothel in the world.

The FBI had been watching the place for years and had a wiretap on the place. But, the raid was led by ONI and the New York City Police. If this had been an actual FBI case, Hoover would have led the raid and taken credit in the headlines. But Donovan and Intrepid were not going to involve an agency that

---

[6] Ibid., 201.

they knew they could not control, and they may not even have known that Hoover had the place staked out. That never became public information at the time and only the FBI files reveal the surveillance and wiretap.

As the case unfolded, Hoover would be asked to investigate. It would be difficult for Hoover to explain why his own agents had not found Walsh, if he had actually been visiting the brothel, when the place had been under observation for years and a wiretap had been in place for six months. The hot potato had now been thrown in Hoover's lap, and this was an investigation he did not welcome.

CHAPTER 18. THE NAZI SPY NEST AND THE CONGRESSIONAL RECORD

The Gustave Beekman case opened in Brooklyn with spectacular tales of orgies, the stuff of supermarket tabloids. There were tales of Nazi spies frequenting the place; the *New York Post* dubbed it the "Nazi Spy Nest." On May 1, 1942, the *New York Post* ran a screaming headline, "Links Senator to Spy Nest," and showed the silhouette of Walsh, which narrowed the identity of the "culprit" to one of the pudgy, older senators. The Washington press corps did not run with the story until they did further research.

Then, Beekman signed an affidavit which identified David Walsh. This provided the legal or journalistic cover the press would need to publicly identify Walsh, and they did so, immediately. Still, no one ran with the story except the Post. Virtually every other editor across the country passed up a story that involved a United States senator, homosexual sex, and Nazi spies; all during wartime. Where was the pack of journalists that Washington is famous for?

If there was a massive cover up, after the story had already been leaked, Walsh would have had to have a protector. It certainly would not be FDR, or the Eastern press, which had been strongly pro-intervention in the lead-up to the war. There was no group that could have an interest in covering up the story that would also have the power to do so.

Where were the attack journalists such as Walter Winchell and Drew Pearson? Most certainly, they would do what they always did: call Hoover first, to get his take on the matter. Since they were both supporters of intervention, they would have had no interest in protecting Walsh. But Hoover would have let both of them know that the FBI had had the brothel under surveillance for years — and never saw Walsh. Virtually all of Hoover's stories were given to Winchell first, as testified by their lengthy correspondence which is contained in FBI files.

Did the Washington press, generally supportive of FDR, draw a line in the sand on this case? Certainly, Hoover held as much sway with the media as FDR did. While the Beekman case continued in state court in Brooklyn, a public announcement was made that Attorney General Biddle would be monitoring the case for the Justice Department. Yet, Biddle's role in the case seems strangely distant for something that had been portrayed as a national security issue. In his memoirs, *In Brief Authority*, 1962, Biddle mentions Walsh twice, and only once does he make any observations about the man. Perhaps, Biddle did not want to admit any role in this sordid affair.

When Biddle was moving to fill a judgeship in Boston, he noticed a comment that Walsh had made about the absence of Jews in judicial appointments in Boston. Biddle quickly got FDR to nominate Charles Wyzanski, "before Walsh could change his mind." He apparently was completely unaware of Walsh's lifelong friendship with Justice Brandeis and his resentment of religious prejudice. Biddle gives himself a pat on the back for "outfoxing" Walsh. He goes on to further describe Walsh. "The first Democrat elected to the Senate in Massachusetts since the Civil War, Walsh, an elderly politician with a soft tread and low, colorless voice, was an isolationist without enthusiasm, whose concealed and controlled anxieties not altogether centered on retaining his job. He was not personally popular in Washington, but he was useful to his constituents."[1]

The attorney general ought to have a sense of the Senate, a body that must confirm judicial appointments; did he truly not know the political positions or passions of this long-serving Senator? Could he possibly believe that Walsh was an "isolationist without enthusiasm"? His comment about being "useful to his constituents" was a common theme repeatedly voiced by the British diplomatic class, but it is odd coming from the Attorney General. If Biddle was so out of touch with who Walsh was, then his role in taking Walsh down may indeed have been minimal. He certainly was doing FDR's bidding. He kept the pressure on Hoover to keep the Boston investigation going, but all Hoover did was create a clear paper trail back to Biddle. J. Edgar Hoover had been gathering dirt on FDR's enemies for years, but he was backing away from the Walsh investigation.

While the Beekman trial received extensive coverage by the *New York Post*, it is difficult to discern what is going on in the courtroom. All of the column space is devoted to Walsh.

On May 4, 1942, the *New York Post* ran a headline, NAMING OF SEN. X IMMINENT. The typeface was larger than the one most newspapers used to

---

[1] Biddle, Francis, *In Brief Authority*, Doubleday & Co, Garden City, NY, 1962, 202.

announce the ending of the war. Speculation was running wild. The *New York Post* called it the "story of the year" and indicated that it was causing a sensation in Washington. A picture of a brownstone building at 329 Pacific St., Brooklyn, was identified as a "House of Degradation." The newspaper reported on the flight of a mysterious "Mr. E.", who was branded as "one of Hitler's chief espionage agents in this country." It describes him as "the suave Nazi agent who gave freely of liquor and food to sailors." The Post's description sounds like the Hollywood productions that Senator Nye wanted investigated, and the writing sounds like something that Robert Sherwood might produce. The timing was certainly of Broadway quality, because May 4 was the same day that the first memo was written on the Boston Shipyard investigation. Senior FBI agent P.E. Foxworth wrote his first memo to J. Edgar Hoover on that date, and identified the source as connected "to the homosexual activities of Walsh (in Brooklyn)... and a special lead that grew out of a remark that a newspaper reporter had made at the Twenty-One Club a few days ago, to the effect that Hitler was going to win the war, and for that reason he was going to do what he could do for a negotiated peace." Walter Winchell was a regular at the Twenty-One Club, a place that very few of the "ink-stained wretches" could afford. Looking back on the conspiracy some 60 years, the brazenness of the participants is remarkable, but it is doubtful they imagined what large footprints they would leave.

The *New York Post* revealed, for the first time on May 4, that three different agencies were spying on the brothel. That fact served to buttress their story but, since they didn't identify the agencies, it was still unclear if the *Post* knew that the FBI was one of those agencies. The *Post* conducted an interview with a "Madame Fox," who identified the Beekman brothel as a favorite of sailors. The interview added color to the story with the implication that she did not use her real name because of her own professional activities.

On May 7, 1942, Walsh's name appeared in bold type on the front page of the Post over the headline of the day: US SINKS 7 JAP WARSHIPS. The juxtaposition clearly suggested that Walsh was a traitor. The article identified three people who had seen Walsh at the brothel: Beekman, Charles Zuber, and a third man only identified as "a runner for Beekman." The cast was building. The *Post* claimed that the government investigative report contained other corroborating evidence but failed to disclose what that evidence was.

On May 15, the *Post* printed Beekman's affidavit. Beekman indicated that the Senator was always in a hurry. "He seldom stayed more than two hours. Sometimes Senator X came in the afternoon, and at other times in the early evening. The senator always made himself at home." Beekman went on to say that

194

he thought the Senator "very interesting" because "the Senator would discuss the topic of the day, current events, and sex."

On May 20, the *New York Post* ran a headline screaming, "WHITEWASH FOR WALSH." They ran an editorial the same day, headed, "The Name is Still Walsh." They went on to say that, "The Senate of the United States spent a whole hour trying to scare The *New York Post*." They attacked the *New York Daily News*, describing it as arch-isolationist. The *Daily News* refused to participate in the smear campaign, giving minimal coverage of the story. The *Post* would go on to attack Attorney General Biddle, even though the FBI files show that Biddle was pushing for an investigation of Walsh in the trumped-up Boston charges, which were running simultaneously with the Beekman trial but which would never become public. Perhaps Morris Ernst felt the Boston case would not be as titillating as the Beekman case.

On May 21, the *New York Post* ran another headline, this time attacking Attorney General Biddle, charging "BIDDLE WITHHOLDS WALSH DATA". Again, the *Post* used typeface that was two inches in height. Was this the beginning of an exit strategy designed to give cover to Biddle to distance himself from the smear? The press stampede had not occurred, and the *Post* was alone in this venture. In the prior day's paper, on May 20th, the *Post* had reported that Biddle had delivered an FBI report that exonerated Walsh to Senate Majority Leader Alben Barkley. Hoover was still hiding from publicity, doing his best to keep a low profile, as was his boss, but Hoover was getting the credit for clearing Walsh, at least on Capitol Hill. Did Hoover make his boss, Biddle, bring the report up to Capitol Hill? The *Post* alleges that Beekman was brow beaten to recant. It goes on to state, "Senator Barkley was followed to the floor by four isolationists-Clark of Missouri, Wheeler of Montana, Tobey of New Hampshire, and Nye of North Dakota, all of whom violently attacked the *Post* for publishing the charges against Walsh. And there, after half an hour angry tirade, the matter ended. Despite the gravity of the charges against the *Post*, the Senate took no action against the newspaper." With Morris Ernst of ACLU fame serving as General Counsel for the *Post*, and running this operation down to its finest details, did the *Post* really think that the United States Senate had any legal options?

While Judge Samuel Liebowitz controlled the courtroom, the actual events of the Beekman trial bear little semblance to the media trial occurring daily in the *New York Post*. Liebowitz made sure that no contradictory information came out of the Beekman prosecution. However, he was unable to control the real 'wild card' in the prosecution, J. Edgar Hoover. In the Boston Shipyard investigation, the unnamed "very able lawyer" had mentioned federal venues in Boston, New

York, and Washington while it was threatening the FBI, trying to get them to initiate action against Walsh. Hoover would not budge. The local prosecutions would have to go forward against Beekman, Zuber, et al, but the charges only involved running a public nuisance. The so called Nazi agents appear to be phantoms, since none were ever identified by their real names, and none ever appeared in Judge Liebowitz's courtroom.

The *Post* ran mug shots of Beekman, which would make him an unlikely candidate for *Gentlemen's Quarterly*, and on May 20, he would be identified as a 'Sweating Witness'. Walsh would find his name sharing newspaper space with some of New York's most unsavory characters, but within the confines of Liebowitz's courtroom, he is always identified as 'Senator X.' Judge Liebowitz agreed to go lightly on the defendants if they cooperated to identify the United States Senator involved. Senate Majority Leader Alben Barkley's statements allege that Beekman only gave the initial affidavit because of threats of prosecution, and that his defense attorney had struck a deal with Liebowitz.

On May 20, Senator Bennett Clark (D-Mo) alleged that Morris Ernst and Judge Liebowitz were in league together, that they had previously served on the bench together. Senate Majority Leader Barkley corrected him. "The senator had mentioned Mr. Morris Ernst whom I do not know. I know that there is such a lawyer. I was told by a certain person that he had been informed Ernst sat on the bench with the judge in the Brooklyn case. I asked the Attorney General about it and he said that statement was incorrect, that some time during this episode, when these statements were made, Mr. Ernst was present as attorney for the *New York Post*. ....I am informed that he was supposed to be present in his capacity as attorney, probably to determine whether the statement should be published. I do not know what happened, but that is the information I have." Senator Barkley placed Morris Ernst at 'the scene of the alleged crime' when the questionable affidavit was developed. The *New York Post* had gotten the scoop of the year, using their own words to describe the story, and their legal counsel had 'sourced the Nile', being present at the creation of the affidavit. While Attorney General Biddle had denied that Ernst and Liebowitz sat on the bench together, Biddle failed to reveal what he undoubtedly knew, as the nations chief law enforcement officer, that Ernst and Liebowitz had worked together on the infamous Scottsboro Trials, with Liebowitz, in effect, being on Ernst's payroll at the ACLU.

Senator Clark then made charges against Walter Winchell, who up until then, appeared to have no involvement. Winchell had no connection to the *Post*, which was a competitor, but he did share a close relationship with Dorothy Schiff during the early 1940's, their relationship souring in later years. However, Senator

Clark provides no evidence, other than to cite Winchell's outrageous conduct by appearing before congressional panels in his Reserve Naval Officers uniform as he ripped into various and sundry officials for their lack of commitment to FDR's war plans. Winchell was on the payroll of the Office of Naval Intelligence, the same ONI that participated in Walsh's 'outing'. While Clark's charges appear to be nothing more than Washington grapevine talk, the files of Dorothy Schiff provide a rather startling self-congratulatory Western Union telegram. It confirms that Winchell, despite J. Edgar Hoover's warning, played an active role in smearing Walsh.

Who was Walter Winchell, and what were his motives? In 1942, he was identified with the "little guy," attacking celebrities, politicians, and big business. By the early 1950s, he had metamorphosed from the liberal representing the working class to the old scold who found a Communist under every tree. In effect, Winchell had reinvented himself every step of the way to become a star in the journalism field. He was also unstable. His mother committed suicide by jumping from the 10th floor of her hospital room. His son had placed a revolver in his mouth and pulled the trigger. In Winchell's case, mental illness did not skip a generation. As a consequence, it can be difficult to discern motivation. The man who had brought misery into the lives of so many celebrities and politicians had a perpetually miserable home life.

A Western Union telegram from Dorothy Schiff Backer dated April 3, 1942 indicates that her relationship with Walter was simply business. The mailgram reads: "Delighted to hear from Leonard Lyons that you are planning to mention the *Post*'s tabloid plans for Monday in your Sunday broadcast. Many thanks and best wishes. Dorothy S. Backer." The *New York Post* had just converted to tabloid style, and Winchell was helping to plug the change. On April 6, Schiff sent Winchell a brief telegram, "Thanks a million."

On June 1, 1942, she sent Winchell a disturbing letter, thanking him for sending her a copy of a letter that he had received from a reader. The contents of the letter aimed at Walsh, and the self-congratulatory tone of Schiff's cover letter indicates that they may have been co-conspirators in the Walsh case. Winchell may have been warned by Hoover, and simply decided to trade information to Schiff for a favor down the road. Winchell covered the story with much more restraint than the *Post*.

> Dear Walter:
>
> Thanks for sending me the letter. We have had scores just like it.
>
> Let's get together at the Stork Club some night.

Sincerely,

The letter that Winchell had forwarded reads as follows:

Dear Walter:

Exposing Senator Walsh isn't all that should be done. He should have been kicked out of circulation a long time ago.

This bird is another "Oscar Wilde," and if you want to get his history, send your investigator up to New England and you'll hear plenty.

Check up on the dive he lived in at the Hotel Lenox, furnished in purple velvet, it has house flowers scented to please the most fastidious customer.

Check on his association with L.C. Pryor better known as "Elsie." These two degenerates should have been decapitated long ago. This bird Walsh never grew hair on his face in his life. "Get It."

And at Louis' Café in the back of the Tremont Theatre, these babies used to gather their victims.

Everyone in the sporting world and also the political in Boston knows of this birds habits, But Boston being Catholic and Irish controlled, you don't and won't see any newspaper pick up anything detrimental to their own.

Keep up the good work, all decent people are with you. Run him out of public life. Keep 'em flying.

Yours for clean living,

This letter perhaps says more about Walter Winchell than the anonymous person who wrote it. The fact that Winchell would select this as a sample of the correspondence he had received on the Walsh case reflects on Dorothy Schiff as well, and her response to the letter erases any doubt that she would find the letter objectionable. The letter writer, Schiff, and Winchell would never imagine that Walsh liked the color purple in part because of his deep attachment to his alma mater, the College of the Holy Cross, whose official color was purple.

The Nazi Spy Nest Case would end up being a "show trial" worthy of other nations the US likes to criticize. This trial was being run by the liberal elite. Beekman's attorney had struck a deal with Judge Liebowitz so the public would never know what actually happened in the courtroom. The only trial New Yorkers would ever hear about was the "trial" in the *New York Post*. Editor Ted Thackrey had been keeping a low profile and Dorothy Schiff Backer was still using the name of her prior husband; and the *Post* continued to hide behind Dorothy's skirt.

However, Winchell's and Thackrey's names would pop up in another venue, *PM*, an upstart liberal New York newspaper. *PM* became the most expensive New

198

York newspaper ever printed, and used color technology as early as 1939. It became the darling of the liberal set and drew some of the most established liberal names, but almost all of them were pro war. It remains today a point of fascination for those who study journalism, and the mystery of how such an expensive newspaper could get financing as war was approaching never seems to have raised the suspicions of its liberal supporters. Ernest Hemingway, I.F. Stone, and Dr. Seuss could all afford to write for *PM* and, having a substantial budget to work with, it was a superior newspaper. But where did the money come from? Marshall Field III, heir to the Field Department Store fortune, is said to have owned and financed it. His liberal credentials are somewhat obscure. He was a committed Anglophile who enlisted in the Army in World War I, a war he could have avoided. The newspaper closed its doors in 1948, as the Cold War loomed.

With the mysterious financing of the *New York Post*, including the hidden ownership issues, and the financing of *PM* in 1939, New York City got its first two liberal voices and both papers boasted about it. While other papers were tightening their budgets, these two startups (the *Post* had been around longer, but had converted to tabloid format) were displaying the latest technology in the newspaper business. They were ardently pro-war and cultivated the literati of that era. Writers like Dorothy Thompson, ardently Anglophile, and her husband Sinclair Lewis, had no trouble getting a forum at either publication. Communists who were anti-war when the Non-Aggression Pact was signed between Hitler and Stalin now found an open microphone for urging intervention when Hitler invaded Russia. Dorothy Schiff's stable of liberal writers would become legendary but it is doubtful they ever knew the union-busting role played by the ACLU or the unhealthy relationship that existed between Intrepid and the newspaper management. Thompson's name appears so often in the intelligence files of various government agencies that it is difficult to discern if she is an "independent" writer or a paid British agent.

While funding a new start-up is never easy, *PM* refused to accept advertising (its position being that it owed its allegiance to those who paid for the paper). It professed its responsibility to its readership so often that it begins to sound like propaganda. This highly impractical stance should have alarmed any professional in the newspaper business, and the continued fascination with *PM* by journalists today highlights how unusual it was. When FDR was investigating America First, he wrote a memo to his Press Secretary, Stephen Early, asking, "Who is paying for all this?" But, he did not ask many questions when these two newspapers were singing his praises.

Marshall Fields started a newspaper in Chicago, the *Sun Times*, to compete with the anti war views of Robert McCormick's *Chicago Tribune* at the exact same time he was starting *PM* in New York. He was certainly doing Great Britain a big favor at a time of great economic uncertainty by starting two very costly operations that were strongly pro-British. Was Fields taking money from the British? He was not known to be a particularly good businessman, and the two publishing endeavors, coming when they did, seem highly risky as business ventures.

Even the Office of Naval Intelligence was asking questions about Winchell's role in leaking information to *PM* regarding two employees at Sikorsky Aircraft. Winchell had been a thorn in the side to some in ONI. As a reservist, he had a direct pipeline to the President. ONI files charge that Winchell had leaked the story to *PM*. Why he did not use the story himself is not explained. However, Winchell often gave stories to other news outlets, and then picked up on them in his own column. In effect, he was the originator of the story, and then played the casual observer in his follow-up column. The ONI files show the displeasure of Sikorsky officials, who defend the patriotism of the two professionals employed there, one of whom was Russian. While Winchell promised to clear all future stories with his commander, there is no indication that any action was ever taken against him.

Thackrey showed a cozy relationship with *PM*, even though they were competing for the same liberal audience. After the war, Thackrey would use PM's presses to launch his own newspaper. Whether British money was used in both newspaper operations may never be known, but the closeness between the *New York Post*, *PM*, and British agent Intrepid has been noted by historians too numerous to mention.

Was British intelligence concerned about the liberals' allegiance to the Allied cause? Or had they simply given up on conservatives? It appears to be a little of both. George Gallup had been commissioned by the British to do constant polling and he was perhaps unfairly criticized for it. It was Gallup himself who had indicated as late as 1940 that 86% (the high water mark) were opposed to entrance in a European war. The *New York Post*'s attack on the *New York Daily News* as being "arch-isolationist" was simply a political maneuver. The *Daily News* had plenty of company across the country, as most hometown newspapers shared the same position. Great Britain's greatest propaganda challenge lay with people like the poor Yankee farmer from Western Massachusetts, the farmers who voted in droves for the Catholic Walsh. They were a stubborn lot.

Great Britain appears to have targeted a younger generation, a more malleable generation that had not read history, a generation that might be more interested in the jazzy tabloid style of the *New York Post* or the more erudite style of *PM*. All Great Britain really needed was a major daily in New York and Chicago that could feed stories to the newspapers of smaller cities and towns — newspapers that did not have the staff to cover foreign affairs. Whether Great Britain helped pay the bills may never be known because of the Official Secrets Act. With the dissolution of the Soviet Union, Russia opened up the KGB files. It is time for London to do the same. When distinguished United States senators are questioning how the *New York Post* is financed, matters have moved beyond the realm of conspiracy theorists.

At the conclusion of the Walsh "trial," the Knights of Columbus called for prosecution of those who had libeled Walsh. On July 17, the *New York Times* began jousting with Ted Thackrey, picking up on the Knights of Columbus efforts to seek justice on Walsh's behalf. While Dorothy Schiff's name had figured prominently at the start of the trial, editor Ted Thackrey was now asked to respond. The *New York Post* did not get the media stampede they expected when they first smeared Walsh, and now they were feeling vulnerable.

> Ted O. Thackrey, editor of the *New York Post*, said today he was "amazed and shocked" at the actions of the directors of the Knights of Columbus in urging the Justice Department to prosecute those responsible for publication of the story concerning US Senator David I. Walsh (D-Mass.), a prominent Catholic layman.
>
> The resolution adopted at the quarterly meeting of the Knights of Columbus board of directors at Milwaukee and announced yesterday at the organizations headquarters at New Haven, also requested that the post office refuse its facilities to the Post, which carried the story....Thackrey said in a letter to Joseph F. Lamb, supreme secretary of the K. of C. : "I am both amazed and shocked to discover that your board of directors has deliberately lent the name of your vast and powerful religious order to such ill-informed attack, without knowledge of the facts and with apparently no effort to obtain them....In view of the failure thus far of the senator to take action in his own behalf, it seems to me peculiarly unfortunate that the Knights of Columbus....should lend itself and its name to such an obvious effort to create a religious issue where none existed and where none has been suggested. The intent to use an organization such as yours in the entirely unwarranted attempt to intimidate, on unsound and unjust grounds, a newspaper fully aware of its rights and obligations cannot succeed.

The United States Senate had railed against attempts by Great Britain to divide the country by using false organizations like the Fight for Freedom Committee, and Senator Burton Wheeler, in the Walsh hearing, had charged that the attempt to divide the country along religious lines was reprehensible. Thackrey's description of the Knights of Columbus as a "religious order" was unlikely to placate the Knights of Columbus. No one in the United States Senate doubted that Great Britain was treating Walsh as "just another Irishman."

In an editorial in the Catholic Review, edited by the Jesuit Fathers, dated June 5, 1942, the editor called for drastic action "…..so that no revival of this conspiracy, with another public official as its intended victim, can possible be attempted." Even the normally staid Jesuits were charging conspiracy in their official publications. Despite the rancor about religion and ethnicity, it was Walsh's Anglophile colleagues in the Senate who were most supportive of Walsh and fully supported the Jesuits' position.

The Brooklyn "Trial" had ended with no one understanding the role played by Attorney General Biddle, and the United States Senate would now take up the case. Biddle, who was trained in the law, clearly understood that Congress had been blackmailed, yet he was a willing participant in the scheme to smear Walsh and it was Biddle who single-handedly pushed for the Boston Shipyard prosecution despite Hoover's warnings that it was bogus.

On June 5, 1942, well after Biddle knew the Brooklyn case was groundless, he wrote a memo to Hoover asking him to continue with the South Boston Works investigation. The Nazi Spy Nest Case went nowhere because the press (other than the *New York Post*), refused to cooperate. Biddle must have known that the prominent lawyer mentioned throughout FBI memos was the same attorney in the Nazi Spy Nest Case. FBI memos had derisively referred to the activity as "just another shot in the dark" to stir up unfavorable publicity on the senator. Another memo of the same period written by J. Edgar Hoover indicated that "it is just another gesture on the part of [name deleted] to accentuate 'the smear campaign carried on by the *New York Evening Po*st.'" On May 27, Hoover wrote directly to Attorney General Biddle regarding the South Boston Works investigation, saying, "Please be advised that the source of this information is [name deleted], who, as you know, was also the source of this information concerning Senator Walsh's alleged connection with the house of degradation operated by [name deleted] in New York City."

Hoover's May 27 memo established that Biddle knew who the source of the information was, and certainly he knew the motives: to destroy another member of the United States Senate. The memos back and forth between Hoover and Biddle show the nation's chief law enforcement officer as FDR's chief political assassin, unable or unwilling to protect the Constitution. Despite Hoover's negative image these days, FBI documents show Hoover and dozens of agents working feverishly to protect the United States Senate. It was Morris Ernst who had described Hoover as head of the nation's "secret police." It is a strange irony of history that it was the head of the "secret police" who tried to stop a conspiracy of the ACLU, the Attorney General of the United States, the *New York Post*, and British Intelligence.

202

On August 7, 1942, Biddle's Executive Assistant, Ugo Carusi, wrote to Hoover pushing for further investigation. "In connection with the attached, the Attorney General suggests that [name deleted] be asked to disclose more about the information which he had, and its source so the investigation may proceed without further delay." The Boston Shipyard investigation had been mocked by everyone involved, from FBI agents to Naval officers. Even the MIT engineers who were interviewed by field agents chuckled that "Walsh would have objected … because we are all Republicans." Yet as late as August 7, 1942, Biddle continued to push hard. His behavior looks irrational when compared with two hundred pages of FBI memos; but perhaps FDR was putting too much pressure on him.

Hoover had warned Biddle in regard to violations of the rights of Japanese citizens, but Biddle was unable to stand up to Roosevelt. Writing just five months earlier, on February 2, 1942, Hoover said: "The necessity of mass evacuation is based primarily upon public and political pressure rather than factual data. Public hysteria, and in some instances, the comments of the press and radio announcers, have resulted in a tremendous amount of pressure being brought to bear on Governor Olsen and Attorney General Earl Warren."

On February 17, 1942, Biddle wrote to Roosevelt. "A great many west coast people distrust the Japanese, various special interests would welcome their removal from good farm land and the elimination of their competition....my last advice from the War Department is that there is no evidence of imminent attack and from the FBI that there is no evidence of planned sabotage."[2] Biddle seems to present the seizure of Japanese property from the view of a political consultant rather than the chief legal mind of the country. He cites the political pressure of special interest groups to seize good farm land, and assures FDR that there is no threat being reported by the FBI or the War Department. He never provides Roosevelt with any legal or moral framework other than to inform FDR that he has the power, as Commander-in-Chief, to seize the land and imprison the Japanese.

While the FBI records show agents frequently making moral judgments about the motives of witnesses and the quality of the information they are getting, Biddle's memos are sterile. The dozens of FBI agents working on the Walsh investigation make unrestrained comments throughout memos, seemingly unafraid of what Hoover might be thinking. They may have felt unrestrained in their comments because they knew that the OSS was running the smear operation; and the OSS was an organization that Hoover loathed. Colonel William Donovan's

---

[2] www.geocites.com/athens/8420/politicians.html.

name, and the OSS, appear in virtually all the field memos written in the Walsh investigation. Given Biddle's active involvement in spying on America First, and his presence at meetings of ONI, OSS, and the FCC whose sole purpose was to spy on America First, it is easy to conclude that this was Biddle's operation. His attempts to keep the investigation going long after both the press and Capitol Hill had slammed the door shut bring into focus both his moral and his political instincts, which appear to be wanting at this juncture. Biddle was not a politician in his own right, and he was not a legal luminary — just one of many lackluster appointments by FDR.

On May 20, 1942, the United States Senate took up the Walsh investigation. Biddle's name was in the news, but Hoover was hiding in the rushes. Alben Barkley, Majority Leader in the Senate, responded to allegations made against Senator Walsh. The Congressional Record contains the full text of Barkley's statements, which essentially exonerated Walsh, laying the blame on "mistaken identity." When the full Senate took up the issue, there was still an unusual silence from the press corps. Mistaken identity?

The public statement laid out a course of action and described what action had already been taken. While Hoover had been hiding from the headlines in this case, he apparently had not been hiding from Capitol Hill. Barkley announced that there would be no Senate investigation and he lauded Hoover for conducting a thorough investigation.

Walsh's career in the Senate was over. He could keep the seat warm until the next election, but his power would be gone. Walsh had received support from all of the power brokers in both parties, as well as Hoover, but the damage had been done. There was no explanation forthcoming other than "mistaken identity." All of the players in Washington, including the press, recognized this as a blatant attack on the power of the senate by destroying Walsh's career, yet no one asked any questions. Knowledgeable people understood this had to have been done by FDR and his British friends.

The text of Majority Leader Alben Barkley's statement in the United States Senate follows, as printed in the Congressional Record, Proceedings and Debates of the 77th Congress, Second Session, Volume 88, No 97, Washington, Wednesday May 20, 1942. (Eighty-four senators responded when the roll was called.)

MR. BARKLEY. Mr. President, will the Senator from Wyoming yield to me?

MR. O'MAHONEY. I will be very glad to yield to the Senator.

MR. BARKLEY. Mr. President, I wish to state to the Senator from Wyoming and the Senate that I ask the privilege of making a statement at this time about a matter which involves the highest privilege of the Senate and the highest privilege of a Member of the Senate.

On May 1, 1942, the *New York Post* carried a story which grew out of a trial of a case in the State court in the City of Brooklyn where a man by the name of Gustave Herman Beekman was under indictment and under trial for an offense too loathsome to mention in the Senate or in any group of ladies or gentlemen. It involved a house, which he conducted and operated in Brooklyn, which was known and is described as a house of degradation. He was convicted in state court presided by Judge Liebowitz. Following his conviction, before sentence was pronounced, he issued what was alleged to have been an affidavit involving a Member of the United States Senate as a frequent visitor to the house which he operated. Based upon that affidavit, or the alleged affidavit, the *New York Post* on Friday, May 1, carried a headline which occupied practically the whole front page, which reads: Links Senator To Spy Nest.

Then it has some photostatic copies of the signature of Gustave Beekman. On the third page of this issue of the *New York Post* is the headline as follows: Senator linked to spy nest, which lured servicemen.

The article proceeds to describe the place, name of the street, and the number of the house. The article contains the charge that a Member of the United State Senate had been frequently seen in this place talking with an alien that was suspected of being a spy in behalf of the Nazis, while the article indicated that the conversation which was supposed to have taken place between this Senator and this German was not audible. No one could testify to what was said, or on what subject anything was said.

The article contained a silhouette of the Senator involved in the charge, blank as a tombstone, which, in all probability, might, in the imagination, fit any one of a dozen or more of this body or men outside this body, just a white silhouette of a man's head.

This publication was brought to my attention by the Attorney General of the United States, Mr. Francis Biddle, and it had been brought to his attention by reason of the intimation in New York made to agents of the Department of Justice, the Federal Bureau of Investigation, that there might be a violation of the Espionage Act on the part of those who resorted to this place, which soldiers and sailors now and then have frequented. The intimation was that these boys were plied with liquor in order that they might become garrulous and reveal the whereabouts of ships from which they had disembarked or upon which they might re-embark for future movements.

The only interest the Department of Justice had in the matter, of course, was to ascertain whether there had been any violation of the law regarding alien activities.

The Attorney General called me up over the telephone, and told me of the publication and wanted to talk to me about it. I told him I should be glad for him to do so, especially as it involved a Member of this body. He himself did not come to see me that day, but he sent one of his assistants, Mr. Cox, a very reliable and efficient assistant in the Attorney General's Office who told me about the publication and the implications involved.

I told the Attorney General, as well as Mr. Cox, that I would like to confer with the Senator from Oregon (Mr. McNary), the minority leader, about what was the best course to pursue, inasmuch as this matter involves the integrity of the Senate. Certainly the Senate of the United States was interested in knowing whether any Member of the body was guilty of any violation of the law involving the safety and welfare of this country, whether he was, as intimated in this article, conniving with the enemies of his country, plotting against its security, its safety, and its welfare.

I talked with the Senator from Oregon, and the two of us agreed that the best course to pursue was for the Department of Justice informally, without any action on the part of the Senate, without any official request from the Senate, to make an investigation, and reveal the facts, and that the Senate's course thereafter should be determined by what the facts turned out to be. I advised the Attorney General of the result of my conference with the Senator from Oregon, and the Attorney General stated that he would proceed accordingly.

Friday, when this article first appeared, which named no Senator but carried the white silhouette, was the 1st of May. A few days later, early in the following week, I think on Tuesday, although it may have been Monday, Senator Walsh, who had not been named in this article, called me over to the telephone, and said he wished to see me. He had been told by the *New York Post* on that day they were going to publish his name as the Member of the Senate involved in this charge.

Senator Walsh came out to my house, and we had a long conference about this matter. He told me then what appeared later in the paper, that he had told the representative of the *New York Post*, when he was called up and advised that they were going to name him, that the whole story was a diabolical lie, and if they published it, that would be what they were publishing. That afternoon they came out in a story and in an editorial naming Senator Walsh of Massachusetts as the Member of the Senate involved in this charge.

Senator Walsh was visibly agitated, as anyone laboring under such a revolting charge would be. I advised him that unless this article appeared in other newspapers than the Post, I doubted the wisdom of his rising in his place in the Senate to make any comment on it, at least until the Department of Justice had investigated it, and he agreed. That course was pursued.

In the conversation between Senator Walsh and me he stated he had never in his life been in this place, or any similar place, that he had never been to Brooklyn in his life, except on three occasions, and at those times he went there to deliver public addresses before audiences of the public.

The day before yesterday, the Attorney General called me over the telephone and said that their investigation had been completed, that it entirely exonerated the Senator from Massachusetts; and that he had in his possession, and wished to submit to me for such use as I might think proper to make them, statements taken by special agents of the Department of Justice, the Federal Bureau of Investigation, showing me facts with reference to the matter. Yesterday afternoon, following the session of the Senate, the Attorney General, Mr. Biddle, and with him one of the special agents, whose name I shall give in a moment, came to see me, and they turned over to me copies of the original documents now in custody of the Attorney General.

A statement of the facts in this case present a weird and fantastic story. I do not deem it necessary to go into any details in describing the house, or the charges made, or the practices that were carried on prior to the conviction of Beekman, the man who operated the house. This Gustave Herman Beekman had supposedly made an affidavit, after his conviction, which was supposedly made after some sort of inducement that if he would tell the whole truth and reveal the names of those who were described as some of the top notchers who frequented his resort, he might receive leniency by way of punishment on the conviction which had just been secured in the State court.

I have here a record of 25 pages, which I shall not insert in the Congressional Record, because it contains disgusting and unprintable things which should not be in the Record. Nor shall I give it to the press, because the statements have no more business in the public press than they do in the Congressional Record. Besides that there are some confidential matters and names involved which I do not think it would serve any purpose to now publish.

In the statement submitted to the Department of Justice, by this man Beekman, he states he did not know what was in the original statement secured from him; that it was not read to him; that it was prepared by his lawyer who had defended him on the trial in the State court; that he did sign it because his lawyer advised him to sign it, but that he did not hold up his hand and swear to it, although the document on its face shows that it was sworn to. He states also that he did not make the statement with any knowledge that it was to be made public or that there was to be any publicity whatever about it; that he made it because his lawyer advised him to make it. In the statements made by not only Mr. Beekman and by others who were frequenters of this resort, they show that there was a man who came to this place about the time and during the time it was alleged in the original affidavit or statement, whatever it may be called, that the Senator of Massachusetts had been to this place. The Department of Justice has submitted to me a photograph of the man who was actually there, and I will submit to any Senator or to anyone else who wants to inspect the photograph, that it looks no more like the Senator from Massachusetts than I look like Haile Selassie. The only similarity is that they are both large men, weighing about the same, perhaps within a few years of the same age. I have four of these photographs. I have the name of the man, which I shall not reveal, because I do not think any purpose could be served by revealing his name, but he is not from Massachusetts, he is not from New York; he lives in New England, but not in Massachusetts.

After the statements were made by Beekman, who made the original statement involving the Senator from Massachusetts, and by a man named Zuber, who also made a statement involving the Senator, and by one or two others, they were shown his photograph, and all of them stated that Senator Walsh was not the man to whom they referred. The photograph of Senator Walsh was also submitted to them, and they all stated that he was not the man they had ever seen in this place. While it is not a very good likeness, not a flattering likeness of the Senator from Massachusetts, it certainly is enough like him to indicate that it is a picture of an altogether different man than the one identified as the man who visited this place.

After these statements were made by Beekman, and by Zuber, and by a man named Fox, and by one or two others, the agents of the Department of Justice visited the man whose picture this is, and they took a statement from him, in which he admitted he was the man; that he had visited this place time after time for purposes which I do not reveal, at the very times and during the very periods which the original affidavit of Beekman indicated as the dates on which the Senator from Massachusetts was claimed to have been seen there.

Of course, it is all fantastic. It is almost incredible.

The Department of Justice in its investigation has gone into the matter as thoroughly and as completely as possible. They have taken statements from everyone who had alleged to have made a statement in regard to this whole matter. All of them unanimously and separately — not together, but separately — stated that none of them had ever seen in or near or around this place, or at the other place from which he had moved, any man corresponding to the photograph of the Senator from Massachusetts.

These things are unpleasant even to talk about, but the Senator from Massachusetts, and the United States Senate, and the country, are entitled to the facts, they are entitled to the statement that I am making based upon an investigation made by the Department of Justice.

I want to congratulate the senator from Massachusetts upon the calm demeanor which he has exhibited in the face of this contemptuous and contemptible charge. The senator from Massachusetts and I have disagreed many times in the floor of the Senate about matters of policy, both foreign and domestic. We disagreed — and many of us did — on the foreign policy of the United States prior to the attack on Pearl Harbor on December 7. But I want to say for the Senator from Massachusetts, that regardless of those disagreements as to policy prior to our entry into the war, the senator from Massachusetts has performed his duties as Chairman of the Committee on Naval Affairs, and his duties as a United States Senator, in a manner indicating his patriotism, and his loyalty, and his devotion to the interests and welfare of the United States. When this charge was made in this publication and was bandied around, handed from hand to hand, and whispered from mouth to mouth, there was not a Senator in this body who did not know at that very moment that the escutcheon of the Senator from Massachusetts, so far as his performance of his duties was concerned, so far as any effort on his part to connive or consort with, or converse with, or conspire with anybody who is the enemy of the United States, was unsullied.

The Senator from Massachusetts indicated in his first conversation with me that unless this article appeared generally in the newspapers of the United States and was confined to this particular newspaper in New York City, he would not exercise what obviously was his right, to rise to a question of personal privilege and discuss it, at least until the Department of Justice has concluded its investigation.

I wish to say to the credit of the newspapers of America that, so far as I know, no other newspaper in the United States carried this story. It may be that one or two other newspapers somewhere carried an intimation of, or a resume of, the story involving in some vague way some member of the United States Senate without naming him. I did not see any such publication. I am advised that with the possible exception of one or two newspapers somewhere whose identity I cannot give, the rest of the newspapers ignored it completely. Of course, I cannot speak for all of them, and I do not know, because I have not seen them all, but that is my information.

This whole situation is unfortunate, but it was not brought here by any of us. It was not initiated by the Department of Justice. It was brought to the attention of the Department because of a trial in the state court in the city of Brooklyn. I am advised by the Attorney General that the Department has completed its work and has custody of the original documents of which I have copies.

Unpleasant as this episode has been, it is a pleasure to be able to state, as I had anticipated from the beginning I would be able to state, that from the beginning to end there was never the slightest foundation or basis for the opinion, charge, or suspicion that the Senator from Massachusetts was the man involved in the descriptions which were given in this publication on May 1. I shall not go into the questions of motives, I cannot read the mind of any human in an effort to ascertain his motives. I do not know. Therefore, I make no intimation, but I am sure every senator and every man in the Government of the United States, including the Department of Justice, felt the same way about it. Their confidence has been confirmed by the investigation to which I have referred.

Mr. President, that is about all I have to say. It is most regrettable that for any reason or any motive a Member of this body, or any American anywhere, high or low, should be involved in such a malicious, degrading charge, or that a Member of one of the legislative bodies of this Nation should be accused of conspiring with alien enemies against the welfare and safety of this country. Nobody acquainted with the senator believed the charge. I hope as a result of this fair, impartial, and exhaustive investigation made by the Department best equipped to make it, those who have been responsible for it will see to it that justice is done, even in their midst, with respect to this despicable accusation against a Member of this body.

Mr. President, I feel compelled to retain these documents that I have received from the Department and withhold them from the Record and the press. The statements I have just made are borne out by these documents. I am not in a position to say they will be available if anybody wishes to inspect them at the Department of Justice. I think the Senate will rely on my statement that these documents amply and overwhelmingly justify the complete and thorough exoneration of the Senator from Massachusetts of any suspicion of ever having engaged in any activity which could have justified any honest man in making the assertion that he was ever there.

MR. WHEELER. Mr. President, will the Senator yield?

MR. BARKLEY. I yield.

MR. WHEELER. I wish to congratulate the FBI, under Mr. Hoover, for carrying out the investigation, and bringing the truth to the country. If the investigation had been conducted by private individuals, there might be the suspicion that such individuals were biased in favor of one person or another; but I am sure that nobody in the country will say that the Attorney General of the United States, or the FBI under Mr. Hoover, was prejudiced in favor of the Senator from Massachusetts. On the contrary, they have rendered a great public service to the nation in making this investigation. I also congratulate the Senator from Kentucky for the statement which he has made in bringing about the exoneration of the Senator from Massachusetts.

MR. BARKLEY. I thank the senator from Montana. I think it was infinitely better for the Department of Justice, through the Federal Bureau of Investigation, rather than the Senate itself, to have made this investigation. The Senate might have been prejudiced in behalf of one of its Members. Nobody can lay a charge of partiality at the door of the Department of Justice.

From the very beginning of this matter, from my first conversation with the Attorney General until my last conversation with him and his representatives, all they have sought to do was obtain the truth; and they have done so.[3]

The above represents a complete copy of the Congressional Record. It is the only investigation that has ever been done of the Nazi Spy Nest Case. Senate Majority Leader Barkley made a specific reference to December 7, intimating that

---

[3] Dinand Library, Walsh Archives, College of the Holy Cross, Congressional Record.

the reason for the attack on Walsh was related to his anti-war stand. Barkley then yielded to Burton Wheeler, the only other senator connected to the antiwar movement who had more visibility than Walsh. The very liberal Wheeler praised the FBI. Wheeler, the senator who was destroyed by slanderous insinuations in the Congressional Franking Case, was praising Hoover "for bringing the truth to the country." Barkley termed the charges "weird and fantastic" and he ridiculed the notion that the picture represented Walsh (in that generation, a picture of Haile Selassie's absurd regalia was guaranteed to spark laughter from children and adults alike). He spent considerable time discussing Beekman's lawyer, suggesting that Beekman was "conned" into signing a document.

The FBI investigation was conducted at breakneck speed. Part of the reason for that was the fact that the FBI had the place staked out. They certainly had a dossier on the men who frequented the place, and Hoover, ever cautious, would want to make sure that, indeed, Walsh, whose homosexuality had been suggested by *Time* magazine in the 1930s, had never visited the place.

It certainly was an unusual day in the news business. Majority Leader Barkley was speaking in the well of the Senate about sex, lies, spies, and the contemporary equivalent of videotape, and was indicating that if no newspaper ran the story other than the *New York Post*, then he doubted the wisdom of the Senator "rising in his place…to make any comment upon it." And no one did. The silence was deafening. The press exercised remarkable restraint. The media acted in concert, unusually so; it is as if they said, enough is enough. With enough high officials pushing, one solitary Irish-American homosexual could be knocked down; but the reporters had drawn a line: this was too blatant a lie, too bald-faced a propaganda stunt, and too much character assassination to circulate.

The raid on the brothel could have been embarrassing for Hoover, because he had the place bugged and had made no arrests. The raid was conducted by Mayor Fiorello LaGuardia's police officers and the Office of Naval Intelligence. Meyer Lansky indicates that the tip came from Washington. It remains unknown whether Intrepid knew that Hoover was watching the same place. It seems unlikely. "Wild Bill" Donovan and the OSS were running the operation, according to FBI files, and it was led by the unnamed "very able lawyer." Hoover's surveillance may have been directed more at the OSS than any homosexuals and German spies.

Despite popular myth, very little German infiltration occurred either by spies or fifth columns. While Hoover always took great credit for this, and the FBI record was quite good, the fact is that the Germans managed to make relatively few attempts. Other than the Norden bombsight case, German intelligence was a failure. On the other hand, Russian and British spying was beyond any control. The best Hoover could do was try to keep them somewhat in check.

On May 21, 1942, Walsh's hometown newspaper, the *Worcester Telegram & Gazette*, printed the Nazi Spy Nest story. The editor felt obliged to explain why they had sat on the story for three weeks and he mentioned an anonymous letter-writing campaign that pressured them to publish the story. The newspaper strongly defended Walsh and defended its own actions in refusing to print the story, labeling it as trash. The *Worcester Telegram* devoted just one page to the story, while lamenting the fact that it had to print it at all. It began with the editor's note, in boldface.

> The story about Senator Walsh has been current in newspaper offices for some weeks and has been a great embarrassment to us. The *New York Post* first brought Senator Walsh into it by name and it has been given somewhat wide circulation mouth to mouth throughout Massachusetts. Here in Worcester we have been condemned in person and by letter anonymously for not printing the story. We have refrained from printing it because it was not the type of story we cared to print. We did not believe it was true, but even if we did so believe we would not print it. The position of the Editor of these newspapers is, as he has said to questioners that it is a grievous thing to print such a charge against any man, and more particularly, it is grievous to print it about a man who has been Governor of Massachusetts and is now a United States Senator. However, it has now reached the point where Senate Leader Barkley felt obliged to make a public statement on the floor of the Senate. This we must print as it is an exoneration of the Senator. While this may have been necessary in Senator Barkley's opinion, we think it is unfortunate because it gives wider circulation to the original charges, which will be known from the Atlantic to the Pacific-Editor.

The headline read: "CHARGE WALSH ACCUSATIONS PART OF 'SMEAR' CAMPAIGN — 'Senators Score Those Behind Unjustified Malicious, Degrading Claims in New York As FBI Completely Exonerates Mass. Democrat.'" As kind as the *Worcester Telegram* was in its reporting, it also began Senator Walsh's political obituary. In a separate article, the headline read, "Walsh Has Had Long, Distinguished Career." Walsh was already being talked about in the past tense. The newspaper editor was a realist.

In Washington, liberal Senators Nye and Wheeler were asking for a further investigation. Yet, their questions were not pointed at rightwing reactionaries, or even conservative Republicans. Despite the obvious involvement of the OSS and Intrepid, the wrath of the senators would be concentrated on a group of Americans whose patriotism was questionable. Senators Nye and Wheeler clearly understood that Great Britain was involved, but they expressed more concern over a shadowy group of fellow-citizens who were bent on damaging representative government. Sometimes, conspiracy theorists are right. And, while the United States Senate would not vote to further the investigation, time would prove that there had been a conspiracy, indeed. While Walsh had run a protracted battle to prevent convoying and to bring the US Navy back closer to the Atlantic Coast, German U-boats were operating just outside America's harbors, sinking merchant ships at an alarming rate. That story was hushed up by what has been called a "free" press.

As the "diabolical plot" unfolded, disturbing connections were found (although most of them were not revealed until much later). On May 21, the *Worcester Telegram* described the odd background of Dorothy Schiff Backer, "who gave up a life of social activity at 39 to become the only woman newspaper publisher in New York." In other words, she had never worked a day in her life until she was 39. The article mentions that she backed the Broadway production of *Abe Lincoln in Illinois*. It would take an unusually astute reader (or journalist) to recognize that Robert Sherwood, FDR's speechwriter, was the playwright who received financial backing from Backer — the same Robert Sherwood who helped Intrepid on the destroyer deal. The newspaper was purchased by Backer's husband in 1939. At least, that is what the *New York Post* said. Backer was a New York society ne'er-do-well; it is not clear that he had the resources to buy the *Post.* During the debate in the Senate, Senator Burton Wheeler charged that the paper had been bought with a loan from the Federal Reserve Board. Was the Federal Reserve Board ever in the loan business? Was the paper bought as a propaganda tool for Great Britain, with the backing of FDR? The *Worcester Telegram* also mentioned that the paper had been established in 1801 by an advocate for increased federal power, Alexander Hamilton. Walsh's career was destroyed by an instrument created by the archenemy of his hero, Thomas Jefferson.

While the debate raged, conservative Senator Tobey (R-NH) strongly defended Walsh. This emotional defense of a liberal, coming from a conservative New Hampshire senator, illustrates the integrity and collegiality of which the senate is capable. Senator Bennett Clark (D-MO) asked for an investigation of Walter Winchell, who had been regularly slandering members of Capitol Hill, even appearing in his Navy uniform to make his verbal assaults. However, Winchell does not appear to have played an overt role in this *New York Post* enterprise. J. Edgar Hoover had warned the media that this was a smear campaign, and certainly would have warned Winchell as well.

The campaign was orchestrated by the general counsel of the *New York Post*, Morris Ernst. Senator Bennett Clark asked that Ernst be summoned to appear before the senate, derisively referring to him as "the great reformer." Ernst was a darling of the liberal set for his defense of free speech cases, rising to fame as a defender in the case involving James Joyce's *Ulysses*. He was eminently qualified to defend the scandal sheet, *New York Post*, from libel. The ACLU, which normally(perhaps nominally) defends free speech, was now defending something more expensive: paid speech. The National General Counsel of the ACLU was running a propaganda campaign with British money.

Ernst's friendship with FDR was well known. Senator Bennett Clark was quoted in the *Worcester Telegram* on May 21 as follows: "I have been informed by a very reputable newspaperman whose information is usually correct that Mr. Ernst brought the story to Washington and went to the White House with it, in an attempt to interest the highest authority in Washington in an effort to smear the Senator from Massachusetts. To the credit of the President and his advisors, Mr. Ernst's suggestions were entirely rejected." The trail had been immediately traced to the White House; Roosevelt could not deny that contact had been made. Senator Bennett Clark appeared incensed, but nevertheless took the president off the hook.

Could it be that Senator Clark naïvely believed that FDR would not be involved? FDR did not have the most reputable background in these matters. Jonathan Alter, writing for *Newsweek* in the 2003-2004 presidential election season, reminded readers of who Roosevelt really was. In March of 1932, according to Alter, FDR was described by newspapers and by Democratic Party brokers as an "unprincipled lightweight." FDR called in the image makers in the New York City press and went on to victory at the polls, but the man himself never changed. His loathing of the Senate Naval Affairs Committee, and its gay Chairman, was so palpable that it is impossible to believe that FDR did not give his approval to this operation.

FBI records show two different trails back to the White House. Attorney General Biddle was pushing the investigation and "Wild Bill" Donovan was running the operation. FBI records document extensive OSS involvement and Donovan was a direct report to FDR. Was the "very able lawyer connected to the OSS," name deleted, Morris Ernst?

Ernst had another job and apparently received money from diverse sources. From 1930 to 1954, Morris Ernst was general counsel for the American Civil Liberties Union. In his capacity as general counsel, this champion of free speech forwarded all membership files to J. Edgar Hoover.

Thus, while liberals paid their dues, Big Brother was watching. Ernst was also fingering liberal journalists who joined the organization, particularly in the New York chapter, labeling them as communists. They were promptly fired. A lid was kept on the newspapers, and union-busting activities were funded by liberal, dues-paying members. Morris Ernst, as General Counsel for the *New York Post*, was also representing the management team, a consortium of New York newspapers, in bargaining with the newspaper unions.

213

Curt Gentry describes the relationship of Ernst and Hoover in *J. Edgar Hoover, The Man and the Secrets.*

> Ernst billed himself as a defender of civil rights, but he was a one man secret police organization, obsessed with power, and he was taking money from everybody. When Hoover was criticized in 1940, Ernst secretly went to his defense. Adolf Berle noted in his diary entry for March 22, 1940, [Morris Ernst] is very angry with the press attack ... J. Edgar Hoover has run a secret police with a minimum of collision with civil liberties, and that is all you can expect of any chief of secret police.

> When Morris Ernst was interviewed in 1975, the year before his death, his memory was already failing. He admitted to having been Hoover's personal attorney, but couldn't remember in exactly what capacity he'd served him. He did recall, however, "the grand and glorious nights at the Stork Club," with the man he said he perhaps admired more than any other. Hoover apparently objected more than once to Ernst's characterizing himself as his "personal attorney." Yet in 1971, Hoover told David Kraslow, then of the *Los Angeles Times*, that Ernst had been his personal attorney for many years. One occasion on which Hoover consulted Ernst in a professional capacity is known — when he was considering a possible libel action against Time and sought Ernst's legal advice.

Gentry shows that Ernst neutralized criticism of the FBI within the ACLU. He also:

> reported on private conversations and he gave Hoover copies of personal letters he had received from such FBI critics as journalist I.F. Stone, the columnist Max Lerner, Congressman Wayne Morse, and FCC Chairman Lawrence Fly (who had clashed with the FBI Director over the issue of wiretapping). He led the fight to have veteran Communist Elizabeth Gurley Flynn removed from the ACLU's board of directors. He was instrumental in having the ACLU adopt the position that there were 'no civil liberties issues involved' in the Rosenberg case. He even offered to become the attorney for the two accused atomic spies, not so much to help them (he'd already decided that Julius Rosenberg and his wife, Ethel were guilty) as to assist the FBI.[4]

While Senator Bennett Clark was demanding the appearance of Ernst before the Senate to determine how deeply he was involved in this conspiracy, issues of a free press were being discussed.

> Senator Wheeler waved a copy of the New York *Herald Tribune* [which refused to print the story] which contained an ad for the Citizens for Victory Committee, which was soliciting contributions for the fight against Hitler, Hirohito, and Mussolini. Wheeler charged that the only reason to raise those funds was for advertisements that smeared Capitol Hill. In his speech before the Senate, he mentioned the Fight for Freedom Committee, which Intrepid, in his memoirs, admitted was a bogus front. Wheeler raised the issue of free speech. "Some persons talk about stopping some newspapers [those that were not supporting FDR ardently enough] in the name

---

[4] Gentry, Curt, *J. Edgar Hoover, The Man and the Secrets*, W.W. Norton, New York, London, 1991, 233-234.

of unity. And yet, I say to my friends, the members of the Senate, that this newspaper and some other newspapers are doing more to stir disunity in the United States of America and they are doing more to break down the confidence of the people in their government of the United States than anything else that can possibly happen could do.

The WASP, Wheeler, introduced the religious and ethnic angle into the equation. From Intrepid's viewpoint, Walsh would always be a Catholic target, and the anti-Semitism and anti-Catholicism of the British Empire remained virulent throughout the war. FDR's own motivations were perhaps different, although his patronizing approach to Henry Morgenthau and economist Leo Crowley because of their non-WASP backgrounds and his clear prejudice against blacks (expressed in the destroyer-base lease deal) leave room to believe FDR's antipathy for David Walsh was partly religious and ethnic. It was Walsh's misfortune to be all the things that FDR wasn't. Walsh was discreet; FDR was profligate. Walsh was loyal to his friends; FDR had none (his most ardent supporters decried his lack of loyalty). FDR would strike a deal with the devil; Walsh was a terrible horse trader. FDR was a patrician Hudson Valley landowner of Dutch extraction; Walsh came from a Catholic industrial town. Walsh was a liberal in 1900, FDR became one when the Great Depression hit. Walsh was gay. FDR was...promiscuous at least, with a very busy sex life and not the monogamous marriage that has been portrayed.

As for J. Edgar Hoover's role, despite the involvement of his personal attorney, Morris Ernst, Hoover wanted no part in the scheme to undermine Capitol Hill. Ernst was a freelancer, selling out to anyone who had power and money. Hoover understood that. Author Curt Gentry explains that Hoover dumped Ernst from his special correspondence list as soon as he retired in 1954 as general counsel to the ACLU because he was no longer useful, and Hoover had established a relationship with the Washington, DC head of ACLU, who continued to spy for Hoover. Apparently, the ACLU had more than one corrupt man in their midst.

> Even more important is what Ernst didn't do. The nearly quarter century during which he served as general counsel of the American Civil Liberties Union encompassed such epochal events as the Smith Act roundups; the federal loyalty investigations; the Hiss, Rosenberg, Lattimore, and Oppenheimer cases; blacklisting, and the anti-Communist witch hunts of the House Un-American Activities Committee and Joseph McCarthy. Yet never once did Morris Ernst criticize, question, or even closely examine the FBI's pervasive role in these and dozens of other related matters, almost

all of which involved serious violations of constitutional rights.[5]

Perhaps Hoover refused to participate in this plot because he wanted to undermine Intrepid's operation. It was well known that Hoover wanted only one sheriff in town. Hoover also had a much better sense of politics than did the Anglophiles. He would certainly not run the risk of incurring the wrath of Capitol Hill just to please FDR, for an operation that was not even his. Intrepid would have gotten credit for it, anyway. Hoover's conduct was consistent. He protected his turf and did not stray too far from it.

The British blackmail attempt on Assistant Secretary of State Adolf Berle had occurred just ten weeks earlier. On February 13, 1942, deputy director of the FBI, Edward Tamm, was warned that Berle was being tailed by Intrepid's agents. The FBI had its hands full trying to protect US officials and their aides from treacherous acts by Great Britain when it was supposed to be Germany that was the enemy.

Berle was being tailed in order to find some kind of incriminating evidence that could be used to blackmail him into silence. The United States Senate had, indeed, become strangely quiet. Was it because they wanted to show solidarity for FDR, or was something else going on? The Walsh story demonstrates that the British Empire would stop at nothing, would employ any tactic, to meet British objectives which included goals for the continuation of imperial policy.

> [T]he empire was not to be propelled through foreign interference into a revolutionary post colonial era, but through an orderly process in which Britain's hegemony would be maintained in the form of commonwealth. Since the Americans could not be expected to acquiesce in such a policy, they would have to be resisted and frustrated in what they did want, which was economic hegemony.
>
> At the same time, however, "C" was authorized by the War Cabinet to maintain a strong active service [spy] in the United States, where the object of all British activity was to maintain lend-lease policies untrammeled by political obligations, impose British control on strategic policy, and ensure that Britain obtained a powerful voice at the peace conference.[6]

This language was reminiscent of World War I. Unpaid war debts were the main reason for Britain's unpopularity in the Senate, especially, and ironically, with conservative WASP senators. Now, in World War II, the strategy was to get assistance from Lend-Lease, "untrammeled by political obligations." Does this mean not paying back, in cash or otherwise?

---

[5] Ibid., 235.
[6] Brown, Anthony Cave, "C," *The Secret Life of Sir Stewart Menzies*, MacMillan Publishing, New York, 1987, 390

General George Marshall was already experiencing the British determination to control strategic policy. As far as having a powerful voice at the peace conference, there could be no bigger threat to the attainment of this goal than Senator Walsh. Walsh had voted against the League of Nations at the conclusion of World War I because he felt it continued the colonial status quo; it would have to be different, this time.

While the attempt to smear Assistant Secretary of State Berle was being investigated, Attorney General Francis Biddle was asked to prepare a report. When he asked the White House where to send it, he was instructed to send it to the representative of Lloyd's of London in Chicago. "It was well known that Lloyd's had a superb intelligence service."[7]

When companies solicit insurance quotes, often on an annual basis, it is quite common to make applications to all the major insurers, particularly for large policies. The insurance applications are quite detailed and corporations must list all their major assets, including their value. This data may involve trade secrets; did the US companies contacting Lloyd's know that they were turning over confidential commercial information to an arm of British Intelligence?

The head of British intelligence since World War I, Vernon Kell, was virulently anti-Catholic. Churchill removed him in 1940, but by then much of the agency was colored by his outlook and his actions. "Kell would never employ a Catholic or someone without an entirely stable home life. He justified his discrimination by saying the Roman Catholic Church had the best intelligence service in the world, and he had no intention of letting it penetrate the Security Service. The importance he placed on a staff member's family life, he felt, was simply common sense: If an officer could not run his own life, how could he be entrusted with the security of a nation? By contrast, Sir David Petrie, the D-G appointed to replace Kell in November 1940, chose a practicing Catholic solicitor, Richard Butler, as his Personal Assistant. Among the flood of recruits of mid-1940 were journalists, intellectuals, playboys, and even homosexuals — men whom Kell would never have considered."[8] Whether or not that represents a positive step, it meant that now journalists from the *New York Post* — even Catholics — might be eligible for employment. This "enlightened" approach even included hiring the more virulent strand of "practicing" Catholics.

America First knew that any ethnic minorities would have their patriotism questioned, and packed the organization with White, Anglo-Saxon Protestants.

---

[7] Ibid., 489.
[8] West, Nigel, *MI 5*, Stein & Day, New York, 1982, 331-332.

The FBI files on America First, all 2,900 hundred pages, reflect FDR's determination to bring them down, but instead it appears a security blanket was thrown around the organization. The FBI field agents wrote glowing reports on how patriotic the organization was.

The FBI report of February 7, 1941 listed the background of the board members of America First. The Treasurer was J. Sanford Otis, Vice President of the Central Republic Bank of Chicago. Members of the national board included Hanford MacNider, a banker and former National Commander of the American Legion; General Thomas Hammond, retired US Army officer, and president of Whiting Corporation; J.C. Hormel, Hormel Meatpackers; Clay Judson, Attorney with the law firm of Wilson & McIlvaine, former president of the Chicago Council of Foreign Relationships and a member of the board of trustees of United Charities; Dr. Anton Julius Carlson, Professor at the University of Chicago and a member of the American Civil Liberties Union (the FBI report called him "extremely liberal"; William Castle, Jr., a former Assistant Secretary of State and Ambassador to Japan; Irvin Cobb, nationally known speaker and author; Janet Ayer Fairbanks, a former member of the executive committee of the Democratic National Committee, published author, and active in the cause of "women's suffrage"; John Flynn, noted economist and writer (for the *New Republic*, and a critic of Roosevelt); and — with no biographical background listed — Henry Ford.

The membership of the America First Committee was proof that loyal Americans, whose patriotism was beyond question, agreed with Walsh's position that US foreign policy had to pursue US interests first, and that it was right to "question authority" when the authorities are going astray.

The FBI report concludes with descriptions of General Hugh S. Johnson, Thomas McCarter, former Attorney General from New Jersey, and "nationally known political woman" Alice Roosevelt Longworth. The FBI agent does not appear to realize that she is the niece of Teddy Roosevelt. The board of this anti-war group is almost entirely WASP, and includes two generals and the past National Commander of the American Legion. The FBI files also contain a letter from FDR, in a memorandum for Stephen Early, asking: "Will you find out from someone — perhaps the FBI — Who is paying for this?" FDR asked Hoover to "follow the money" regarding a board consisting of Ford Motor, Sears and Roebuck, and Hormel Meatpacking. America First did not call many minorities to serve (for different reasons than the British front organization, Fight For Freedom Committee). America First knew that minorities would have their lives destroyed. The Fight For Freedom Committee did not want minorities to serve because they might possibly be viewed as advocating for their own people, thus diluting the propaganda message. But, no one could doubt that these WASPS serving on America First placed their loyalty to the United States first, not to a former mother country.

The work of the FBI field agents gave Walsh his only protection, as an individual, from an otherwise totalitarian administration run by FDR. The hundreds of pages in Walsh's FBI file and the nearly 2,900 pages on America First in all cases exonerate Walsh; but they could not protect his political career.

Hoover was given the thankless job of following up on FDR's request for further investigation of America First. On March 1, 1941, Hoover responded with generalizations and a note that, "If it's the President's wish that a more exhaustive investigation be made relative to the means by which the America First Committee is financed, I hope you will not hesitate to call upon me to conduct such investigation." Perhaps he muttered under his breath, "Call Intrepid."

The FBI files reveal intense and continual pressure on Hoover from the White House. The field agents seem to have been oblivious of the political impact of their work. If FDR had seen most of the 2,900 pages of their reports, he would have been outraged. They are almost completely praiseworthy in every instance regarding America First. Apparently, Hoover and his subordinates did not mention that what FDR actually wanted was damaging information.

A report dated June 10, 1941 by agent J.F. Sears reports on "infiltrating" a meeting of America First in Philadelphia. That must have been easy to do — the crowd spilled out into the street, and cheered the talks given by Senator Walsh, Charles Lindbergh, and author Kathleen Norris. Each time the President's name was mentioned, "a loud boo went up from the crowd."

Another report from that date describes a counter demonstration run by Fiorello LaGuardia. LaGuardia had sent his men down to Philadelphia, with little success. The FBI reports, "There appeared to be just as many people outside the arena as there were inside, and it was the general opinion that the America First Committee was gaining in strength and that undoubtedly there were more people present for the America First Meeting than there were for the LaGuardia protest meeting the night before." There was, however, one troubling sign. The America First speakers were making "quite a point of the fact that the national radio companies had refused the facilities of their broadcasting systems for a nation-wide broadcast of the meeting and stating that everything possible was being done to prevent the America First Committee from presenting their views to the American people." While this anti-war rally was hugely successful, it was denied access to the media and did not receive the publicity of prior rallies at Madison

Square Garden in New York City.

While J. Edgar Hoover's closest subordinates knew they were conducting a massive political surveillance operation, they were only willing to go so far. On May 3, 1941 E. A. Tamm received a request from Marvin McIntyre, Secretary to the President. McIntyre stated that he was a good friend of General Robert Wood, Chairman of America First, and indicated that he had discussed a particular letter with Wood, but that Wood had not provided him with a copy. He was requesting that the FBI get him a copy. Without waiting for Hoover's approval, Tamm responded by saying that if he was a friend of Wood, he could ask him for a copy himself. Tamm would not have sent such a response to the White House unless he knew Hoover would back him up.

One FBI report of February 9, 1942, written by Colonel Philip Thurber, G2, reports on a private meeting in the home of Edwin Webster, Sr., who is identified as a "Wall Street banker with Kidder, Peabody." This same Webster naïvely submitted his membership roster to J. Edgar Hoover to be sure he had no subversives in his New York Chapter. Webster had no idea the agents were in his house; Hoover certainly had no need to review his roster. Private comments attributed to Charles Lindbergh at this house party include the observation "that Great Britain was responsible and that she should have joined with Germany in destroying the yellow danger and Bolshevism. If such a move had been made, it would have put America in a better position to fight Japan." This quote is remarkably similar to Louis Kilzer's thesis (in *Churchill's Deception*)that the Hess affair was related to a purported agreement for England and Germany to team up against Russia; and no one was closer to the "appeaser" set than Lindbergh, who lived in London before the war. That a friend of the appeasers would help to discredit a patriotic American organization is another indication of who was infiltrating whom, and to what extent. The power of propaganda would help Great Britain dispose of its former friend, Lindbergh.

Senator David Walsh's FBI file shows no bribes, no kickbacks, and no homosexual sex with German spies. What the files do show is FDR and the OSS (the agency Americans wrongly assumed was accomplishing heroic feats of espionage in Europe) silencing Capitol Hill. Everyone on the hill, including the press, knew that, but the public would never know.

Sadly, the alleged "right-wing reactionaries" were right. FDR destroyed the liberal opposition in the Senate with tactics that most Americans associated with his partner in the war effort, Joseph Stalin. Taxpayer dollars were spent convincing Americans that "Uncle Joe" was an ally; and taxpayer dollars were spent extolling the virtues of Churchill and Roosevelt. No such funds were made available to inform the electorate that they had a much bigger friend in Senator David Ignatius Walsh.

CHAPTER 19. REQUIEM

The heroic aspects of America's participation in World War II are often viewed with great nostalgia; however, the reality of that era is quite different. Racial and ethnic prejudices added fuel to the fires of World War II. The friction with Great Britain was not coming from the extreme fringes; it was coming from the center. Father James Gillis, editor of the *Catholic World*, in a speech on September 22, 1941, charged that the foreign policy of the Administration had become, in reality, one of "offense, designed to help preserve the British Empire." Mainstream publications regularly painted Great Britain in an unflattering light, one that suited its actions throughout the centuries. On that September day when Father Gillis was speaking, the necessary arousal of the public to the threat of Hitler could not be accomplished because of Great Britain's lack of credibility. The public was right to be suspicious. British actions during the war do not enhance the image of the British Empire, no matter how much propaganda was turned out by their friends.

FDR's incursion in the Pacific delayed the salvation of Europe still further. His shabby treatment of Prince Konoye's moderate government was based in part on racial condescension. Japan's misguided attack on Pearl Harbor across 3,000 miles of ocean may have been based on imperial hubris. Each underestimated the other. Had the voices of anti-war senators not been snuffed out by insidious propaganda, the beginning and ending of World War II could have been quite different. The anti-war movement was not built by pacifists but by committed patriots who continued to push for the build up of a strong navy, army, and an emerging air force.

The attempt by Great Britain and FDR to destroy Congress hit a roadblock in David Walsh. FDR could not get Congress to go along with the increasingly long shopping list that Churchill wanted filled. Intrepid was loaned out to FDR, to destroy the opposition in Congress. Intrepid trained the OSS; planted spy Roald Dahl in the White House along with fellow spy Robert Sherwood, FDR's speechwriter; bought off as much of the media as they could; blackmailed government officials; and murdered prominent United States citizens. This book focuses on Walsh, but he was just one vote, and one voice. How much money Great Britain spent rigging US elections will never be known, but Great Britain's active participation in smearing Nye, Wheeler, and Walsh has become clear — they were all liberals, who would have questioned Great Britain at the peace table. Great Britain had to resort to character assassination with Nye, Wheeler and Walsh because they could not be bought off with money. Conservative critics were easily branded rightwing reactionaries, and were easier to marginalize.

The army arrayed against David Walsh was vast: Intrepid, as a stand-in for Churchill, "Wild Bill" Donovan, as a stand-in for FDR, the *New York Post*, as a stand-in for the Anglophile press, Fiorello LaGuardia, who controlled the prosecution in New York, the mob, headed by Meyer Lansky, and a front organization called the American Civil Liberties Union. Senator Bennett Clark spotted the sham in 1942, derisively referring to Morris Ernst as "that great reformer," yet the ACLU kept him on until 1954, and when he retired, Hoover immediately found a replacement. Are liberals always naïve? This was not a genteel age, an age of truth and justice. If FDR had not undercut George Marshall's urge to invade Europe sooner rather than later, perhaps twenty million civilian lives would have been spared. But the United States had no control of strategy in Europe. As far as Japan, perhaps the atomic bomb would never have been dropped. When scientists who had worked on building the bomb were working feverishly to stop the deployment of it, they approached Charles Lindbergh and asked him to speak out against it. His response was that his name had been so tarnished he felt he would do their cause more harm than good. America's participation in the war might have started quite differently and ended quite differently. But FDR listened to nobody — at least, no American. Intrepid kept an eye on him in the White House; despite FDR's willing participation, 10 Downing Street felt the need to know what he was thinking every day. What if an aide actually convinced him of a policy that could threaten Great Britain's interests? By the war's beginning, the White House inner circle was reduced to Harry Hopkins and the strange coterie of women that Churchill met on his trips to Washington.

There is some chance that the *New York Post* was quick to spread the story simply out of its own pervasive Anglophilia; but Roosevelt was close to George Backer, the publisher of the *Post* — so close that on election night, 1940, Backer was among the Roosevelts' house guests. As FDR's speech writer Robert

Sherwood wrote,

> On election night [the 1940 election], after a stand-up supper at Mrs. Roosevelt's cottage, we drove through the Hyde Park woods, beloved by Franklin Roosevelt, to the big house to listen to the election returns.... My wife and George Backer and I joined Hopkins in his bedroom. He had a small $15 radio similar to the one he later gave Churchill. He had a chart and he had been noting down a few returns, but most of it was covered with doodles. The first returns early in the evening indicated that Willkie was showing unexpected strength and Hopkins for a time seemed really worried; I have been told that early in the evening even Roosevelt himself was doubtful of the outcome, but I saw no signs of that.[1]

This was the mysterious 1940 election that bypassed the two heavily favored Republican candidates, Taft and Dewey. While FDR was able to distance himself from the sordid affair, as time passes the closeness of all the participants in the scheme to smear Walsh becomes clear, and all roads lead back to the White House.

If Senator Burton Wheeler's charges are to be believed, more than xenophobia connected these people, for money played a vital role. Backer was taking money from FDR, Sherwood was taking money from Backer (to finance his plays), and Ernst was taking money from everybody.

Senator David Walsh may not have realized immediately that his career was over. He was still in office, but no public official can survive even such a hint of scandal. He had no way of publicly refuting the charges. It did not matter that it was all made up, and every Washington insider realized that, including the press. Walsh had served almost as long as Churchill, having begun public service as a state representative in Massachusetts in 1899; but now, his influence would wane in the Senate.

The voters back home in Massachusetts, the party activists, had no way of knowing that the great liberal champion, FDR, had led the fight against Walsh. It was all too fantastic. Why would Roosevelt take out a fellow liberal Democrat? A rightwing conspiracy might do it, perhaps, but not FDR. Therefore, it was whispered, the charges must be true; in fact, everyone knew he was gay. This was a political era when the voters did not much care what went on in the bedroom, as long as it stayed in the bedroom. FDR could carry on a lifelong affair with Lucy Mercer Rutherford and Dwight Eisenhower could carry on with Kay Summersby, but it was important to keep it discreet. The news media generally would not print such stories, either. But, Walsh could not respond to the charges, because he could

---

[1] Sherwood, Robert E., *Roosevelt and Hopkins, an Intimate History*, Harper Brothers, New York, 1948, 200

not admit to homosexuality. The "whispered rumor" won the day.

Walsh had not been exposed simply because he was high on FDR's enemies list; that simply made it possible. When Senate Majority Leader Barkley discussed the Walsh case with FDR, Roosevelt suggested that Walsh should do the honorable thing and kill himself. The palpable hatred expressed by FDR may have been rooted in FDR's failings in his early professional career before the Senate Naval Affairs Committee. His conduct before the committee in 1919 resulted in a finding that FDR had perjured himself, and in an affair that, ironically, revolved around homosexuality.

David Walsh was destroyed after Pearl Harbor, after the hot war had begun, because Great Britain was looking forward. Great Britain wanted a strong hand at the peace table, and Walsh's strongly anti-colonial views had been expressed at the conclusion of World War I. When he first entered the Senate, he fought against the founding of the League of Nations because it was designed to maintain the colonial status quo. He fought for Philippine independence.

Walsh did not need the ACLU on his side. He subscribed to the thinking of another Massachusetts native, Henry David Thoreau: whenever he spotted a "do gooder," he walked the other way, "lest they do their good to me."

David Walsh did not commission polls to determine what he stood for. He stood with the workingman and woman, who did not trust big government, particularly big government overseas. He stood with the poor Yankee farmers from the western part of the state, and they rewarded him with their votes. He alienated both of the Democratic presidents under whom he worked. He stood with Justice Brandeis, not with Attorney General Biddle. He stood with Senator Burton Wheeler, a Yankee from Massachusetts via Montana, not "Wild Bill" Donovan of OSS fame.

He was, according to the *New York Times*, the unparalleled fisher of votes in Massachusetts. He attracted votes from Protestants and Catholics alike. David Walsh clubs existed in nearly every Massachusetts city and town; they had to, because the big city machines never supported him.

David Walsh wrote the first minimum wage law in the United States, the Walsh-Healy Act. He advocated for the first welfare system by speaking up for widows and orphans in an era when it was not popular, before the Great Depression. As Governor of Massachusetts, he started the first extension program at state colleges, which allowed people in the working class to take college courses. The year was 1913.

He decried the "Rape of Nanking," before it had a name. He was greatly influenced by giants in the US Senate, both liberal and conservative, who were staunch isolationists; men like William Jennings Bryan, who had stood up to Wilson when he broke his pledge to the voter not to enter World War I, and conservatives like Henry Cabot Lodge. He was a steadfast believer in the right of self-determination, a position that put him on the road for a clash with the British.

The principle of "self determination" was an idea that came to the shores of Cape Cod with the English settlers called Pilgrims, a dissident group, themselves. It spread to Rhode Island, when settlers broke away from the Massachusetts Bay Colony; and later with the establishment of Connecticut at the Charter Oak, and again, when Catholics settled Maryland, and the Quakers settled Pennsylvania. It spilled into the Ohio River Valley, and continued spreading into the Western territories. The people who settled these territories lived close to the land, never trusted big government, and sent to Washington people like David Walsh and Henry Cabot Lodge from Massachusetts, and Thomas Walsh and Burton Wheeler from Montana, and William Jennings Bryan, the "Silver-Tongued Orator" from Nebraska, and Gerald Nye from North Dakota, and Hiram Johnson from California. They did not trust Washington, never mind London, Paris, or Berlin.

Great Britain never grasped the concept of "self determination," at least, not for others. The damage done by Intrepid and Churchill to American institutions at a perilous hour is clear evidence that Great Britain never accepted what happened in 1776. They burned the White House down in the War of 1812; and they captured it again in the summer of 1940 — with the willing collusion of many US citizens. FDR failed to protect the White House. None of the handpicked pals who surrounded him as the war approached ever distinguished themselves on matters of foreign policy. The New Deal brain trust was long gone. Churchill had his plans, and personnel; FDR's plans were vague and uncertain. His arrogance in thinking he could charm Stalin with his smile was delusional. The void of leadership would be admirably filled by the "long, gray line" of West Point and the not so gray characters of Annapolis. It would turn out to be not so gray after all.

The FDR that is shown in American statues and official history is iconic, legendary, in every sense. The FDR that is revealed in contemporary documents was insecure, venal, petty, untrusting of others, unwilling to give credit to others, unable to accept the counsel of others. His moral failings were many; his loyalties nonexistent. He tried to match wits with Germany and Japan, but his biggest enemy was an unfaithful ally who had been a major participant in the schemes of Europe for centuries and whose concern was to keep as much of the spoils of war as possible. It was an old game, and they were very good at it.

In the final analysis, FDR was used, and then thrown away. Winston

Churchill did not even attend his funeral. That would appear to sum up the vaunted FDR-Churchill partnership.

> Winston Churchill, ... when the president was alive, had always been eager to come to Washington. He had made great professions of friendship, writing as recently as March 18 that 'our friendship is the rock on which I build'; and that he would never forget how Roosevelt had comforted him over the loss of Tobruk by giving him 300 Sherman tanks. But now he would not cross the Atlantic to mourn his ally....When he wanted something from Roosevelt, the trip was worth it. For a ceremonial function, it was not.[2]

FDR came into the game with a Secretary of State whom history has described as slow and methodical, and he kept him for three terms. Harry Hopkins, his chief advisor in the White House, was a social worker by training and his health was worse than FDR's. When this social worker served as Secretary of Commerce in the 1930s, during the country's worst economic crisis, the business community was appalled. As chief gatekeeper of the White House during World War II, he was even less qualified. The history of World War II is replete with stories of American generals who led the nation in battle, who made almost all the right decisions, whose education and training were second to none. There are few stories about heroic civilians in FDR's administration, because at the senior levels there weren't any. There are no stories about brilliant foreign policy decisions, because there weren't any.

FDR's liaison partners included the British Ambassador to Washington, Lord Lothian, a man who was singing the praises of Nazi Germany before the war began. He died before the war was over; as a Christian Scientist, he refused medical treatment. On the intelligence side was William Stephenson, Intrepid (assisted by his lieutenant, Richard Ellis, who confessed to selling secrets to the Russians and Germans). His critics say he bragged too much, even though he waited thirty years to publish his memoirs. They claim he took the credit of others. He did. Indeed, he had plenty of help. The King of England was pleased. William Stephenson was knighted after the war.

In America, those who had brought down Walsh received less honor. When Harry Truman (the third of FDR's Vice Presidents) assumed the Presidency, he was not looking for "yes" men. He brought in a heavyweight as Secretary of State, George Marshall; everyone had confidence in him. He knighted nobody. He fired Attorney General Biddle, whom Truman never liked. He fired Donovan and abolished the OSS, an agency that the military had never trusted. According to Adolf Berle's diary, Marshall disliked Donovan so much that it showed on his

---

[2] Morgan, Ted, *FDR: A Biography*, Simon & Schuster, New York, 1985, 769.

face.

There are no statues on the mall in Washington honoring a true patriot, David Walsh. There was no memorial to World War II Veterans until just recently. Why ? They never demanded it. They just wanted to return home to Main Street. Walsh overcame tremendous prejudice based on his religion. He stood up under unbearable pressure, fully cognizant of the storm swirling around him. He knew the daggers would come; he just did not know who would be wielding the fatal knife. He remained constant to his beliefs for his whole career — something few politicians can say. He had ample opportunity to sell out to FDR, but refused to bend. He was resigned to serve in the loyal opposition in the Senate. While FDR took all the bows for the New Deal legislation, it was the Senate who produced the laws, based on ideas that had been debated since the turn of the century.

Walsh's beliefs were formed early in life in Clinton and nurtured later by the Jesuits at the College of the Holy Cross. It was his Jesuit friends who encouraged him to visit the Philippines in 1918, and the Jesuits who informed him of massacre inflicted in the Chinese city of Nanking by invading Japanese troops. As he became aware of a world much larger than Europe and America, he remained convinced that isolation was America's best policy; but his interest in world affairs was far broader than that of the Anglophiles who ended his career. There are no statues to Walsh in Washington, but the citizens of Massachusetts did erect a statue in his honor in the most appropriate of places. Every Fourth of July, as the Boston Pops finishes its performance, as the fireworks explode, the statue of Senator David Walsh is illuminated on the Charles River Esplanade.

As for the British? Their closest ally, FDR, "continued to respect England. A great people, brought up in a great tradition, he told his doctor, Ross McIntyre, one night at dinner at the White House. Often an irritating people by reason of conviction of superiority so ingrained and perfected by time as to transcend mere egotism, and a shrewd hard-bargaining people, aggressive territorially and in every trade relation; nevertheless a steadfast people, a people kin to us by blood, holding the same ideals, and our assured ally in the event of war."[3]

There is some evidence that the British actually like that definition. When the movie *Mrs. Miniver* was released in Great Britain, audiences were upset at the depiction of the English in quaint villages. They wanted to see the British lion roaring. They did not realize this was a propaganda film aimed at the American market, so the kinder, gentler Britain was being portrayed. With the empire gone,

---

[3] Ibid., 505-506.

Britain has now been condemned to play the role in the film they so despised.

David Walsh faced one last battle back home, in Massachusetts. Before leaving Washington for the last time, he had a chance to vote for Philippine independence, in July, 1946. Life had come full circle. He returned for his final campaign against a worthy opponent, the returning military veteran Henry Cabot Lodge, Jr., who had quit his senate seat to enlist. Walsh had no chance.

His sisters urged him to retire; he brushed off the suggestion and still projected confidence that he could win. Hannah and Julia headed off to the White Mountains, leaving the house free for him in his campaign. They did not have much of a vacation, however. Hannah Walsh died of a heart attack in September — leaving a check on the table for $500.00 as a contribution to David's campaign. She and Julia must have been worried the whole vacation about the election; the thought of her brother's impending defeat would have been unbearable. Walsh lost by 300,000 votes.

He received many letters from supporters, afterwards, many of them connected to the United States Navy. One letter was from Admiral Richard Byrd, navy aviator and navigator, and explorer of the North and South Poles. Byrd wrote as follows:

Dear Senator:

I want to tell you what a great sense of personal loss I will feel at your absence from the Senate.

It is a very sad situation for your friends down here who admired you for so long. All of the older officers in the Navy Department feel as I do. The day we learned of your defeat was a day of mourning.

Your contribution to the Navy and the country has been of inestimable value to our national security and no man can say that you did not serve your state and the Navy and your country with the highest ability. We know you were caught up in a chain of circumstances and a tide of feeling that swept the country against which even a man of great accomplishments like yourself could not have stood up.

In other words we know that if the people had voted on your record and your contribution to the country there could not have been any question as to the outcome. Your many grateful friends in the Navy Department join me in sending you our very best wishes.

Sincerely,
Dick Byrd [4]

The letter is both a tribute and a tacit acknowledgement that Byrd, a friend

---

[4] Wayman, Dorothy G., *David I. Walsh, Citizen-Patriot*, Bruce Publishing, Milwaukee, 1952., 342-343.

of both Walsh and FDR, knew what had happened to Walsh. Byrd, an American hero from the 20th Century, America's century, knew all the battles Walsh had fought for the United States Navy.

In May 1947, David Walsh made a visit to Stephenson's home country, Canada, but not for a purpose Intrepid would have approved, for he chose a Francophile destination. He had made a habit of taking,

> a closed retreat, three days of silence, meditation, and prayer at the Jesuit retreat house, Campion Hall in North Andover…He proposed to his lifelong friend, Judge Connelly that it would be pleasant to take Mrs. Connelly and Miss Julia for a motor trip to Montreal and a pilgrimage to the famed shrine of St. Anne de Beaupre.
>
> It was a good trip with old friends, and Walsh enjoyed it, but the long steps up the shrine seemed to tax his strength. "When he came back, I could see that he did not feel well, but he wouldn't say anything," remembers Elizabeth Cooper….He was listless for a few days and then seemed to have a summer cold.[5]

On June 8, his sister Nellie died of a cerebral hemorrhage. On June 9, David Walsh suffered a stroke; by June 11, he was gone. On his bedside table lay the Psalms of David; he had been reading the Seventieth Psalm. "How many times must David Ignatius Walsh have read and found comfort in the words of David, the Sheperd King:

"I am become unto many as a wonder; but thou art my strong helper….My enemies have spoken against me…let them be confounded and come to nothing that detract my soul…Thou hast taught me, O God from my youth….and unto old age and gray hairs: O God forsake me not.

How great troubles has thou shown me, many and grievous and, turning, thou hast brought me back to life and hast brought me back again from the depths of the earth.

My lips shall greatly rejoice when I shall sing to thee; and my soul, which thou hast redeemed." [6]

Congress, after standing silent for too long, took radical action to help prevent the kind of abuses suffered by David Walsh, and with very little debate between liberals and conservatives. Rather than limit the powers of the Supreme Court, as FDR had tried to do, they limited the power of the president — but not the presidency; an occupant of the White House would be limited to two terms. The decision to amend the constitution without debate showed a unity of purpose between conservatives and liberals, but also smacked of the elitism. While their purposes were lofty, the decision not to tell the country why such extreme action

---

[5] Ibid., 345-346.
[6] Ibid 346

was necessary, smacks once again of a troubling pattern used by the liberal elitists, Communists, and British Imperialists. The ordinary folk along Main Street can't handle the truth.

David I. Walsh died at mid century. His first campaign was in a horse and buggy. He participated in the debate over the League of Nations. He fought colonialism his whole career, and fought for Philippine independence as early as 1900. He authored most of the 1930's legislation regarding the rights of the worker, legislation that survived the New Deal. He stood up to FDR's assault on the Supreme Court with the Court Packing Plan. He fought our participation in World War I and II. He witnessed the arrival of the atomic age. More importantly, this isolationist helped escort America onto the world stage gradually, and helped escort Great Britain off.

Congress, after standing silent too long, finally took radical action when they amended the Constitution. They never fully bought into the messianic qualities of this aristocrat, who, like all politicians, was in the right place at the right time.

David I. Walsh's timing was exquisite as well. He was born on what would later become Veteran's Day, and he was buried very close to the center of Clinton, Massachusetts, on Flag Day. His statue on the Charles River Esplanade is not far from where the Pilgrims landed. It is illuminated once a year on the Fourth of July, as the Boston Pops Orchestra concludes with the 1812 Overture, as the fireworks explode. While perhaps not his choice of music, the rest of the score he would likely approve of. It is unlikely that any of the celebrants of the Fourth of July activities on the banks of the Charles River have any idea of the granite monument that looms behind them, standing on the edge of darkness overlooking his flock. He was in that position much of his life, standing alone.

As for the WASP's who were the backbone of the America First Committee, a roll call is needed. WASP's who knew that anyone who served on America First would have their patriotism questioned. WASP's who knew where their allegiances lay. WASP's who remembered why their forebears left England in the first place. WASP's who aspired to the ideal of citizen participation, like the poor Yankee farmers of Western Massachusetts who voted for Walsh in every election. WASP's who thought it was American to "question authority."

A partial list is as follows:

General Robert E. Wood, J. Sanford Otis, Thomas Hammond, J.C. Hormel, Hanford Macnider of the VFW, Clay Judson, Dr. Anton Julius Carlson, R. Douglas Stuart, William Castle, Jr., Irvin Cobb, Janet Ayer Fairbanks, Alice Roosevelt Longworth, Thomas McCarter, Bishop Wilbur Hammaker, Amos

Pinchot, Dr. George Whipple, Major Alford Williams, Mrs. Burton Wheeler, Mrs. Bennett Champ Clark. World War I Ace,Eddie Rickenbacker.

"Hear, Hear."

POSTSCRIPT

FDR's actions and his complicity with the leaders of a foreign nation during wartime suggest how tenuous the notion of democracy can be, and how duplicitous governments can be. While I have traced all leads right back to the White House, they go out the back door and lead almost always to Columbia University. The misconduct of government officials can be the fuel of conspiracy theorists and in FDR's case, his official actions were often worse than imagined conspiracies.

FDR was a Columbia University Law School dropout. The campaign against Walsh and others was dominated by Columbia University faculty and graduates, including William Donovan. The propaganda campaign was orchestrated by British money paid to Professors Hugh Highet and Helen Highet, and others too numerous to mention. British Security Coordination essentially "leased" the Classics Department at Columbia and from there they influenced public opinion.

Rexford Tugwell, a Columbia University professor and original member of FDR's brain trust, authored the first biography of the President. His close friend Raymond Moley, a fellow Columbia University professor, was credited with writing FDR's first major speeches. Although he later had a falling out with FDR (a common occurrence), he was also known to be a committed Anglophile.

Historians have given great credit to the William Allen White Committee for arousing Americans to aid Great Britain; that, in effect, was a front, as well. Although it was portrayed as a citizen effort led by William Allen White, the editor of the *Emporia Kansas Gazette*, it was actually run by Columbia University professors. The heartland was a bastion of liberalism, and the campus propagandists gave all the by-lines to the editor from Emporia, Kansas, to indicate that prairie patriots bought into this program. (Before the American Revolution, Columbia was called King's College. Could it be that the Anglophile connection has never been severed?)

The first inkling that the William Allen White Committee was a fraud came from William Allen White, himself. Historians often fail to mention that White resigned in disgust when the war had barely begun. They rarely mention that he opposed going forward with the destroyer deal without congressional approval. FDR opted to go forward by executive order. White also opposed FDR on convoying.

At that point, FDR unleashed an attack. Great Britain had used White shamelessly, but when they could not use him any more, they did not ease him out of his position. Fiorello LaGuardia used an ethnic slur in an attempt to destroy him, a term that much of the world would consider a compliment but that resonates with particular rancor in an Anglophile world. He equated White to a Frenchman, and a traitor to boot. "On December 26, 1940, Fiorello LaGuardia went public with a letter attacking White, 'When the going was good for the allies, you and others were strong in saying what you would do. Now that the going is bad, you are doing a typical Laval."[1] This was a reference to the French Foreign Minister who was associated with the Vichy government. Since White was a newspaper editor himself, he would have no difficulty reading between the lines. Now, he noted "policy direction [that] deeply troubled him...since the committee, was more or less bearing his name. White now described the Committee to Defend the Allies as a dreadful responsibility that has been a shadow on [his] heart."[2] Heaping insult upon injury, the board named LaGuardia honorary chairman. White dutifully submitted his resignation

According to the Seeley G. Mudd Transcript Library at Princeton University, White said he resigned because of the lack of democratic procedures. To counter this criticism, the Committee to Defend America by Aiding the Allies expanded its board to 600 members. That may have been an effective propaganda move to counter White's charges, but a board that large also serves to obscure who the real players are, and who was really behind the board's actions.

White had some suspicions, but unfortunately he died before completing his autobiography. Other reputable sources were able to finish the story. The Washington office of the William Allen White Committee was run by Donald C. Blaisdell. Arguably the most important field office in the United States, it was run by enthusiastic volunteers — at least, that is what history books say. Blaisdell,

---

[1] Committee to Defend America by Aiding the Allies, Seeley G Mudd Transcript Library, Princeton University

[2] Ibid.

also a former Columbia University professor, and roommate of Rexford Tugwell, and friend of Raymond Moley, was in fact on FDR's team. White probably suspected as much.

The Truman Library provides Blaisdell's own admissions. A shadow government was making decisions, beyond the checks and balances represented by the Congress and the Court. FDR was operating outside the framework of the constitution and federal law, using shadow employees paid with taxpayer dollars but working for a foreign power. Congress knew it, but never managed to make the case without sounding paranoid, and never successfully drove home the point that Roosevelt's actions were criminal in nature. On June 20, 1940, Senator Walsh had threatened criminal prosecution over the delivery of brand new torpedo boats to Great Britain, vessels that had long been promised to the United States Navy. However, charging a president with "criminal acts" is more a political battle than a legal one and FDR, aided by his friends in the press, was able to outmaneuver Walsh in the only courtroom that mattered: the court of public opinion.

In an oral history interview for the Truman Library conducted in 1973 by Richard D. McKinzie, Blaisdell almost casually admits that he was on the Department of Agriculture payroll the entire time he ran the Washington office of this supposedly "volunteer" group. McKinzie started the interview by asking a simple question, that is, how did Blaisdell's career jump from Agriculture to work on the United Nations? (Blaisdell was assistant to Assistant Secretary of Agriculture, M.L. Wilson when he started working on the Committee to Defend America by Aiding the Allies.)

> The short space of time after I left Agriculture (but not the payroll), in 1940 in June, until I went to the Department of State in late December 1941, all of that time I spent in my activities for the Committee to Defend America by Aiding the Allies. A Washington office was established. Livingston Hartley and I ran it.

> One or two others who were involved in this were able to persuade Mr. White to become titular head of it; that's what it was because he never was a very active person organizationally, or anything of that kind. He lent his name to it and his prestige, and I was involved in that in Washington. In December 1941, I went to work for Lynn Edminister in State to get supplies to Great Britain. This is one of those cases where they used an innocuous name to veil a very important significant strategic operation. They called it the Office of Lend-Lease Reports; this was like the Manhattan Project a little later on [also run by Columbia University]. The idea was to use a completely innocuous title to cover up something of much greater significance.[3]

Blaisdell did not leave the Department of Agriculture payroll until he

---

[3] Truman Library, Oral History Interview, Donald C. Blaisdell, interview conducted by Richard D McKinzie, 1973.

transferred to State in December, 1941, when his services were no longer needed to get the US into the war. Blaisdell describes the secrecy surrounding his work aiding Great Britain. Mckinzie, the interviewer, is incredulous and makes statements in the form of questions. He asks, "Chief of Staff of the Commander in Chief Admiral Leahy didn't have a staff in the White House...A staff who could be looking at the thing in terms of grand strategy including post-war reconstruction? Leahy didn't have any staff?"

Once again, the same pattern appeared — the White House had no staff to lead the US in World War II; yet, the tip a shadow government emerges, criminal in nature. Monies appropriated for the Department of Agriculture were used for a private committee working to help a foreign power. Whom did they report to? Later, in 1941, the Committee to Defend America by Aiding the Allies merged with the Fight for Freedom Committee, a committee that Stephenson, in his Intrepid memoirs, admitted was a British propaganda front.

The use of government employees on such activities was a clear violation of both Neutrality Acts. Blaisdell's description of the secrecy surrounding the activity gives ample evidence that the participants knew it was criminal. FDR had many willing helpers, carefully screened and largely selected from among Columbia University graduates. They identified with grand old England, more than with their own country.

Blaisdell talked about his work on post-war reconstruction, including his work in establishing the United Nations — years before Congress would even consider it. Without wandering into the realm of conspiracy theories, one has to acknowledge that a number of writers, mostly of an Anglophile bent, have proposed some form of Atlantic union. Blaisdell mentions working with Livingston Hartley, an author who proposed such a union. Was Great Britain floating these ideas, perhaps thinking that a gullible former colony would go along with another "League of Nations"-type gambit where Great Britain would have six votes for America's one? Lord Northcliffe did describe the US as a "nation of sheep." Great Britain has been unable or unwilling to integrate herself into Europe. This insular, island people have been far more isolationist than Americans could possibly be.

There was, and in some quarters still is, a strain of thinking in the US that colors all things British with an allure of aristocracy, before which all things American seem provincial and crude. This sense of inferiority was part of what drove the traitorous acts of so many who were connected to the media. The American intelligentsia of that era, particularly the writing crowd, thought that anything worthwhile came from London, if not Rome, Paris, and Berlin.

Jews, like other minorities, were allowed to be foot soldiers in the British

236

Empire as long as they did not ask to have a say in policy matters. Lise Namikas, writing for Historian, says "the need to appear representative of the American mainstream led the committee to ignore minorities such as Black Americans and to discourage Jewish Americans from membership because of their reputation as 'war mongers' and supposed interest in serving narrow ethnic concerns."[4] Another view would be that they were not Anglophile enough. However, some were. Dorothy Schiff apparently was, and besides, she owned the *New York Post*.

According to Jeffrey Potter, in *Men, Money, and Magic*, Dorothy's first marriage to Richard Hall was in the Episcopal Church, otherwise known as the Church of England. Dorothy describes her grandfather's house as resembling the Court of Saint James. Her parents had sent her to London on several occasions, hoping that she would marry someone respectable.[5] In August, 1931, on a voyage to London, she met the renowned baron of the British press, Lord Beaverbrook. Through her affair with him, she met Winston Churchill, Leslie Hore-Belisha, and Randolph Churchill. Dorothy's horizons broadened suddenly and dramatically when a new man came into her life, or more accurately, she was ordered into his. He was the renowned British press lord, Lord Beaverbrook born William Maxwell Aiken and knighted prior to his peerage....The press lord and future publisher [Dorothy] were together almost constantly the rest of the voyage.... Later, she would became Roosevelt's paramour, a relationship that would last for years. As a consequence, there were not a lot of secrets between 10 Downing St and 1600 Pennsylvania Avenue.

Dorothy Schiff left 256 boxes of papers, upon her death, to the New York Public Library. Included are Jeffrey Potter's transcripts, initialed by Dorothy Schiff. Her romantic relationship with Roosevelt is covered in great detail, including a letter written by FDR detailing their joint purchase of property next to the Roosevelt estate.

The affair with Lord Beaverbrook, Minister of Munitions in World War II, reveals the incestuous relationship between the power elite in London, Washington, and New York. The Communists were right about one thing: it was about class; it was, indeed, about a class struggle. Dorothy Schiff could overcome her Jewish background as long as she played the game according to the rules of the Anglo elite. Those rules included a requirement that one have plenty of money.

---

[4] Historian, Summer 1999, Lise Namikas, "Committee to Defend America and the Debate Between Internationalists and Interventionists, 1939-1941."
[5] Potter, Jeffrey, *Men, Money, and Magic*, 1976, Coward, McCann, & Geoghan, New York, p. 80, 81, 84

Dorothy Schiff described Roosevelt's view of Joseph Stalin in terms similar to Daisy Suckley's. Both women, who had no formal education beyond high school, apparently remembered FDR's impression so clearly because they were dumbstruck by FDR's naiveté. Schiff, who dropped out of Bryn Mawr after one semester, offers the opinion that FDR was not very bright. Schiff describes her relationship with FDR.

> I had made a very good beginning with him. In what became kind of a court relationship, I never did talk about myself; not a word. He wasn't interested in me but in having what he thought was a well dressed young woman around with whom he could be comfortable and ramble on to. My clothes were New York designer things then, and he was amused by my John Fredericks hats, which I haven't worn for years. He didn't see many people who were well dressed, and the ones around him weren't even attractive. There just wasn't any competition, not that I was thinking of that. There was a class thing, too. He was a snob — horrible word, and I wish I could think of a better one — and he liked women who were well bred and brought up. Ladies is the word, I guess. I was a rich kid of the right kind — not the robber baron type — and had been to the right schools. As to being Jewish, C.P. Snow wrote that once you reach a certain financial level, people don't think of you as anything but very rich. At thirty-three, I was twenty years younger than he — young enough to be attractive to ... well, he liked the ladies.[6]

While FDR and Dorothy's affair blossomed, Schiff eventually saw through the smoke screen of FDR's radiant smile. "Before long I began to wonder if he was really of first magnitude and if it wasn't merely the sun-god quality which gave people confidence. His conversation was mostly trivial, there were all those juvenile stories being repeated endlessly, and he wasn't well informed on anything except naval history and current political issues which are dead now. I missed the intellectual and sophisticated world of Max [Lord Beaverbrook] that I had known in London"[7]

Dorothy's devastating comparison with her other lover, Beaverbrook, shows FDR, as a less than towering intellect, and her descriptions of the men around FDR are even more devastating. She describes Harry Hopkins as "the social worker he really was" and describes Sam Rosenman as a person who "let himself be treated as a law clerk."

When Dorothy Schiff's biography was published in 1976, the book received explosive pre-publication publicity regarding her sexual trysts with FDR. *Time Magazine* gave it extensive coverage in its June 7th, 1976 edition, but at the

---

[6] Ibid., 136.
[7] Ibid., 169-170.

last minute, Schiff hired Attorney Morris Abrams, a savvy political operator. Schiff denied the charges were true. Apparently Schiff was getting considerable pressure not defame FDR. Her author, Jeffrey Potter, was stunned at her denials, and insisted that taped transcripts existed.

Yet upon her death, she left her papers to the New York Public Library, and included are Potter's paper transcripts, with each page initialed by Dorothy Schiff. The interviews with Jeffrey Potter indicate her joint purchase of property with FDR next to Hyde Park, the so called 'Red House' which was to be their retirement villa, and further indicates a motor trip back to Hyde Park by Jeffrey Potter, Dorothy Schiff, and Franklin D. Roosevelt, Jr., to reminisce about Hyde Park. Again, this appears to be another affair that was well known to the Roosevelt children, and would cause further humiliation for Eleanor. Dorothy Schiff expresses her remorse for embarrassing encounters with Eleanor as Schiff and FDR spent time together at Hyde Park.

Dorothy Schiff recalls getting a call from the White House while she was at a party hosted by Herbert Bayard Swope, editor of the *New York World*. Swope was a member of the Century Club, and it was Swope who fixed her up with George Backer. It was a call to visit Hyde Park, and Dorothy's description of her visits there mirror Daisy Suckley's descriptions of the Hyde Park routine.

"FDR's Hyde Park visits, when Dorothy usually joined him, were scheduled every month or six weeks, The visits usually followed a set pattern, beginning with Saturday lunch at "Granny's", which Dorothy remembers meant just the three of them except occasionally when they were joined by a relative or Missy LeHand....I think she thought I was safe for her son because I did not want anything and everyone else did. She might have been worried if she thought I could hurt him politically. As to other designs he might have had on me, she wouldn't have cared. She loathed Eleanor and would have arranged things for him so he could have what he wanted. Her main concern was to get him to Hyde Park as often and as long as possible, and I was a draw." [8]

Dorothy Schiff's description of that incestuous age is not all that surprising, as the upper classes had a tendency to keep misbehaviour within the family, or certainly within the classes. It would have been far more frowned upon if such misbehaviour involved someone of the lower classes. Theodore Dreiser's *An American Tragedy* was based on just that premise. While Dorothy indicates that "Granny" helped provide cover for her son to cheat on Eleanor, she indicates that Eleanor clearly knew, and that FDR had flaunted it in her face. Dorothy

---

[8] Ibid., 140-141.

further indicates that her husband, George Backer knew, and approved of her affair.

"George was overwhelmed by the President, and it was he who really sold me on him. George saw it all in a *droit du seigneur* way, his wife being tapped by the lord of the manor. He was proud of it, and it gave him tremendous prestige with his friends. Alexander Woolcott, for the first time impressed by me, tried to get in the act by having himself invited to the White House by Mrs. Roosevelt. Those thirty-six million votes, or whatever it was, and the power it meant dazzled George."[9]

Author Jeffrey Potter asked Dorothy Schiff was effect the sexual relationship with FDR had on her marriage.

"Dorothy's answer was immediate. "A lot." For George, it was more than having a wife who impressed his friends by the connection. He was able to feel that, however peripherally, he was making an impression on history. FDR was much more than just the founder of the New Deal. A master of political timing, he was the symbol of hope for the nation, even if Al Smith had said, when asked to support FDR in his campaign for Governor of New York, "Frank just doesn't have the character for a job this big." [10]

Al Smith's judgment of FDR's character would be an accurate one. However, all the public ever saw was the radiant smile. The propaganda version of FDR would be handled by his classmates at Columbia, and they would keep extremely busy writing fictional accounts of virtually every aspect of the war, as well as domestic legislation. Again, the troubling pattern emerges that the ruling class had determined that, because times were so bad, the American public could not be told the truth. This patronizing approach was just a rationalization, because the ruling class has never found a convenient time to include the American public in decision making. The American public had been relegated to the level of women in society. After all, women had only been allowed to vote for twenty odd years. They could cook the meals, take care of children, fix the drinks, and make themselves available for sex, observe the political scene, but don't ask for power. In FDR's life, they did observe the political scene, and their observations are priceless.

George Backer's mental health began to deteriorate, and their marriage fell apart. Dorothy described him faking a British accent, and even George's friends mentioned it to her.

---

[9] Ibid., 146.
[10] Ibid., 147.

"In Dorothy's view George was undergoing a major personality change at this time, and it was one that she did not understand.....he seemed affected, and began speaking with a British accent. His close friend, Samuel Chotzinoff, with whom he wrote a play said, "What the hell's the matter with George-where did he get that accent"? [11]

Author Jeffrey Potter provided copies of FDR's letters to Dorothy, written on White House stationery, asking Dorothy for a $9,000 deposit on "his" and "her" cottages for their retirement years at Hyde Park. The date of the letter was April 5th, 1938. In a few short years, FDR would be asking for Dorothy's assistance to destroy the anti-war movement, and David Walsh in particular.

Dorothy Schiff expressed mixed feelings about not following through on FDR' demands to build their retirement home when FDR wanted it done. While she pined for the social life in London, she presents a patronizing view of FDR.

"My timing on the Red House was off. I didn't build it when the President wanted me to, and by the time I did, it was too late. By then, I think he had given up on me. He wanted the house to be built, of course, and to have me in it, but it was all for him. Once I saw this, I was no longer the child and he the father. Somehow, next I seemed to have become the provider, though not a mother figure. Before long I was kidding him about a new girl he was supposed to be very keen about, Princess Marta of Norway...Of Course, I didn't know then he was still seeing Lucy Mercer, who being married, had to keep in the background."[12]

It is doubtful that she knew of FDR's relationships with Missy Lehand or Daisy Suckley, since most of her discussions of those two seem very friendly. She may have had no idea how many women FDR was involved with. She spent many social occasions at Hyde Park with both of them.

While Dorothy's affair with FDR was winding down, she offers more of a glimpse at FDR's relationship with Churchill and Stalin, and again the comparisons mirror the observations of other women in Roosevelt's life. Her comments hardly suggest an FDR-Churchill partnership, at least not in the talent department. Her comments are eerily similar to Daisy Suckley's observations about FDR's naivete towards Stalin, but a bit more damning.

"The President was provincial compared to the cosmopolitan Churchill and felt terribly inferior despite commanding so much more power. Of course, in addition to being intellectually superior, Churchill exhausted him by keeping him late a night with his verbal pyrotechnics and brandy. Churchill knew more about

---

[11] Ibid., 148.
[12] Ibid., 173.

even Civil War battles than the President, and in literature would quote such writers as Swineburne, while the President could think only of Longfellow....Ludicrous as it may seem, he thought Stalin spoke the same language. The President thought he was great, was crazy about him. He said they were brothers in being for the common man and that they spoke the same language. Now it seems idiotic, but probably gave him relief from the feeling of inferiority he had about Churchill. I used to hear endlessly that the two of them would gang up on this ghastly Churchill, who was so superior. It was always Uncle Joe this, or Uncle Joe that.....I never heard the President talk about anyone else that way. It was if they were the naughty boys ganging up on the teacher."[13]

Her next husband would be another extreme Anglophile, Theodore O. Thackrey, whom she suspected was a British spy. When she confronted him on it, he denied it. In fact, she was well aware that London was putting newspaper writers on their payroll in the Far East and Thackrey had been an editor in Hong Kong; she must have suspected they were active among US newspapers, as well. She was suspicious of Thackrey's involvement with the Zionists and suspected Menachim Begin was a spy, but failed to spot Dr. Chaim Weizmann as a spy for Great Britain. A letter in the Dorothy Schiff Collection at the New York Public Library dated June 21, 1941 written by Weizmann to Lord Moyne at The Colonial Office, gives clear evidence that Weizmann was spying for Great Britain. The letter, or tome would be more descriptive, six typewritten pages, details conditions in America, especially amongst American Jews. Could Great Britain be promising world Jews, and Americans in particular, that it would grant that British colony, Palestine, its independence when the war was over, if Jews "cooperated" with Great Britain? The detailed report is a groveling attempt to satisfy Great Britain, yet Weizmann himself expressed doubts that he could trust the British to keep their end of the bargain.

> But things have been moving rapidly in these three months that it is difficult to understand the static attitude of the British Government with regard to the arming of the Jews in Palestine and to a Jewish army, particularly in view of the picture which the Arab world presents today. We feel deeply that appeasement, which may have disappeared from the English mind as far as world politics is concerned, has found its last stronghold in the attitude of the our British statesmen toward the Jews. The Arabs have betrayed and are betraying, — and in the term "Arab" I include Egypt; therefore they must be appeased. The Jews are doing the impossible under difficult circumstances to render every assistance: therefore they can be ignored. All this seems so utterly absurd, short-sighted and un-English that I sometimes wonder whether this fear of the Arabs in not merely a feint which covers — subconsciously

---

[13] Ibid., 183.

perhaps — something much deeper, namely, fear and suspicion of the Jew. This is an ancient experience to us dating from Pharoic times! I am conscious that perhaps I am generalizing a little too severely, but I am giving you the general impression created in the Jewish mind and also on a great many Americans whom you can count amongst the best friends of England, foremost amongst them a person like Dorothy Thompson.[14]

Weizmann clearly understood that Great Britain was promising the Arabs the same thing, creating a balance of power that will leave both of them weak and with Britain in charge. Menachim Begin learned his lessons from the Irish. When the Easter Uprising occurred in 1916 in Dublin, Great Britain rushed its top diplomats to Ireland and promised that if Ireland remained loyal until World War I was over, Ireland would be granted its freedom. Irish leaders agreed. When World War I was over, 400,000 Irish men had marched to their death, or returned maimed for life. Then, Great Britain reneged.

Michael Collins quit his career in London and returned to Ireland to lead his country into battle, thus providing a new generation of leadership. Using guerilla tactics and a gun, young Collins would drive Great Britain out of Ireland. The Irgun had studied his tactics, and Menachim Begin was not about to repeat the mistakes of the Irish by trying to negotiate with Great Britain.

Dorothy Shiff's contribution of her personal papers provides immeasurable insights to history. Among her papers is an announcement of her wedding to Theodore Olin Thackrey: "among the guests at the wedding were Mrs. John M. Schiff, wife of the bride's brother, Lieutenant John M. Schiff, Jr. U.S.N.R., who is stationed in London, Mr., Mr. and Mrs. James Warburg, Mr. and Mrs. Cornelius V. Starr, Mrs. Irving Berlin, Mrs. Anna Rosenberg, Diana Forbes-Robertson (Mrs. Vincent Sheehan), Miss Elsa Maxwell, Mr. and Mrs. Morris Ernst and Mr. and Mrs. Edgar Ansel Mowrer."[15] The list documents an interesting nexus of people connected to the very mysterious 1940 election campaign of Wendell Willkie, but appears in an even stranger light when read in conjunction with a letter written by Ted Thackrey dated October 19, 1942.

When Wendell Willkie was campaigning to keep his name in the news for a planned run in the 1944 elections, Ted Thackrey offered the support of the *New York Post*, and funds. That meant the *New York Post* was making the news rather than reporting on it. And whose money was it? Thackrey was not independently wealthy and Dorothy Schiff gave no indication that she was financing Willkie. In

---

[14] Chaim Weizmann letter to Lord Moyne, June 21, 1942, Dorothy Schiff Collection, New York Public Library, Box 256

[15] Nuptials and Mr. Willkie announcement, Dorothy Schiff Collection, New York Public Library, Box 88.

the letter in question, Thackrey promises extensive campaign coverage, and indicates "the offer of staff and clerical help was a genuine one. A telegram from you will bring them.... If other syndication plans have not appealed to you, we should be glad to undertake the handling of copy to at least one newspaper in every community in this country where a newspaper is published, on an entirely non-profit basis. I suggest that may be the most effective method of assuring adequate publication. I know that there could be a considerable money value both to you and any syndicate if your impressions were bartered on a commercial basis, and I feel equally sure that neither you nor we have any desire except the most widespread understanding of our need for closer and more forthright relationships with other people of the world who aspire as we do to democracy. Please let me know if we can serve you in this respect or in any other."

Ted Thackrey corresponded with Willkie about his plans to start a political party, the Liberty Party. "I suspect that if we start now there will be adequate time to organize thoroughly in every state before 1944. Without involving you in any way at this stage, unless you wish to be involved, I should be glad to know whether you believe we should start proselytizing now for the formation of the nucleus of a national Liberty Party here, or whether you think the timing would be off. Personally, I believe now is the time."[16]

The 1940 election has been viewed with great suspicion by many observers because Willkie came out of nowhere to win the nomination, having been a Republican for only two years, and also because it appeared his candidacy was generated by the Eastern press. This letter reveals that the *New York Post* was more involved in politics than Willkie was, almost as if the *New York Post* were hiring a candidate.

Ted Thackrey, a busy big city editor, should have been too busy to organize a new political party. Furthermore, the money trail is suspicious. US senators were charging that Schiff bought the newspaper with money from the Federal Reserve Bank during the Walsh hearings. Was this just Washington gossip, or fact? How does one get a loan from the Federal Reserve Bank? Dorothy Schiff's hidden ownership of the *New York Post* raises a distinct possibility that the senators were onto something. Dorothy Schiff's husband, George Backer, had been publicly identified as the owner. It wasn't until she divorced him that it became known that the *New York Post* was owned by her father, Jacob Schiff. Even when Dorothy Schiff, a college dropout, was hired as Publisher in 1942, without one day of newspaper experience, the Schiffs continued to hide their ownership interest. The

---

[16] Theodore Olin Thackrey, letter to Wendell Willkie, October 19, 1942, Box 88.

glass ceiling had been shattered by a female college dropout with no experience, yet the media never asked how, or why. What was the need to hide the ownership interest? Was British money involved? The 1940 election went down in history as the strangest Presidential election ever, and the *New York Post*'s role in that election was unusual, to say the least. It could not support 'favorite son' candidate Thomas Dewey, the darling of the liberal wing of the Republican Party.

When Judge Samuel Liebowitz heard the David Walsh case, in a courtroom in Brooklyn in May, 1942, the Senator was not even there. But Walsh's tormentors were all there. Morris Ernst, General Counsel for the *New York Post* and the ACLU, Dorothy Schiff, owner of the *New York Post* and mistress of FDR and of Great Britain's Minister of Munitions, Lord Beaverbrook, Fiorello LaGuardia, Mayor of New York (who was in control of the detectives who were making the charges), and William Donovan, head of the OSS, who was coordinating the whole operation.

Judge Liebowitz was not an obscure judge. Liebowitz rose to national fame during the Scottsboro Trials. While previously well known in the New York area, he was hired by the American Communist Party to defend the Scottsboro Boys. The American Communist Party was more interested in making political hay with the American left, and spent much of their time denigrating the NAACP as being too main stream. The American Communist Party was considered the laughingstock of the American political scene, but the Scottsboro Case gave them respectability.

The Jewish Journal of Greater Los Angeles describes Liebowitz as a careerist. "'Like many mainstream Americans, he was not sympathetic to the black cause,' said Barak Goodman, a writer director of the 2001 Oscar-nominated documentary Scottsboro: An American Tragedy, '....and he hated Communists. He simply wanted to advance his career'."[17] He had taken the Communists' money and it provided him with a measure of fame, but a strange episode ended his relationship with the party. Two of the attorneys for the Communist Party were arrested and accused of bribing a witness; yet, Liebowitz was not charged. He denounced his co-counsels before the evidence was in, and the American Communist Party was thrown off the case. Criticizing co-counsels in a legal case is very unusual behavior. Liebowitz asked the court to transfer the defense to the ACLU and the court approved the change; thus, Liebowitz began working with Morris Ernst. Ernst was having weekly dinners with J. Edgar Hoover at the Stork

---

[17] Pfefferman, Naomi. Jewish Journal of Greater Los Angeles. "Case Lost/Insight Gained." March 30, 1901.

Club. It seems likely that Hoover would have assisted in disposing of the Communists, thus denying them the headlines they were trying to generate. The ACLU would now garner the headlines. Perhaps it was the ACLU, working covertly, that assisted the FBI in disposing of the American Communist Party. Whether the ACLU's actions were patriotic or self serving, their treachery was remarkable, particularly for an organization claiming to be the premier organization fighting in the trenches for free speech.

Franklin Delano Roosevelt left nothing to chance. The conspiracy was complete. This left wing conspiracy was eating its own. There were no reactionaries present in the courtroom, no rightwing generals, no John Birchers. Perhaps, liberalism is not always progressive, connected to the people, connected to Main Street. David Ignatius Walsh, Gerald Nye, and Burton Wheeler were all destroyed. The ones who survived were the liberal elite in New York City, the socially connected, the Anglophile do-gooders. They were never "outed." The purge was complete. No wonder liberalism is dead.

To this day, one rarely can read of the courageous achievements of these men of the Senate, and their House colleague from Montana, Jeannette Rankin. Jeannette Rankin was the only person in the House to vote against the declaration of war on Japan; the only member of the house wearing the 'pants'. Rankin was trying to tell America that something did not seem right; that Congress was voting without sufficient facts; but the only people listening were in Montana. They erected a statue in her honor on the Mall in Washington.

One historian who attempted to tell the public the truth was Charles Beard; he was persecuted for it, every step of the way. The very liberal Charles Beard was smeared by the supposed liberal leader of his day, President Woodrow Wilson, during the debate on World War I. Charles Beard was perhaps the most prominent historian on the American presidency during the first half of the 20th century. Beard was Chairman of the Department of Government at Columbia University, the bastion of Anglophile thought. Two of the professors he had hired were fired for opposing US entrance into World War I. Beard resigned in protest. The most eminent US historian of the 20th century was never hired again by any university. Attorney General Palmer had listed him among the most dangerous radicals in the United States, and he was under FBI surveillance much of his life. At least, this left him the academic independence to stand against FDR's machinations with the Supreme Court and his foreign policy, and allowed him to devote his time to writing.

Senator David I. Walsh, Charles Beard, Jeannette Rankin, and Senators Nye, Wheeler, Tobey, and Clark all had their voices silenced by a propaganda

POSTSCRIPT

campaign as insidious as any threat America has ever faced. The din of the campaign was so powerful it could destroy American icons, and rob Americans of their heroes.

Charles Lindbergh is another hero that has been taken from America. Generations have now been taught that he was anti-Semitic. Yet, at the FBI headquarters in Washington, one may find hate letters calling Lindbergh a "Jew lover." The letters allege that, "Everyone knows that Harry Guggenheim is paying for his aviation research." In the Pulitzer Prize winning book, *Lindbergh*, Scott Berg quotes Harry Guggenheim as saying, "Slim has never had the slightest anti-Semitic feeling." Guggenheim wasn't just his benefactor; they were friends.

The two most cited examples of Lindbergh's anti-Semitism are his acceptance of the Order of the German Eagle, and his 1940 Des Moines, Iowa speech in support of America First. Berg explained that the award had been arranged by FDR's ambassador to Germany at the time FDR was trying to smooth over relations with Germany, and that Lindbergh had no idea he was receiving the award until he arrived at the American Embassy.

In the speech at Des Moines, Iowa, Lindbergh asked Americans to ignore the plight of the Jews, who he said were advocating their own cause. Unfortunately, that was the prevailing belief in those times and it was very like the claims that were thrown in the face of Walsh every time he advocated anything regarding Irish affairs. It affected every ethnic group. To advocate for your own people was considered un-American, unless your people were English. Lindbergh in his speech was espousing exactly the foreign policy of FDR; while Lindbergh's speech was given in 1940, Roosevelt's policy towards Jews did not change, even in subsequent years when more information about the holocaust was available to him.

What is remarkably absent from the written record is any criticism from the American Jewish community. All the attacks on Lindbergh came from Anglophile newspapers, and only after he took an anti-war stance. Harry Guggenheim asked him to refrain from talking to the press, explaining to him that his words would surely be twisted.

Lindbergh spoke against war in November, 1939, and he was contacted by student activists soon after. A small group of Yale University law students were recruiting students and recent graduates of universities throughout the country "to enlist the support of those who feel as we do, that the policy of the United States should be hemisphere defense rather than European intervention, and who are willing to work for the adoption of that policy."[18] The student anti-war movement that met with Lindbergh that day could not have been more centrist; it included future President Gerald Ford, future Supreme Court Justice Potter Stewart, future Peace Corps Director Sargent Shriver, and future Ambassador Eugene Locke.

But, it was FDR who had media access and FDR's interventionist stance that won the day. However, it would not win the war, for FDR had prepared the country poorly. Military conscription had passed by only one vote, and America and Congress were badly divided. Ethnic distrusts had been stirred. The United States Navy was badly under-funded. Admirals watched as brand new ships were sent to the British Navy, under documents calling for a transfer of moth balled hulks. Brand new Liberators, fresh off the assembly line, were sent to Churchill while Army Air Force officials stewed. When General Douglas McArthur left the United States Army to take up a military post in Manila in 1939, horses were still being used. When Pearl Harbor was attacked, Admiral "Bull" Halsey noted that he was sadly short of scout planes. Admiral Richardson had resigned his command at Pearl Harbor one year before the attack, claiming it was a sitting duck. Churchill's own admission before the House of Commons that FDR had promised to enter war in the Pacific was never passed on to naval commanders. FDR's civilian leadership and preparation for war, despite his determined stance to embroil the country in the fight, was weak and indecisive. He did not mobilize civilian leadership; he divided it. He did not mobilize public opinion; he left that job to Great Britain. He did not infuse his Cabinet with new talent. He never proposed a plan to go to war, and consequently could not prepare his military commanders.

Despite poor civilian leadership, the American military, operating under a significant handicap, responded magnificently. General George Marshall boldly proposed to invade Europe just six months after Pearl Harbor. Former military leaders and heroes cautioned America about going to war, especially with inadequate preparation; but once war came, they knew how to draw up a strategy. President Eisenhower in his farewell address in 1960 warned of the growing "military industrial complex." Senator David I. Walsh, and Nye, Wheeler, Lindbergh and others, warned of a "media complex" but could not get a forum for their views. The anti-war movement in America in 1940 was studded with military heroes; true patriots. When such respected voices are not only muted but destroyed, one wonders what has become of "American democracy." Why are those who urge peace, even if they are clean shaven, always treated like a national security threat?

---

[18] Berg, A. Scott. *Lindbergh*. Berkeley Books, NY: 1998. p. 411.

When armistice was declared, Charles Lindbergh visited Germany. "I feel ashamed of myself, of my people," Lindbergh wrote in his diary, "as I eat and watch those children. They are not to blame for this war. They are hungry children. What right do we have to stuff ourselves, while they look on — well-fed men eating, leaving unwanted food on our plates, while hungry children look on. What right have we to damn the Nazi and the Jap while we carry on with such callousness and hatred in our hearts?" "Yes, I know," Lindbergh told himself, "Hitler and the Nazis are the cause. But we in America are supposed to stand for different things."[19]

With Roosevelt's death, Lindbergh noticed a shift in attitude in Washington. According to Berg, it did not happen overnight. It took one week. "But, as he wrote to a friend in America First in the second week of the Truman administration, 'I....found a general feeling that there will be a definite turn in the direction of constitutional government from now on.' And he would later report to General Wood, 'the vindictiveness in Washington [has] practically disappeared as far as I was concerned.'"[20]

Great Britain, with the use of propaganda and the control of an Anglophile news-gathering operation, was able to disrupt the democratic process and destroy American icons in the process. The successful propaganda campaign pitted one group against another, as many senators had charged, and libeled anyone who questioned their policies. The pervasive use of sex, spies, and videotape in Hollywood was not aimed only at David I. Walsh. It was aimed over the heads of Congress directly at the American people. Propaganda was a date rape drug designed to win over an unsuspecting public. The photos of unsavory characters that were used on the front page of the *New York Post* pale in comparison to the films being produced by Hollywood. The movies paid for by British Intelligence were beamed into 'every theater near you'. Hollywood had never been an Anglophile town; it belonged to ethnics like Joe Kennedy and Jack Warner. Britain would have to buy their way into town because no amount of backslapping would help since a "good ole boy" network did not exist. British taxpayer dollars would simply buy the movies that Great Britain needed. While there was a huge outcry about the Hollywood investigation during the red scare 1950's, the general public has never heard about the very responsible, thoughtful investigations of Hollywood in 1941. Had Pearl Harbor not turned the country's attention away, the public would have learned about Great Britain's financing of propaganda movies.

---

[19] Ibid., 466.
[20] Ibid., 463.

Intrepid succeeded just in time.

There is a veritable cottage industry in books singing the praises of the FDR-Churchill partnership. It is high time someone picked up the torch from historian Charles Beard and started telling the world the truth.

As for the ACLU, Morris Ernst's continued desires for money caused conflict with his close friend, Roger Nash Baldwin, the founder and Director of the ACLU. Baldwin had to rely on Ernst and others for legal direction, since he was not, himself, a lawyer. Their falling out was related to work that Ernst was doing for Dictator Rafael Trujillo. Ernst, while playing the role of civil libertarian, had no qualms about taking money from the most repressive dictator in the Caribbean.

Yet Baldwin's qualms about the way Ernst made his money was perhaps colored by his political outlook. Ernst had developed a reputation as being anti-communist whereas Baldwin could hardly be considered such. Baldwin had no compunction regarding taking money from the Soviet Union. Baldwin, another WASP Anglophile do-gooder, demonstrated a flirtation with Communism that outlasted even ethnics Emma Goldman and Elizabeth Gurley Flynn. Whereas Goldman and Flynn were in your face Communists, the only difference between them and Baldwin appears to be integrity. Goldman and Flynn never tried to hide their Communist beliefs or affiliation. At the same time, both would later admit they were wrong about the Soviet Union, and would attack the atrocities being committed by Lenin and Stalin, as early as the 1920's. Baldwin would remain a "fellow traveler", defending the Soviet Union right up to 1939, until the signing of the Non-Aggression Pact. The fact that the Communists could sign a treaty with the biggest fascist in Europe left Baldwin vulnerable to critics on the Left, and Baldwin became more circumspect about his open support of Communism.

An unholy alliance had developed between the British Foreign Office and the American Communist Party in the successful attempt to destroy the anti-war movement in the United States. David Walsh had been attacking Communists his whole career. The American Left would lend more than a helping hand to dispose of Walsh. They would become the chief instrument in Walsh's political demise. While Stalin had no qualms about dealing with Hitler, when the Non-Aggression Pact became history with Hitler's invasion of the Soviet Union, he quickly embraced America's unfaithful ally, and mobilized the American Communist Party to support Great Britain and the Soviets in their goals and objectives. It was Walsh's misfortune to be a target of the most ruthless empires of the Twentieth Century.

Baldwin made his money the old fashioned way, quietly taking money from the Soviet Union. It only became public when he was indicted for it. The complaints did not come from right wing prosecutors, but came from disillusioned members of the Kuzbas Commune. The members had been recruited to go to a utopian paradise, but a capitalistic real estate agent could not have written a more misleading pitch. Because of the flood of complaints from commune recruits who had paid to travel to the Soviet Union, the New York City District Attorney requested and indictment of Baldwin for larceny, and on April 17th, 1923, a New York Grand Jury approved it. While he beat the charges, the trial was an embarrassment amongst the American Left. Further, it revealed some unseemly details that would have discredited the entire civil liberties effort, had it gotten more widespread coverage in the media.

"In an oral history he later completed for Columbia University, Baldwin acknowledged he had handled various sums of money, so-called Moscow gold, on behalf of the Kuzbas colony and the Russian Reconstruction Farms. One check for $1 million, was drawn on a bank in Manhattan by the Soviet government, in consideration of the good public relations the colony and farms engendered. It was passed on to Baldwin and two other trustees of a fund established to purchase equipment. Had word of such a transaction gotten out, Baldwin acknowledged, it might have come back to haunt him."[21]

The ACLU remained one more organization dominated by Anglophiles of dubious allegiance to the United States who allowed ethnics to serve, but only if you contributed to the perceived goals as set by Anglophile leaders. While Jews and Catholic were welcome, their demise would often occur when they were no longer of value to the organization. The purge of Elizabeth Gurley Flynn from the national board came about because of her honesty about her Communist affiliation. Her ousting remains a stain on the ACLU today because her demise came about only because she insisted on her right to freedom of speech, that is, to openly admit she was a Communist. When she was ousted, she asked the board why Baldwin himself should not be ousted, because he had secretly supported the Communist cause. Her attempt to exercise free speech would have been defended by the most ardent conservative. Flynn was being thrown overboard because it was no longer convenient to have her on the board.

In the 1920's, when Abraham Cahan, a stridently anti-Communist editor of the *Jewish Daily Forward*, questioned where money was going for Russian relief efforts, charging that it was going to propaganda, he was subject to a vicious

---

[21] Cottrell, Robert, C. *Roger Nash Baldwin and the American Civil Liberties Union.* Columbia University Press. New York: 2000, p. 175

attack by the ACLU. Nonetheless, the ACLU pretended to do an investigation of Cahan's charges, but incredibly enough, had Walter Nelles, an attorney sit on the investigating committee with Baldwin. Nelles apparently was simply monitoring the investigation for his law partner, who represented the agency being investigated, the Friends of Soviet Russia.

"In mid-October committee members issued a report fully exonerating the Friends of Soviet Russia, declaring that it had carried its work out with dedicated commitment to famine relief. Nelles declined to sign the report because he had a potential conflict of interest involving the appointment of his law partner as counsel for the Friends of Soviet Russia." [22]

Given the nature of the ACLU, conflict of interest should have been one of the first considerations in putting together an investigative board, but control of the outcome seems to have been the first consideration. This appears to be another 'show trial' by the American Left, designed to placate those in the left that were concerned with this issue.

Emma Goldman, perhaps the United States most prominent Communist, criticized Roger Baldwin's failure to renounce the Soviet atrocities.

"Emma Goldman suggested to Baldwin that "dear old [Theodore] Dreiser had a much more penetrating eye than you or many others-he at least saw some evils-you saw nothing." Admitting that he did not condemn the evils in Russia in the same manner as comparable ills elsewhere, Baldwin argued, "Such protests might be used by the common enemies of us all-the capitalist and imperialist press." Baldwin then asserted, "I prefer a working class dictatorship to a capitalist dictatorship, and in this practical world you come pretty near having to choose." [23]

Baldwin's pro-communist, pro-Stalinist rhetoric may have simply been patter amongst his friends in the Left, but Goldman's criticism is startling and appears heartfelt. Baldwin also had ample opportunity to clarify his political leanings, and his prolific correspondence throughout his life left plenty of opportunity for course correction. There weren't any. While many in the left expressed misgivings when the Soviet colossus was revealed for what it was, Baldwin never did. His opposition to the Soviet-German Non-Aggression Pact appears more political than heartfelt; he was simply embarrassed with his friends in the American Left. The ACLU would next embrace the causes of the British Empire to destroy the American anti-war movement.

While the *Chicago Daily Tribune* would remain ardently anti-war in its

[22] Ibid., 171.
[23] Ibid., 194.

steadfast support for America First, it would find its old enemy, the ACLU, working secretly for the goals of an aging British Empire. The Anglo-elite that ran the ACLU had determined that aiding the British Empire was the best way to aid Joseph Stalin. Writers for the *Tribune,* the leading anti-war newspaper of the WWII era, would not find this surprising because they had exposed the ACLU as early as 1933, when they denounced their behavior in the Scottsboro Trials. The NAACP had originally agreed to defend the Scottsboro Boys, but their legal representative, the famed Clarence Darrow, resigned from the case because he refused to work with the Communist attorneys hired by the ACLU. While the NAACP and Darrow refused to work with Communists, and withdrew from the case, since the American Communist Party was paying for the defense, they would generate favorable publicity for the communist cause. The ACLU would have no second thoughts about working with the Communists, and when the courts in subsequent years threw the American Communist Party off the case, and appoint the ACLU as sole counsel, suspicion always remained among the American Left about possibly treacherous conduct by the ACLU.

"The Tribune then pointed to a recent speech by Baldwin, in which he had termed political democracy flaccid and called for a united front of communists and liberals to battle fascism. The paper denounced the very idea of such an alliance.

"A union of communists and genuine liberals would be a union of the snake and the bird. The Civil Liberties union is such a union. Liberals who support it are either gullible or they are not liberals. There are no civil liberties remaining except where political democracy exists, and so long as the Civil Liberties union is run as it has been and is, by enemies of democracy, its title is a flagrant hypocrisy which can no longer deceive any but liberal sentimentalists befogged by mere phrases. Even these ought to be shocked at its methods in the Scottsboro affair." [24]

The alliance of Churchill's government with the ACLU was more natural than one would think at first glance. The ACLU provided a coupling of communists like Baldwin, and anti-communists like Morris Ernst, who could provide a united front to destroy Churchill's foes. The counterbalance of Baldwin and Ernst at the top of the ACLU was best described by a former ACLU staffer. Roger Cottrell, in *Roger Nash Baldwin and the American Civil Liberties Union*, quotes Lucille Milner, who worked for Baldwin for many years, describing Ernst as the smart 'fixer'. Indeed he was, and despite the publicity he generated in representing James Joyce's *Ulysses*, his reputation was earned outside the courtroom, not inside. Baldwin on the other hand was a dreamer, unfortunately

---

[24] Ibid., 164.

more interested in imposing his dreams on others. Ernst was not nearly as 'altruistic'.

Lucille Milner, Baldwin's secretary for 25 years, and a committed civil libertarian in her own right, resigned in 1945, and criticized Baldwin's defense of the right, especially the purging of Elizabeth Gurley Flynn. The issue, again, was free speech. How could an organization that champions free speech, purge the only honest member of the national board, a woman who openly admitted she was a Communist? Baldwin had another agenda now that the war was on, which was to couple Joseph Stalin's Soviet Empire with British Imperialism. Despite his deeply help Communist beliefs, he could not do this openly. His differences with Elizabeth Gurley Flynn were strategic, not philosophical. The Anglo elite's flirtation with Communism is troubling, but perhaps not irreconcilable. Virtually all of the major figures in spy cases from the World War II era were from the Anglo elite. What is troubling was how few WASP's were prosecuted. Most became cooperating witnesses, and were not charged. Guy Burgess, Donald McClean, and Kim Philby were allowed to flee despite long standing evidence of their treasonous activities in Great Britain. In the United States, Elizabeth Bentley and Whittaker Chambers were allowed to be cooperating witnesses, and Alger Hiss was given a relatively light sentence considering his high position, while lower level spies Julius and Ethel Rosenberg were executed. It is not hard to conclude that the Rosenbergs did not have the class protection afforded WASP's. British scientist, Klaus Fuchs, who was stationed at Los Alamos, was far more of a spy threat, yet his British citizenship seemed to assure him a lighter sentence than the Rosenbergs. The twin evils of the 20th Century, Communism and Imperialism, both believed in big government, and both suffered from top down elitism. It was the elite that would determine what was best for the masses.

While the ACLU did do an investigation of Baldwin and Ernst's ties to the FBI, many on the left charged it was a whitewash. The ACLU made sure it received no headlines at all, and showed no accountability to its membership. Baldwin was forced out by the ACLU national board, and they announced his retirement on January 1st, 1950. However, they allowed him to maintain various and sundry honorary titles, thus assuring the public would never be aware of the treachery within the ACLU. It appeared to be a harmonious break.

"Although Baldwin was out as ACLU Director, its long standing orientation as a largely Waspish organization did not change. Baldwin's successor, Patrick Murphy Malin, who taught economics at Swarthmore College, was a member of the eastern elite, and had attended an Ivy League university, working in the field of international human rights, believed in pacifism, and was independently wealthy, thanks to his in-laws, the Biddles of Philadelphia."[25]

While the Biddle family proved to be the most destructive force in gutting David Walsh's constitutional rights during the debate on WWII and destroying his career, with Attorney General Biddle's conduct stooping to a criminal level, a Biddle family member would determine what's best for the liberal left as the United States entered the Cold War era. Ethnics were invited in to provide 'color' to the organization, but were quickly thrown overboard when it was convenient. WASPS seemed to approach civil rights as if it was a parlor game, not a constitutionally given right in America.

Author Robert Cottrell quotes Roger Nash Baldwin that "because of the world's imperfections...only a man of "respectable native stock"-like its architect- could have guided the civil liberties movement." [26] More shocking is his admission upon being forced out of the ACLU, that he would not ask the organization to pay for his Century Club membership. Perhaps he did not want the ACLU to know that he had continuously belonged to the Century Club since 1927. The Century Club membership, long linked to the mysterious 1940 election, where Wendell Willkie, a Democrat for just two years, received the Republican nomination for President over two well known Republicans, Taft and Dewey, also had a member dabbling in civil liberties. They must have thought it quaint. One can almost imagine Roger Nash Baldwin telling the membership that he was inviting two guests for the luncheon speakers program today, Emma Goldman and Elizabeth Gurley Flynn. Why do conspiracy theorists have to make up the same old tired conspiracies, when there is so much fertile territory to plough through?

It is not without considerable irony that Great Britain, the country that lays claim to spreading its language throughout the globe, albeit aided with gunboat diplomacy, cannot tell us who its greatest practitioner was; William Shakespeare. Who was he? A Catholic? A noble? A commoner? Was he Christopher Marlowe? Is he a composite of three people? The latest book on Shakespeare, *Players, the Mysterious Identity of William Shakespeare*, by Bertram Fields, has been released with excellent reviews, but as usual, there are more questions than answers. The country obsessed with the British mystery genre has foisted it on us through PBS. Perhaps it will go main stream some day. Culture is a powerful thing. Will transparency ever become a staple of British culture? Apparently reality shows are not their cup of tea. An Irishman has finally found something good to say about Great Britain.

---

[25] Ibid., 326.
[26] Ibid., 332.

INDEX

257

263

Select Bibliography

Aglion, Raoul. *Roosevelt and de Gaulle, Allies in Conflict, A Personal Memoir*, The Free Press, New York, London, 1988.

Beard, Charles. *President Roosevelt and the Coming of the War*, 1941, Yale University Press, 1948.

Berg, A. Scott. *Lindbergh*, Berkley, New York, 1998.

Berthon, Simon. *Allies at War*, Carroll & Graf Publishers, New York, 2001.

Biddle, Francis. *In Brief Authority*, Doubleday & Co, Garden City, NY, 1962.

Brown, Anthony Cave. *'C', The Secret Life of Sir Stewart Menzies*, MacMillan Publishing, New York, 1982

Cole, Wayne S. *Roosevelt & the Isolationists, 1932-45*, University of Nebraska Press, Lincoln and London, 1983.

Cull, Nicholas. *Selling War*, Oxford University Press, 1995, New York, Oxford, 1995.

Curley, James Michael. *I'd Do It All Again*. Prentice Hall, Englewood Cliffs, NJ, 1957.

Davis, Kenneth. *FDR: The War President, 1940-1943*, Random House, New York, 2000.

Day, David. *The Great Betrayal*, W.W. Norton, New York, London, 1988.

Eisenberg, Dennis & Dan, Uri, Meyer Lansky, *The Mogul and the Mob*, Paddington Press, 1979.

Gentry, Curt. *J. Edgar Hoover, The Man and the Secrets*. W.W. Norton, New York, London, 1991.

Griffith, Sally Foreman, *The Autobiography of William Allen White*, second edition, revised & abridged, University Press of Kansas, Lawrence, KS, 1990

Harrington, Dale. *Mystery Man, William Rhodes Davis, Nazi Agent of Influence*, Brassey's, Dulles, VA, 1999

Kilzer, Louis. *Churchill's Deception*, Simon & Schuster, New York, London,Toronto, Sydney, Tokyo, Singapore, 1994.

Konoye, Prince. *Memoirs*, courtesy of University of San Francisco Library

Lash, Joseph P. *Roosevelt and Churchill, 1939-1941*, George McLeod Limited, Toronto, 1976.

Manchester, William. *American Caesar*, Little, Brown, Boston, Toronto, 1978.

Manchester, William. *The Last Lion, Winston Spencer Churchill, Visions of Glory, 1874-1932*, Little, Brown, Boston, Toronto, 1983

Manchester, William. *The Last Lion: Winston Spencer Churchill; Alone, Vol. II, 1932-1940*, Dell Publishing, New York, 1988.

McCullough, David, *Truman, A Touchstone Book*, Simon & Schuster, New York, London, Toronto, Sydney, Tokyo, Singapore, 1992.

Morgan Read, James. *Atrocity Propaganda, 1914-1919*, Yale University Press, 1941.

Morgan, Ted. *FDR: A Biography*, Simon & Schuster, New York, 1985.

Moss, Norman. *Nineteen Weeks, America, Britain, and the Fateful Summer of 1940*, Houghton Mifflin Company, Boston, New York, 2003.

O'Toole, G.J.A. *Honorable Treachery*, Atlantic Monthly Press, New York, 1991. OK, 1939.

Packard, Jerrold. *Neither Friend Nor Foe*, Charles Scribner's Sons, New York, 1992.

Perisco, Joseph E. *Roosevelt's Secret War*, Random House, New York, 2001.

Peterson, H.C. *Propaganda for War*, Univ. of Oklahoma Press, Norman,

Philby, Kim. *My Silent War*, Dell-Grove Paperback, New York.

Pogue, Forrest C. *George C. Marshall, Organizer of Victory*, New York, Viking Press, 1973.

Pool, James & Pool, Suzanne. *Who Financed Hitler*, Dial Press, New York, 1978

Potter, Jeffrey. *Men, Money & Magic*, Coward, McCann & Geoghegan, NewYork, 1976

Renwick, Sir Robin. *Fighting with Allies, America and Britain in Peace and War*, Times Books, Random House, New York, 1996.

Roosevelt, Elliott and Brough, James. *The Roosevelts of Hyde Park, An Untold Story*, G.P. Putnam's Sons, New York, 1973

Rusbridger, James & Nave, Eric. *Betrayal at Pearl Harbor*, Summit Books, New York, 1991.

Sherwood, Robert E. *Roosevelt & Hopkins, an Intimate History*, Harper Brothers, New York, 1948

Stevenson, Sir William, *A Man Called Intrepid*, The Secret War, Harcourt, Brace, Jovanovich, New York, London, 1976.

Stinnett, Robert B. *Day of Deceit*, The Free Press, New York, 2000.

Theobald, Robert A. *The Final Secret of Pearl Harbor*, Devin-Adair Company, Old Greenwich, CT, 1954.

Ward, Geoffrey C. *Closest Companion*, Houghton Mifflin, Boston, New York, 1995.

Wayman, Dorothy. *David I. Walsh, Citizen-Patriot*. Bruce Publishing,

Milwaukee, 1952.

West, Nigel, *MI 5*, Stein & Day, New York, 1982

Other Sources

Dorothy Schiff Collection, New York Public Library

FBI Reading Room, Federal Bureau of Investigation, Washington, D.C.

Historian, Summer 1999, Lise Namikas

Jewish Journal of Greater Los Angeles

National Archives, Washington, College Park, New York Regional Office

Seeley G Mudd Transcript Library, Princeton University

The New American, John T. Flynn: Principles First, Vol. 16, No. 3, January 31, 2000, by John F. McManus

Truman Library, Oral History Interview, Richard McKinzie, Interviewer

Walsh Archives, Dinand Library, College of the Holy Cross

Walsh, David I. FBI Personal file, Freedom of Information Act Request, Federal Bureau of Investigation, U.S. Department of Justice

Worcester Telegram & Worcester Evening Gazette